Canada
in the New
Global Economy

*Problems
and Policies*

INGRID A. BRYAN
Ryerson Polytechnical Institute

John Wiley & Sons
Toronto ■ New York ■ Chichester ■ Brisbane ■ Singapore

Canadian Cataloguing in Publication Data

Bryan, Ingrid A.
    Canada in the new global economy : problems and policies

Includes bibliographical references and index.
ISBN 0-471-64096-4

1. Canada – Economic policy – 1945–   .*
2. Canada – Economic conditions – 1945–   .
I. Title.   II. Title: Economic policies in Canada.

HC115.B78 1994   338.971   C94–931961–9

Text & Cover Design: JAQ
Acquisitions Editor: Bill Todd
Associate Editor: Madhuvanti Ranadive
Copy Editor: Freya Godard
Proofreaders: Bethany Rae/Edward Ikeda
Illustrations: Randy R.T. Townsend
Printing and Binding: Edwards Brothers

Contents

iii

Preface

A complex set of circumstances face Canadians today: globalization of economic power and technological change, slow economic growth, accumulation of debt at all levels of government, environmental stresses both at the local and the global levels, an aging population, changes in the nature and role of the family, and an increased awareness of gender and racial inequalities. As a result, many families and individuals experience a strong feeling of social and economic insecurity. The world in the 1990s bears little resemblance to the world of 30 years ago, and yet both our policies and our thinking often reflect the social, political and economic conditions of the past.

Economists are frequently accused of not caring about the real world, of not being policy oriented, and of devoting excessive time and resources to the development of abstract, highly mathematical models. As result many students interested in public policy have been turned off economics, because they feel the discipline offers few solutions to the problems of society. While the criticism is deserved, a substantial number of economists in Canada and abroad devote their professional lives to studying real economies and institutions. The wealth of material published on the Canadian economy is truly impressive and gratifying, but it also becomes a challenge for students because much of it is inaccessible to non-specialists. *Canada in the New Global Economy* is an attempt to assist both students and teachers in explaining, analyzing and integrating the major global and local economic issues confronting Canadians.

The book is written from an economist's perspective, but with the intention of making it as readable as possible for university and college students who have a minimum background in the principles of economic theory. It could be used as a textbook in economic policy courses, Canadian issues courses, business and government courses, as well as provide supplementary Canadian materials to studies in international economics, intermediate macroeconomics and environmental economics. Because of the extensive references provided at the end of each chapter, it could also be used in more advanced economics courses. I have written the book around a framework; the framework being an examination of Canada's economic well-being from several perspectives: our standard of living as measured by GDP per capita, our environmental record, our employment record, our record of looking after the poor and disadvantaged in our society, and finally, our competitiveness. The last chapters examine our policies and give some suggestions for improvements.

I owe thanks to my research assistant Mauro Morettin and to my colleagues in the Economics Department at Ryerson: Ali Bolbol, George Carter and Gus Zaks for their assistance in finding materials and in reading some of the chapters. I also want to thank my students in my Canadian Political Economy class for suffering through the early stages of the manuscript, and my non-economist husband Rorke Bryan for reading through the material and offering constructive advice on how to make the book comprehensible for readers with a limited knowledge of economics.

INTRODUCTION
The Global Challenge

This introduction gives an overview of the fundamental changes that are taking place in the global economy and how they affect people in all countries. After reading the introduction you will be able to define globalization, describe the forces behind it, and discuss the effect it may have on Canadians.

Canadian events, problems, and policies can no longer be discussed in isolation from those affecting other countries. It is, of course, unlikely that they ever could, but recent changes in the human and physical environments have created an entirely new, different, and interdependent world. Improvements in communications technology have allowed us to be spectators in the front row of every important world event and sometimes even to be participants in world affairs. During the 1990-91 war in the Persian Gulf, people all over the world could tune in to direct newscasts from Baghdad and Tel Aviv and see live the horror of missile attacks.[1] Television covered the massacre of students demonstrating in Tienanmen square in Beijing and the shooting of children in the former Yugoslavia. Television and the other media are constantly shaping public opinion, and it is public opinion that controls and often unseats governments.

Communications technology has also radically transformed the financial markets. At the touch of a computer keyboard, large sums of money move from one country to another, in search of the highest return. A firm's working capital can be invested overnight in interest-bearing assets in whatever market gives the highest yield. Minute changes in interest rates can trigger large enough changes in the flow of funds to create exchange-rate crises beyond the control of any government. As a result, domestic policies have become increasingly subservient to the whims of the international financial markets.

Production has become multinational to such an extent that it is now almost impossible to define the national origin of a product. A car assembled in Canada may contain parts made in the United States, Japan, Mexico, and South Korea. Even office work is being farmed out to other countries. These trends are features of what has become known as **globalization**. Economists define globalization as "the increasing internationalization of the production, distribution and marketing of goods and services" (Harris, 1993, p. 752) or more precisely, as "the increasing integration of economies through trade and investment flows, and the creation of production in numerous countries through foreign direct investment in order to be internationally competitive" (Dobson, 1992, p. 105).

We have also been made more interdependent by the physical environment. Everyone is affected by the thinning of the ozone layer and by global warming. Dirty air and dirty water do not stop at national boundaries. Species are disappearing at unprecedented rates, jeopardizing the normal functioning of ecosystems and the biosphere. No country acting alone can solve the problems afflicting the environment, but all countries acting together can have a considerable effect.

The following description of the major political, economic, technological, and environmental changes that are facing us will provide a framework within which Canadian problems and policies can be understood.[2]

Political Changes

One of the recent political changes in most industrial countries is a decline in the belief in the ability of governments to govern effectively (Maynes, 1990, p. 39). After the Second World War, there was some confidence that governments were able to influence the future in a favourable direction. Economies were growing rapidly, and people were willing to give part of the credit for their higher living standards to the government. Since then, though, the power of governments has been reduced by globalization, for some multinational companies have annual sales exceeding the gross domestic products of many countries, and changes in domestic policies can cause millions of dollars' worth of assets to leave the country. Instead of trying to protect their citizens from adverse international economic events, governments find themselves having to explain why global realities prevent them from intervening. This loss of power, combined with the slow economic growth of the seventies and eighties, made it obvious that governments could not keep their promises.[3] As a result, governments and politicians are now regarded with skepticism, cynicism, and suspicion.[4]

Another reason for the lack of respect for governments and politicians is a decline in deference to authority in general (Maynes 1990). Most societies require some such deference in order to maintain law and order; otherwise police have to be stationed at every street corner. Previously, deference to authority developed because people could not conceive of any other response. The ruler was often believed to hold power by divine right, and if any person did not show him or her due deference, the reaction was often ruthless. Even today, governments have been known to suspend the rule of law in order to inspire fear in their citizens. Examples of those tactics are show trials and death squads.

But, forced deference is unlikely to succeed (unless supported by a strong, absolutely loyal army) for two reasons: the power of the media and improved education. The media guarantee that atrocities become known almost immediately to the rest of the world. Television in particular has a unique capacity to bring world events into the lives of ordinary people and therefore to mobilize political action. Satellite technology in the hands of privately owned media has greatly limited government control of television coverage and therefore of news. The internationalization of television also makes it difficult for governments to control the news. Other media are also important. Fax machines are said to have been used to inform outsiders of the 1990 Soviet clampdown in the Baltic republics. Tapes of the Ayatollah Khomeini's sermons were circulated and played in mosques in Iran before the overthrow of the shah.

Education appears to have had a humanizing effect on people's ideas of what is acceptable and not acceptable. Human rights have become a matter of great concern, not only among the electorate in North America, but also in other parts of the world. No longer can democratic governments send a generation of young men and women to die in wars for causes they do not embrace. The Gulf War was thought to be a just war, at least in the Western countries, only as long as casualties were kept to a minimum.

Nowhere have these political changes been more swift and radical than in eastern Europe. Within two years, the Cold War came to an abrupt end with the rapprochement of the United States and the former Soviet Union. The Berlin Wall, which had physically separated eastern and western Europe for 30 years, was torn down in 1989 and Germany was reunified. The whole of the Soviet empire in eastern Europe as well as the Soviet Union itself fell apart peacefully, much to the surprise of military analysts.

In western Europe, integration rather than disintegration was taking place. In 1992, the Maastricht Treaty was ratified, strengthening the existing European Community by formally establishing the European Union. This was followed by successful negotiations in 1994 to admit more countries into the Union (Austria, Finland, Norway, and Sweden). The stage was set for the emergence of a new economic and possibly political superpower in Europe.[5] In North America the Canada-U.S. Free Trade Agreement came into force in January 1989, followed by the North American Free Trade Agreement between the United States, Canada, and Mexico (NAFTA) in January 1994.

Though the Cold War is over local wars and civil unrest continue. The collapse of communism seems to have robbed some countries of the ideological bond holding them together, be it communism or anticommunism. There appears to be a general decline in the influence of traditional political parties and a rise in the importance of single-issue groups. There also appears to be a worldwide tendency for ethnic minorities to strive for more cultural, political, and economic influence; a struggle that may or may not be violent; examples of such minorities are African Americans and Hispanics in the United States; French Canadians in Canada; the Flemish in Belgium; indigenous peoples in Canada, Mexico, South America, and Australia; Kurds in Iraq; Tibetans in China; Sikhs in India; and Serbs and Croats in the former Yugoslavia.

Even though the arms race between the superpowers has disappeared after a series of disarmament treaties and the demise of the Soviet Union, the arms build-up in the developing countries continues with the proliferation of chemical and nuclear weapons. The dismantling of the nuclear arsenal of the former Soviet Union is a formidable task, particularly as the Ukraine appears reluctant to give up control over the weapons on its territory. According to *The Economist* (March 14, 1992), the former Soviet Union had 27,000 nuclear weapons, a stockpile of approximately 100-150 tonnes of weapons-grade plutonium, and 700,000 people employed in its nuclear industry. The prospect that either weapons or experts might be employed by terrorists or new nuclear powers is chilling. Israel, Iraq, Iran, Algeria, Pakistan, India, and North Korea either have nuclear weapons or the ability to produce them. The availability of nuclear or chemical weapons in conjunction with the social and ethnic unrest in some of these countries constitutes a an explosive mixture that could destabilize whole countries and regions.

Developments in Science and Technology

In science, the recent advances have been truly spectacular, ranging from new knowledge about the age of the universe to the discovery of the genetic recipe for a human being; from discoveries in the world of elementary particles to the tectonic plate theory that explains the formation of the continents. For the uninitiated, science has become increasingly difficult to understand. Science has also become so specialized that a molecular biologist can probably not understand the work of a genologist and vice versa. The quantum physicists appear to live in their own world, which to most people seems absurd.[6] It is a world in which all particles are waves and waves are particles. "Things" do not exist since they do not have properties until they are measured. Time travel appears to be a possibility — at least in theory.

Though the general public is in favour of allocating public money to basic research, there is probably a fair degree of cynicism and skepticism toward some scientific theories and discoveries. The alleged discovery of cold fusion by two University of Utah scientists, which, had it been true, would have given us almost boundless and thus free energy, and the subsequent failure of other scientists to replicate the findings, did not instill confidence in the ability of science to solve real-life problems. In the sixties the reputation of science was damaged by the claims that nuclear power would be so cheap it would not be worth metering and so safe that any worry about radiation leaks was groundless. Neither of these claims was true. In fact, nuclear power became the most expensive way of generating power, and the Chernobyl accident in Russia dispelled the notion once and for all that nuclear reactors were foolproof.

Science and technology are in principle separable; in practice they are not. Science does not necessarily result in new or improved technology, and technology in its very primitive forms could exist without science. After all, stone-age people were able to fashion tools without, presumably, any knowledge of science. Nevertheless, without basic research, major innovations are unlikely, for new technology flows from discoveries in science. The development of computer technology was made possible by advances in quantum physics. Similarly, without advanced technology, advances in science are unlikely since few discoveries in science are made without the advanced technologies found in today's modern laboratories.

According to Freeman (1987), there are four different types of technological innovations: marginal innovations, leading to small improvements in products and processes; radical innovations that lead to the complete revamping of production techniques in a particular area; technical revolutions that give rise to new industries with their own products and processes; and fundamental changes that transform relations between the technical system, the economy, and society. Most innovations are of the marginal type. However, the last few decades have seen both kinds of technical revolution and changes that have fundamentally changed the way we do things in communications technology, biotechnology, and materials technology.

The invention of the transistor by Bardeen, Brattan, and Shockley in 1947 led to the development of integrated circuits and subsequently to robotics, microcomputers, and satellite technology. The advent of computers and the application of computer technology to production, management, and all aspects of communications have been truly revolutionary. The first computer application in manufacturing was in the machine-tool industry through computerized numerical control (CNC), followed by computer-assisted design and computer-assisted manufacturing (CAD/CAM). The culmination of this development is a fully integrated, flexible manufacturing system, in which a computer can retool the machinery to switch from one product line to another with virtually no downtime. As a result, products can now be custom-made with little effect on cost. Modern industry will have come full circle back to its beginnings in the nineteenth century when most products were custom-made.

Computers are also adding up payrolls, registering students, reserving airline seats, guiding missiles to their targets, and aiding both doctors and mechanics in diagnosis. Computers have also revolutionized communications, more so than we realize. We take for granted the ability to dial almost anywhere in the inhabited world. We can fax a message, a map, a blueprint, or a manuscript also instantly anywhere in the world. We can communicate with colleagues, data banks, and libraries via linked computers. Our credit line can be checked immediately anywhere if we carry an international credit card. Large sums of money can be transferred immediately across borders in search of the highest return. The accelerated pace of advances in integrated circuits, combined with developments in photonics and fibre-optic systems, have vastly expanded the transmission capacity, providing the potential for further economies of scale in the accumulation and use of information (Malmgren 1990).

Large changes have also taken place in biology and genetics, leading to innovations in biotechnology. Biotechnology developed out of findings made in the university laboratories in the 1960s.[7] In 1944 a Canadian, Oswald Avery, was the first to discover that genes were made of DNA, a long string of chemicals, the precise structure of which was not known until 1953. James Watson and Francis Crick at Cambridge University found that DNA was composed of two intertwined strands of four different chemical bases that could be arranged in any order. Connections between the strands could only be made between two specific pairs of chemicals. Later it was discovered that the bases of DNA were arranged into a code that specified the assembly of amino acids into proteins. Proteins are known to be made of 20 amino acids, the codes for which were found to be made up of groups of three of the DNA bases in sequence (codons). Each stretch of codons is in fact a gene. It was not difficult to see that this discovery could have commercial implications. If the genetic code for the manufacture of a desirable protein (such as a drug) could be inserted in the DNA of a living cell, the cell could be used to manufacture the protein; this was an ability it could pass on to future generations of cells. Organisms could also be improved by the addition of new genes (for example genes that improve pest resistance in crops).

Genetic engineering has so far led to the production of human insulin in bacteria, human growth hormone, microbes capable of digesting crude oil, and improved pesticides. Some claim that biotechnology will have an effect on the economy and on people's lives comparable to computer technology.[8] Others are sufficiently worried about its ethical implications to call for stringent controls on its further development. It is clearly possible to tinker with human genetic material by inserting "desirable" qualities or removing "undesirable" qualities — to create a super-race of humans. There are other misgivings about the spread of genetically engineered material in the environment with its often unpredictable effects.

The third major development in technology referred to above is the emergence of new materials.[9] Ceramics and plastics are used in engines as substitutes for metals. Carbon-fibre composites are used in tennis rackets and fishing rods as well as in structural parts of aircraft. Optical fibres are a substitute for copper in telecommunications. Most of the new materials are composites of plastic, resin, ceramics, and powdered metals, reinforced with fibres such as glass and carbon. They can be easily moulded, they are stronger than metals, and they do not rust. These changes provide formidable challenges for countries, like Canada, that produce raw materials.

The potential economic effects of the technological changes on the structure of the world economy will be discussed in the next section after a brief summary of the postwar history of the world economy.

Changes in the Global Economy

The decades immediately following the Second World War were characterized by rapid economic growth and substantial increases in the standard of living in the industrial countries. The United States was by far the dominant economic power. There was optimism about the ability of governments to manage the national economies. Inflation and unemployment were thought to be mutually exclusive. Economics was ruled by Keynesianism, which held that unemployment could be brought under control by either an increase in government spending or a cut in taxes, and inflation by a decrease in spending or an increase in taxes. The concomitant budgetary deficits and surpluses would cancel each other out over the length of the economic cycle.

Nineteen seventy was a watershed year in several respects. The two oil shocks of 1973 and 1979 fed inflationary cycles that had had their origins in the Vietnam War. Inflation and unemployment occurred simultaneously and a new term was coined, stagflation, which seemed immune to standard macroeconomic remedies. In most countries economic growth came to a virtual standstill, and the United States started to lose its dominance of the world economy. The oil-producing countries had a surplus of money. The lending of oil money to developing countries was expanded, resulting in a debt crisis in which several countries, including Mexico, were on the verge of defaulting on their payments.

The recession of 1981-82 was severe and was followed by a period of slow growth and high inflation caused by the large budget deficits during the Reagan administration in the United States. There were two reasons for the large deficits. One was that the military budget was doubled in the early eighties to counter the apparent Soviet threat. The other reason was that the administration believed that tax cuts would generate so much extra activity that the government's tax revenue would actually increase, resulting in a decrease in the size of the deficit. Taxes were cut, but revenue did not increase.[10] Inflation therefore had to be contained by very restrictive monetary policies, resulting in record-high interest rates. These interest rates in turn helped in plunge the world economy into another deep recession in the early 1990s.

World trade in the 1970s and 1980s continued to expand at rates higher than the growth in the world economy, partly because of the reduction in trade barriers resulting from the Kennedy and Tokyo rounds of negotiations under the GATT. Both the Japanese and the German economies posed formidable challenges to the dominance of the United States in the world economy. Japan was studied intensely for clues as to why her economy was performing so well while others were stagnating. Among management experts, Japanese-inspired quality teams and just-in-time delivery became buzz-words. Japan's success was attributed to a well-educated and homogeneous labour force, emphasis on long-term strategies and technology, harmonious industrial relations, and a low level of military spending.

The collapse of the Soviet Union had ramifications for the whole world economy, but their precise nature are not yet clear. Though the developing countries made some improvements in income, literacy rates, and mortality rates, progress was extremely uneven, the most vigorous growth was in southeast Asia among the so-called newly industrialized countries and there were prospects for rapid progress in China and India and perhaps in South America. Indeed, during the Industrial Revolution, Great Britain and the United States took 50 years to double real per capita incomes. The newly industrialized countries are doing this in a decade. Already nearly half of the world's output is accounted for by countries outside Europe and North America (*The Economist*, January 8, 1994). Most of Africa, however, has not fared well and its prospects are uncertain.

The technological changes referred to above have fundamentally changed the structural relationships in the world economy. In particular, they have weakened the links between the industrial economy and the demand for primary products, between capital and trade, and between employment and the industrial economy (Drucker 1986).

The traditional link between manufacturing and primary-products industries was strong and immediate. An expansion in manufacturing was followed by a rise in the prices of raw materials as a result of the increased demand for raw materials. This was no longer true in the 1980s, when raw material prices in real terms were lower rather than higher, even though most economies were expanding (World Bank, 1992, p. 32). This resulted in large changes in the terms of trade for raw material producers and greater difficulties in servicing their external debts.

The probable reason for the weak link between the demand for raw materials demand and industrial production is technology. Changes in technology have allowed manufacturers to use less material-intensive and energy-intensive products and processes. For example, 50 to 100 pounds of fibreglass cable can carry as many messages as a ton of copper cable (Drucker 1986). One hundred pounds of fibreglass can be made with only 5 percent of the energy required to make one ton of copper cable. The use of plastics rather than steel represents a saving of raw materials of approximately 50 percent. The United States used less steel in 1990 than in 1960, whereas the GNP during the same period increased two and a half times (Thurow, 1992, p. 41). The amount of industrial raw material used per unit of production has declined by 50 percent since the turn of the century. The demand for raw materials has also been reduced by environmental laws requiring recycling.

The second traditional link was between capital flows and trade flows. Capital flows were thought to accommodate trade flows and not to be an autonomous force in themselves. If imports were greater than exports and if exchange rates were fixed, capital would have to flow into a country to finance the imports. The country would have to borrow money. According to Drucker (1986), capital flows are now 25 times larger than trade flows. That expansion can probably be attributed to several factors: the deficit in the U.S. balance of payments and the willingness of foreigners to finance the deficit, the two oil shocks with the vast amount of oil money that needed to be placed in lucrative assets, and floating exchange rates, which made it profitable to speculate in foreign exchange. Additional factors were the deregulation of capital markets and the improvements in communications technology making it possible to transfer funds across borders at the touch of a button.

Capital flows have also broken the immediate connection between exchange rates and trade flows. It was believed that, if a country's exports became uncompetitive, the resulting balance of payments deficit would disappear after an automatic depreciation of the currency.[11] Capital flows may now stop this depreciation from taking place, and currencies can remain over- or undervalued for significant periods of time.

The third change is the weakened link between employment and industrial production, caused partly by changes in technology and partly by changes in the nature of the firm and in the nature of employment. Aggregate industrial production can expand with only minor increases in employment because of automation and a shift in the industrial countries from labour-intensive to knowledge-intensive industries. This shift also entails a shift from high-volume to high-value industries, from mass production to specialized production. Ohmae (1990) points out that these developments have increased the proportion of fixed costs in production. Labour (a major component of variable costs) has to a large extent been replaced by machinery, and new activities such as research and development have added more fixed costs to business operations. When most costs are variable management tries to increase profits by cutting the cost of material and wages (hours of work). In a fixed-cost environment the emphasis changes to maximizing marginal contributions to fixed costs by increasing sales, not only locally but also globally.

Reich (1991, p. 104) argues that the main struggle in the previous high-volume industrial economy (which probably lasted until the 1970s) was between the owners of the machinery (the capitalists) and those who ran them (the workers). Peace was achieved in the 1950s when management agreed to labour's demand for higher wages in return for labour's cooperation in turning out an ever-increasing volume of goods, which lowered the per unit costs and created a large middle class that could afford to buy them.

During the seventies and eighties this type of high-volume production was shifted to countries with lower labour costs, resulting in a decrease in demand for blue-collar workers in the industrialized countries. The firms that survived and prospered during this period of change were those that concentrated on serving the unique and rapidly changing needs of particular customers. A new, high-value product may have a life of only 18 months, in which the first six months are spent in perfecting quality and production and achieving economies of scale (Malmgren 1990). The following year will have to generate the necessary revenue to cover the high start-up costs before the product has become obsolete. To stay in business a firm has to introduce new products continuously. In order to do so, the traditional reliance on sales personnel must be complemented, or even set aside in favour of the use of technicians and engineers working with consumers to design new products.[12] There is little need for the traditional blue-collar worker. In the "new" economy, the important industries are microelectronics, biotechnology, the new materials industry, civilian aviation, telecommunications, robots and machine tools, and computers and software (Thurow, 1992, p. 45).

The successful high-value business will have three different but interconnected skills (Reich 1991): (1) to solve problems, (2) to help customers understand their needs, and (3) to link problem solvers and problem identifiers. There must be people who know how to put products together in unique ways and with a knowledge of what the products are able to do. There must also be people who can help the customers understand what they need. All these various skills must be brought together successfully. In the high-value enterprise, the tension is not between capital and labour; rather capital and labour are both subordinated to the claims of those who solve, identify, and broker new problems. As evidence Reich (1991, p. 104) cites statistics showing that in 1920, 85 percent of a car's cost went to pay labourers and investors. In 1990 the proportion was less than 60 percent. The remainder went to designers, engineers, stylists, planners, executives, lawyers, and so on.

The high-value enterprise is becoming increasingly international as the expertise of skilled people from anywhere and everywhere are brought together to contract with low-wage unskilled labour from around the world for the part of production that must be standardized and produced in high volume. It is estimated that in the late eighties half of world trade was performed by multinational corporations and that 30 percent was trade between different branches of the same firm (Paquet, 1990, p. 83).

Reich (1991) argues that there are three main types of employees in the new global economy: **symbolic analysts, routine producers,** and **in-person servers.** The symbolic analysts account for the top 20 percent of incomes. They are the cream of the crop. A person's access to tangible and non-tangible wealth is determined by the value that the global economy places on his or her skills. The symbolic analysts are the scientists, the engineers, the designers, the brokers, the problem solvers, and the problem identifiers. They are the people who are valuable and who will command a larger and larger share of society's wealth. Routine production workers (the traditional unskilled blue-collar workers), on the other hand, faced with a growing pool worldwide of unskilled and semi-skilled workers, will find their incomes slipping and their jobs disappearing.[13] In-person services, (such as those performed by social workers, teachers, waiters, and nurses), which cannot be traded around the world will be sheltered from such competition. However, they will still find themselves in a precarious position. They will face competition from laid-off routine production workers, immigrants, and labour-saving machinery. Income inequality in society will increase.

There is some statistical support for Reich's hypothesis. In the 1970s wage inequalities either fell or were stable in most industrialized countries. But, according to OECD statistics, in the 1980s the wage gap increased in 12 of 17 OECD countries. In the United States in 1980, the highest-paid 10 percent of workers earned 4.8 times as much as the lowest 10 percent. The corresponding figure for 1989 was 5.6. The ratio in Britain increased from 2.5 in 1980 to 3.4 in 1991. The most pronounced increase in wage differentials was between those with a university degree and those without. In the United States the premium earned by workers with a university degree increased from 37 percent in the 1970s to 53 percent in 1989 (*The Economist*, July 24, 1993).[14] The situation in Canada will be examined in Chapter 7.

Changes in the Global Environment

The new global economy is intricately linked with the global environment. Environmental factors will have an important effect on how the world economy will develop in the future. World population growth declined from over 2 percent a year a couple of decades ago to approximately 1.7 percent in 1992. But, given a current world population of 5.4 billion, it means that each year nearly 90 million people are added. The world's population will reach 6.2 billion by the year 2000 and 8.2 billion in another 20 years, after which it is likely to stabilize. Though the world will probably be capable of producing enough food for such a large population, it is unclear if the global environment in the wider sense has the capacity to adjust:

> Ultimately a good environment comes down to human carrying capacity. The use of almost everything and the disposal of almost everything is directly proportional to the number of people on the globe...
>
> If the world's population had the productivity of the Swiss, the consumption habits of the Chinese, the egalitarian instincts of the Swedes and the social discipline of the Japanese, then the planet could support many times its current population without excessive pollution or deprivation. On the other hand if the world's population had the productivity of Chad, the consumption habits of the United States, the egalitarian instincts of India and the social discipline of Yugoslavia, the planet could not support anywhere near its current numbers. Unfortunately, most humans seem to fall in the America-India-Chad-Yugoslavia category (Thurow, 1992, p. 226).

One of the most fundamental challenges facing all of us is how we can give everybody a decent standard of living without destroying the biological communities that sustain us. The environmental stresses are formidable. Most of us are now reluctant to go out in the sun without protective sunscreen because of the increased risk of cancer from the thinning of the ozone layer. Life in some large cities is a health hazard because of air pollution, and much of the world lacks adequate drinking water. Soil erosion and soil salinization are jeopardizing agricultural production in many countries including Canada. Most climate models predict that the world's climates will become warmer because of the build-up of carbon dioxide in the atmosphere, mainly from the burning of fossil fuels. While a warmer climate may sound pleasant for us Canadians, it could cause irreparable and undesirable changes to our ecology, in particular in the Arctic. Species of animals and plants are disappearing at an unprecedented rate because of urbanization and the cutting down of forests, not only in tropical countries but also in Canada. In response, many governments, including our own, are committed to including environmental issues in decision making and have embraced the concept of **sustainable development** (see Chapter 2). Sustainable development is "development that meets the needs of the present without compromising the ability of future generations to meet their own needs" (World Commission on Environment and Development, 1987, p. 43).

Most people are probably in favour of a cleaner environment as long as it does not cost anything. Unfortunately much of the international discussion about the environment is marred by long debates about who is going to bear most of the cost of the clean-up: the rich countries or the poor countries. Costs become the dominant issue in periods of slow economic growth, when the rallying cry becomes jobs *or* the environment rather than jobs *and* the environment. We will return to this important question in Chapters 3 and 4.

Conclusions

The subject of this chapter has been the fundamental changes facing the world and Canada in the political, technological, economic, and environmental spheres, all of which interact and reinforce each other.

In the political arena, there appears to be a general lack of confidence in the ability of governments to solve today's economic, social, and environmental problems. This lack of confidence, combined with diminished power of governments because of globalization and decreased deference to authority, have led to political disintegration in many parts of the world and increased tensions between various interest groups in others. The decline in the power of governments and in deference to authority can be attributed to improvements in education and the massive advances in communications technology that allow information, messages, images, and money to be transferred instantaneously over large distances. Other changes in technology that affect us are advances in biotechnology and materials technology and the use of computers in production.

The changes in technology have in turn led to fundamental changes in the structure of new global economy. It is based on knowledge rather than on materials, resulting in far-reaching implications for the organization of production. Firms have become increasingly footloose, moving production to where there is cheap labour if they need unskilled labour. If some of the firm's operations require a pool of highly trained specialized labour, those operations will be located where such labour is available. Financial capital, which is equally footloose, moves across borders in search of the highest return. The rewards to knowledge will increase, leading to larger income disparities between the skilled and unskilled.

These developments, coupled with the globalization of environmental problems, provide us Canadians with enormous challenges if we want to maintain our standard of living; challenges that will occupy the rest of the book. So far, we have proven ourselves adept at arriving at workable solutions to complex issues. Compared to most other countries, we are lucky. We are blessed with a variety of natural resources, we have a relatively clean environment, and we have a culturally diverse, highly educated population, capable of generating a wealth of ideas and solutions to our own problems as well as to the problems of the world at large. We should be able to rise to the challenge.

TOPICS FOR DISCUSSION

1. To what extent does globalization create different challenges for Canada than for other countries ?
2. Will globalization tear us apart as a country or bring us together?
3. Given that so many problems facing us are international, is there a need for a world government?

RECOMMENDED READING

Richard Lipsey's article in the fall 1993 issue of *Canadian Business Economics* contains an excellent discussion of the likely effects of the new technologies. Drucker's original article on the global economy in the spring 1986 issue of *Foreign Affairs* is also well worth reading. Thurow's book *Head to Head: The Coming Economic Battle Among Japan, Europe, and America* and Reich's *The Work of Nations: Preparing Ourselves for 21st Century Capitalism* were written for popular audiences, and have influenced thinking in both Canada and the United States. They provide interesting contrasts in their discussions of implications of globalization for the United States.

References

Bibby, Reginald W. *Mosaic Madness: The Poverty and Potential of Life in Canada*. Toronto: Stoddart Publishing Company, 1990.

Dobson, Wendy. "The Changed World Economy: Origins and Implications." In *The New World Economic Order: Opportunities and Threats*, ed. Jerry Dermer, Toronto: Cactus Press, 1992.

Drucker, Peter. "The Changed World Economy." *Foreign Affairs* 64 (Spring 1986): 768-92.

The Economist "A survey of advances in biotechnology," April 30, 1988, The queerness of quanta," January 7, 1989; "Snip, bake and glue," July 21, 1990; "Cross-frontier broadcasting: And nation shall speak guff unto nation," May 2, 1992; "The end of the beginning," October 24, 1992; "Rich man, poor man," July 24, 1993; "The new-bathed stars emerge" and "The new world order," January 8, 1994.

Freeman, C. "The Challenge of new technologies." In *Interdependance and Co-operation in Tomorrow's World: a symposium marking the 25th anniversary of the OECD*. Paris: OECD, 1987.

Gottschalk, Peter. "Changes in Equality of Family Income in Seven Industrialized Countries." *The American Economic Review* 83 (May 1993): 136-42.

Harris, Richard G. "Presidential Address: Globalization, Trade, and Income." *Canadian Journal of Economics* 26 (November 1993): 755-77.

Hawking, Stephen W. *A Brief History of Time: From the Big Bang to Black Holes*. New York: Bantam Books, 1988.

Lipsey, Richard G. "Globalization, Technological Change and Economic Growth."

Canadian Business Economics 2 (Fall 1993): 3-18.

Malmgren, Harold B. "Technology and the Economy." In *The Global Economy. America's Role in the Decade Ahead*, eds. William Brock and Robert Hormats, New York: W.W. Norton and Co. 1990.

Maynes, Charles William. "Political Changes in the 1990s." In *Perspective 2000*, eds. K. Newton *et al.* (1990): 39-59.

Newton, K., T. Schweitzer, and J-P. Voyer ed. *Perspective 2000. Proceedings of a Conference Sponsored by the Economic Council of Canada, December 1988.* Ottawa: Ministry of Supply and Services, 1990.

Ohmae, Kenichi. *The Borderless World. Power and Strategy in the Interlinked Economy.* HarperCollins, 1990.

Paquet, Gilles. "Commentary," In *Perspective 2000*, eds. K. Newton *et al* (1990): 80-91.

Purchase, Bryne B. *The Innovative Society. Policy Review and Outlook, 1991.* Toronto: The C.D. Howe Institute, 1991.

Penrose, Roger. *The Emperor's New Mind. Concerning Computers, Minds, and the Laws of Physics.* London: Oxford University Press, 1989.

Thurow, Lester. *Head to Head: The Coming Economic Battle Among Japan, Europe, and America.* New York: William Morrow and Company Inc., 1992.

Reich, Robert B. *The Work of Nations. Preparing Ourselves for 21st-Century Capitalism.* New York: Alfred A. Knopf, 1991.

World Bank, *The World Development Report, 1992.* New York: Oxford University Press, 1992.

World Commission on Environment and Development. *Our Common Future.* Oxford: Oxford University Press, 1987.

Endnotes

1   CNN is available in 137 countries (*The Economist*, May 2, 1992).

2   Many books have been written about these changes. See for example *Perspectives 2000, Proceedings of a Conference Sponsored by the Economic Council of Canada* (Newton *et al*, 1988).

3   The GNP growth rates of non-communist industrialized countries declined from a yearly average of 4.9% in the 1960s to 3.8% in the 1970s and to 2.9% in the 1980s. On a per capita income basis, the growth rate was 1.1 % in the eighties compared to 2.8% in the sixties (The World Bank 1992).

4   A recent *Globe and Mail*/CBC News poll indicated that 64 percent of Canadians felt that our political leaders did not have a vision of the future, nor any idea how to achieve such a vision had they had any (Purchase 1991). A poll by Decima Research as reported in *The Globe and Mail* October 1, 1990 found that 65% of the polled described politicians as incompetent, 57% as unprincipled. The same poll was conducted in 1980, where only 33% thought politicians were incompetent and 28% unprincipled. Bibby (1990, p. 83) reports the results of two Gallup polls, one in 1989 and one in 1979 where the respondents were asked how much

respect and confidence they had in among other things political parties and the House of Commons. The proportion rating high or very high went from 38 to 30% for the House of Commons and from 30 to 18% for political parties.

5 At the time of writing it is not clear what a new power structure in the world will look like. According to *The Economist* (January 8, 1994), the four powers most likely to form a part of a new world order, replacing the old order which was dominated by the United States and the Soviet Union, are in order of probability the United States, China, Russia and Europe. There might also be two additional contenders: Japan and a power centred on the Muslim world.

6 For attempts to explain the new physics, see for example the bestseller *A Brief History of Time From the Big Bang to Black Holes* by Stephen Hawking (1988) and *The Emperor's New Mind. Concerning Computers, Minds, and the Laws of Physics* by Roger Penrose (1989). *The Economist* is also a good source for readable explanations of science. See "The queerness of quanta", (*The Economist*, January 7, 1989) from which the examples of things and waves are taken.

7 See "A survey of advances in biotechnology", (*The Economist*, April 30, 1988).

8 Currently, a new field is in the making: genomics. Genomics is the study of sets of genes rather than individual genes. The new field is developing out of the human genome project which attempts to map all the genes in the human body (*The Economist*, October 24, 1992).

9 See "Snip, bake and glue", *The Economist*, July 21, 1990.

10 The relationship between tax rates and tax revenues was not based on fact. It was thought up after a restaurant meal by an economist called Laffer and became known as the Laffer curve (see also Chapter 9). The whole approach to fiscal policy was christened Reaganomics or supply-side economics.

11 A country with a balance of payments deficit is not earning sufficient foreign exchange to finance its international transactions. The shortage of foreign exchange will lead to an increase in the price of foreign exchange (the exchange rate). The depreciation will make exports cheaper and imports more expensive and will therefore work to correct the deficit.

12 Thurow (1992) believes that sustainable comparative advantage lies in process technology rather than product technology because of the speed at which a new product can be imitated through "reverse engineering". He argues that US managers do not understand production, while German and Japanese managers do, which explains why the United States has lagged behind in the use of process technology.

13 Thurow (1992, p. 53) provides data which indicate that this is already happening in the United States. While real GNP increased by 28 percent between 1973-1990, real hourly wages for non-supervisory workers fell by 12 percent. Weekly wages fell even more (18 percent) because of the increase in part-time employment.

14 For a review of the evidence, see Gottschalk (1993). He also presents statistics for Australia, Canada, France the Netherlands, Sweden, United Kingdom and the United States showing increased disparities in all countries in both earnings

Part One

━━━━━

Canada's
Economic Performance
in the 1990s

THE FOLLOWING SEVEN CHAPTERS WILL OUTLINE, ANALYZE, and discuss the challenges facing the Canadian economy in the 1990s. In addition to the global changes occurring in the world economy, Canada, like all other countries, has to contend with its own unique problems. The 1980s were dominated by the acrimonious debates about the Constitution and free trade. The constitutional debate was an exercise in **rent-seeking**. Rent-seeking is a term economists use to describe attempts by interest groups in society to get a larger share of the national income. The constitutional debate centred on arguments about the allocation of power between the federal government and the provinces, between Quebec and the rest of Canada, between aboriginal peoples and other Canadians. It culminated in the referendum of October 26, 1992 when the proposal for constitutional change was turned down by the voters in most provinces. The constitutional debate did not settle the constitutional issues, and it diverted resources from the solution of other important economic problems.

The other main issue was free trade. The report of the Macdonald Commission (Canada 1985) recommended that Canada should negotiate a free trade agreement with the United States. Subsequent negotiations with the United States were successful and concluded in the fall of 1987. The ensuing debate over the merits of free trade was intense, and the 1987 Canadian election was fought on the issue. The Canada-U.S. Free Trade Agreement came into force on January 1, 1989. Later, Canada took part in trilateral negotiations with the United States and Mexico to form a North American free trade area. These negotiations were concluded in December 1992 but were reopened by the incoming Clinton administration in 1993. Some changes were made, and at year-end all three countries had ratified the agreement. NAFTA came into existence on January 1, 1994.

The initial effects of free trade on the manufacturing sector, combined with the effects of the new Goods and Services Tax introduced in 1989, a large federal deficit and debt, and a worldwide recession, did not make for a happy entry into the 1990s. Canada's unemployment rate increased to 11.3 percent in 1992. Compared to the situation in other recessions, many layoffs were caused by permanent plant closures; that is, the jobs would not return when the economy picked up. It seemed that the world as we knew it had changed fundamentally. As a result many Canadians experienced a deep feeling of insecurity (The National Forum on Family Security, 1993, pp. 1-18).

The question that will be the subject of our discussions is how the Canadian economy is performing and whether or not we can maintain our prosperity. Will the changes in technology lead us into a new period of growth, or are we going to be left by the wayside in the global race for competitiveness? Will environmental constraints diminish our standard of living? Have we left our children with an impossible debt? What should be the yardstick for measuring the success or failure of the Canadian economy?

An implicit goal of economic activity is the satisfaction of human needs and aspirations, that is, the promotion of human well-being.[1] However, in the light of the world's environmental problems, this goal is clearly very narrow unless we interpret human well-being over a number of generations. Sustainability would dictate that we expand the goal to be the satisfaction of human needs and aspirations without compromising the needs and aspirations of future generations.

To define and measure human needs and aspirations, or well-being, is clearly impossible, almost as impossible as arriving at an aggregate or average measure of real happiness. We must devise a method for adding up economic and social benefits over the lifetime of an individual, over different individuals of the same generations and over different generations of individuals (Osberg, 1985, p. 49). A certain level of economic activity may be achieved at the expense of poor people or at the cost of greater economic security. Any judgement of whether or not we are becoming better off as a society therefore depends on the weight we give to economic inequality and insecurity as opposed to economic growth, and to the well-being of current generations as opposed to that of future generations (*ibid.*).

In Part I, we shall look critically at economic well-being in Canada. Chapter 1 will examine the most common measures of economic well-being estimates of income derived from the national accounts as well as some other commonly used indicators. But economic well-being is more than the average person's command over goods and services traded through markets. The environment influences our well-being in many respects. A polluted environment affects our health both physically and mentally. Natural resources also provide a living for many Canadians. The next three chapters will examine various ways in which the environment affects our well-being.

Since most of us spend our lives working, it is obvious both the quantity and the quality of work, as well as the security of work, is important in determining our welfare as individuals. Chapter 5 will examine our record in creating jobs and our unemployment record. In Chapter 6 we will follow Rawls (1971) and argue that a country's success or failure in promoting the welfare of its people must be judged not only by the welfare of its average citizen, but also by the welfare of its poorest and most vulnerable citizens. We shall look at the distribution of income and the incidence of poverty in Canada compared to other countries. Our future prospects will be discussed in Chapter 7.

Will we be able to continue to earn our place in the world economy? What does it mean to be competitive ?

TOPIC FOR DISCUSSION

To what extent has the economic environment changed for Canada since the Macdonald Commission? If you were to head a new royal commission, what would you concentrate on?

RECOMMENDED READING

The definite study of Canada's economic performance and future prospect based on conditions in the early 1980s is in the report of the Macdonald Commission (Canada 1985). The report is over 1,000 pages long, and to read it is a formidable undertaking. However, there is a good summary of the conclusions and recommendations in Volume I.

References

Canada. *Report of the Royal Commission on the Economic Union and Development Prospects for Canada*. Ottawa: Ministry of Supply and Services, 1985.

Canada. Economic Council of Canada. *First Annual Review, 1964*. Ottawa: Queen's Printer, 1964.

Canada. The National Forum on Family Security. *Family Security in Insecure Times*. Ottawa: The National Forum on Family Security, 1993.

Osberg, Lars. "The Measurement of Economic Well-Being." In *Approaches to Economic Well-Being*, ed. David Laidler. Ottawa: The Royal Commission on the Economic Union and Development Prospects for Canada and Ministry of Supply and Services, 1985.

Rawls, J. *A Theory of Justice*. Cambridge: Belknap Press, 1971.

Endnotes

1   The traditional goals for economic policies in Canada (as first enunciated by the now defunct Economic Council of Canada) were full employment, economic growth, price stability, a viable balance of payments, and an equitable distribution of income. (Economic Council of Canada 1964).

1

National Income and Other Measures of Canadian Economic Well-Being

After studying this chapter you will understand both the usefulness and the limitations of national income for measuring economic well-being. You will be familiar with the attempts to design better measures of well-being, and you will be able to explain why there are conflicting data about Canadian economic well-being compared to well-being in other industrialized countries. For example, according to 1990 data, Canada ranked *eleventh* among industrialized countries in terms of gross national product per capita, *fourth* in terms of gross domestic product per capita (adjusted for different purchasing power of currencies), and *second* in terms of the United Nations Human Development Index.

We will begin by examining the measures of economic well-being that centre on national income. To avoid confusion we will make a distinction between utility, welfare, and economic well-being (Osberg, 1985, p. 50). Utility refers to an individual's satisfaction with his or her economic situation at any given time. Welfare is the total utility enjoyed by an individual over a lifetime. Economic well-being is the total welfare of society.

One of the traditional assumptions of economics is that consumers maximize utility, where utility is strictly related to the consumption of goods and services (and leisure). Consumers are assumed to be insatiable in the sense that they will always prefer more goods to fewer goods, even though the additional utility we derive by consuming more of the same good declines. The fourth apple you eat will not give you as much utility as the first. Utility cannot be measured directly for that would involve making a comparison between the utility one person derives from a good and the utility another person derives. If both Dick and Jane say they love apples, can we conclude that they love apples with equal intensity? The utility of one person is also assumed to be independent of that of another. If my best friend, my worst enemy, or my neighbour acquires a Ferrari, my own utility is not affected. There is no envy and no sharing of pleasure.

If one assumes that utility is derived from one's own consumption of goods and services, then one can argue that economic well-being can be measured by the total amount of goods and services produced and consumed in an economy as measured by the gross domestic product (GDP). In this chapter we will look at the limitations of using GDP as a measure of economic well-being and the various suggestions for improving national income accounting. We will also address the question of whether or not an improvement in economic well-being will make us happier. Is economic growth desirable? Finally, we will examine the Canadian data to determine if our economic well-being has improved and how we as Canadians have fared in comparison to people in other countries.

The Calculation and Definition of GDP

National income accounting grew out of the then new economic theories propounded by Keynes during the Great Depression. It was part of a search for a better understanding of the determinants of aggregate economic activity such as output, employment, and the general price level. The current system of national accounts reflects the Keynesian macroeconomic model. According to Keynes, the economy is in equilibrium only when aggregate demand equals aggregate supply. Aggregate supply is the value of all goods and services produced, and aggregate demand is the sum of expenditures on consumption, investment, government expenditure on goods and services, and net exports (the value of exports of goods and services minus the value of imports of goods and services). It should be noted that equilibrium does not necessarily entail full employment. For example, a drop in aggregate demand caused by a decrease in investment spending would lead to an increase in business inventories, a reduction in the production of goods and services (aggregate supply), and an increase in unemployment. The economy will have reached equilibrium at a lower level of output. Similarly, an increase in aggregate demand in the presence of unemployment would lead to an expansion in production and employment until a new equilibrium was reached. It is easy to see why it became crucial for policy makers to have a thorough understanding of the components and determinants of aggregate demand (gross domestic product).

In Keynesian analysis, there are two different ways of measuring the value of the goods and services produced in an economy: the expenditure approach and the income approach. According to the expenditure approach, GDP is the sum of all expenditures in the economy. More precisely,

$$GDP = C + I + G + (X\text{-}M),$$

where C is the value of all the consumption goods and services bought by consumers;

I is all the investment goods bought by consumers (only expenditures on housing are included here) and business; and

G is the value of all the goods and services bought by all levels of government.

Some goods and services bought are imported (M) and should therefore not be counted. Others are exported to foreigners (X) and should be counted. For that reason we add exports and subtract imports from the total (X-M).

The second approach to national income accounting involves adding all incomes generated in the economy. The expenditure on goods and services of all the participants in the economy must by definition be equal to all the incomes generated in the economy (payments to all the factors of production). GDP is the sum of wages and salaries, rents, interest, profits, indirect taxes net of subsidies, and depreciation.

A distinction is made between gross domestic product (GDP) and gross national product (GNP). GNP measures output owned by Canadians and therefore incomes earned by Canadians, while GDP is the value of output produced in Canada. In order to reconcile GDP with GNP, one must add investment income received from non-residents and subtract investment income paid to non-residents. Other common measures of national income are net national product (NNP), which is GNP minus depreciation, and disposable income, which is basically the incomes of individuals after taxes and transfers.

But national income statistics are not perfectly accurate measures of economic activity, because they do not measure the activities in the "underground economy."[1] The underground economy includes illegal activities such as trade in drugs, illegal gambling, and prostitution. The drug trade alone is likely to be valued in billions of dollars. Other activities are not included in the statistics because they are not reported to the authorities, usually to avoid taxes. This appears to be particularly common in the service sector, where some repair people will give a lower price to a customer who pays cash and does not need a receipt.

Estimates of GDP include only the value of market output. Non-market economic activities such as housework or home repairs are excluded from consideration. The housework of paid servants is included in GDP; that of househusbands, housewives, children, and other unpaid household members is not. A meal bought in a restaurant is included, a meal cooked at home is not. Transportation by taxis, rented cars, and buses is included, whereas transportation in your own car is not. The list goes on. The result is that the GDP as a measure of total output may be misleading, particularly if one tries to make comparisons over time or across nations. For example, the unprecedented movement of women into the labour force in the last few decades may have led to a considerable overstatement of the increase in value of output. The care of small children has moved from the households to day-care centres or paid babysitters, the care of elderly relatives to nursing homes or hospitals. Home-cooked meals have given way to fast food.

There are also some offsetting changes. Many people, particularly during economic downturns, are prepared to attempt most types of house maintenance and repairs. And the recent low real price of gasoline may have encouraged people to switch from public transit to private cars.

Leisure is not included in GDP. If an economy can produce the same level of output with less work, one could argue that there has been an improvement in well-being. However, attempts at including leisure are fraught with difficulties, in particular, the calculation of a value for leisure. For example, if leisure is valued at the average wage rate in society and wages increase as a result of improvements in productivity, it implies that over time there is an improved productivity of leisure. That raises the question of how leisure can become more productive. Leisure can mean doing nothing, and to be more productive in doing nothing is a contradiction in terms.

Another difficulty involves the separation between final and intermediate products (Eisner, 1988, p. 1614). Intermediate products are not counted since that would lead to double counting. For example, the value of grain would be counted three times: as grain, as flour, and as bread. For this reason, purchases by consumers and by the government are counted as final, whereas business purchases of goods and services are counted as intermediate (unless they are investment goods or additions to inventories that are also counted as investments). This also leads to anomalies. For example, police services purchased by the government are included in GDP, but the security services purchased by firms are not, because they are considered an intermediate product. Security is presumably necessary for production. However, using the same argument, publicly provided police services could also be considered an intermediate product. We do not get utility from the police, only from the products whose consumption is made safer by the provision of police services. Currently an increase in crime leads to increased GDP if more police services are provided to fight the crime. This increase in GDP hardly signifies an improvement in economic well-being. Police services are **defensive** goods (regrettable necessities) in the sense that they are wants necessary for the satisfaction of other wants. Some of those anomalies would be avoided by excluding the cost of police services from GDP. The same argument could be made for defence and fire protection. And it could be argued that food is obviously a defence against hunger, clothing against cold, and shelter against the weather. However, the classification and exclusion of those goods as defensive would generate much controversy.

Expenditures on investment goods do not include expenditures on training and education (that is, investment in human capital) or expenses related to the creation of new knowledge. This omission contradicts research findings on the determinants of growth. Most studies of the determinants of economic growth attribute economic growth not only to investments in physical capital and growth in the labour force, but also to technological progress and improvements in human capital (Denison 1985). Health expenditures could also be seen as investment in human capital in so far as they lead to a healthier and more productive labour force. However, the conceptual problems of classifying more health and education expenditures as investments are horrendous. For example, some proportion of the costs of attending university is not investment in the future. At least for some students, part of the experience of going to university is having fun. Similarly, how much of health expenditure is maintenance rather than investment? An appendix operation, for example, does not improve future productivity.

There are other inconsistencies in the treatment of investment. The fact that investment goods are included in the national income accounts means that the concept of sustainability is built into the accounts. According to Hicks (1948, p. 172), a person's income is the maximum value that can be consumed in a given period without leaving the person any worse off. Similarly, a country's income is the maximum that can be consumed in a period without leaving it any worse off. If a country saves and invests, it will be better off in the future. If we wear out our capital goods faster than we are replacing them, we are clearly living beyond our means. NNP is meant to measure sustainable income because it is GNP minus depreciation. Is NNP sustainable the way it is calculated? Not really. If a country cuts down its forests, poisons its wildlife, pollutes the air, and fills its rivers and lakes with sewage, is it better off? Most people would argue it is not; the national income figures, however, may suggest that it is. The reasons are twofold: the accounts do not treat natural resources as a stock of capital, nor do they subtract the defensive expenditures necessary to compensate for the negative effects of consumption and production. The grounding of the U.S. supertanker *Exxon Valdez* off the coast of Alaska led to an increase in U.S. GDP of approximately $1 billion (the cost of the clean-up). It is obvious that these types of expenditures are true intermediate products and should be treated as costs of production rather than final products available for consumption (Daly and Cobb, 1989, p. 71).

Natural resources have not figured prominently in neoclassical economics. When economics was developed as a discipline, the scale of human activity was not large enough for scarcity of natural resources to be an issue. The only factors of production that matter in neoclassical economics are labour and capital. Humanly created capital is seen as a close to perfect substitute for natural resources, and therefore the assumption that resources are finite is unrealistic. It is acknowledged, of course, that local scarcities will occur, but it is believed that they can always be overcome with more money and physical capital. "The underlying assumption is that all physical things ultimately consist of the same indestructible matter that is arranged in production, disarranged in consumption, rearranged in production, and so forth. The economy is a closed flow from production to consumption to production again. Nothing is used up, only disarranged." (Daly and Cobb, 1989, p. 194.)

This view of the world is physically impossible because it contradicts the second law of thermodynamics. The first law of thermodynamics supports the circular flow in the economy by asserting the equivalence of matter and energy. Energy (or matter) can neither be created nor destroyed. However, the second law of thermodynamics states that because of entropy the amount of usable energy declines when energy is used. Materials can never be completely recycled. When coal is burnt, it is transformed into heat and ash. It is true that the amount of energy in the heat and the ash is equal to the amount of energy in the original coal, but the energy is too dispersed to be used again, and any process attempting to reconcentrate it would use more energy than it could generate. The whole economic process involves converting raw materials into products and waste materials that can never again be returned to their orignal state. (Daly and Cobb, 1989, p. 194). Each time this process takes place, there is a loss of usable energy.

Capital and natural resources are clearly substitutable within limits, but ultimately they must be complements. Given the environmental crisis that faces us, the complementarity of the two must be recognized. If we assume near-perfect substitutability, Hicksian sustainability would still require us to keep the total amount of capital constant (physical and natural capital). If we run down the natural resources, we would have to compensate for this decline by an equivalent increase of physical capital. On the other hand, if we assume complementarity between capital and natural resources, both physical and natural capital would have to be held intact. Both assumptions require that natural resources be included in in the national income accounts.

Extended Accounts for GDP

There have been numerous attempts at extending the national accounts to give more accurate representations of economic well-being. All of these suffer from the difficulties inherent in such an exercise (Eisner 1988). One of the earliest attempts was by Nordhaus and Tobin (1972), who developed a measure of economic welfare (MEW). They adjusted the conventional accounts by adding imputations for capital services used by governments and households. They included values for non-market work and leisure as well as subtracting the consumption of defensive goods, such as the costs of commuting to work and government expenditures for police, sanitation, road maintenance, and national defence. They also deducted an estimate for the "disamenity" of urban life. They built in sustainability by subtracting not only depreciation, but also the investment necessary to maintain a constant capital-to-output ratio that allows consumption to increase at a rate consistent with population growth and technological progress (Eisner, 1988, p. 1627). Whereas real GNP in the United States had on the average grown by 3.91 percent a year between 1947 and 1965, sustainable measured economic welfare showed an average growth of only 2.07 percent a year.

A similar measure of economic aspects of welfare was constructed by Zolotas (1981). Though he did not go as far as Nordhaus and Tobin in calculating the investment necessary for future consumption, he did subtract estimates for resource depletion and the costs of environmental pollution. On that basis he estimated that the average annual growth rate of real GNP between 1950 and 1977 to be 3.45 percent, while the increase in the economic aspects of welfare averaged 2.02 percent (Eisner, 1988, p. 1635). Other attempts surveyed in Eisner (1988) include those by Jorgenson and Associates, Ruggles and Associates, and Eisner and Associates. In general, the extended accounts suggest a relatively smaller role for business in economic activity and a much expanded role for the non-market sector. This is particularly the case if one includes estimates for investments in health, education, and research performed by households, non-profit institutions, and government.

An index of sustainable economic welfare for the United States was developed by Daly and Cobb (1989) who included income distribution, the depletion of natural resources, and the value of non-market labour. They did not include an estimate for leisure because they considered the conceptual difficulties to be insurmountable. They found that the average annual increase in their index from 1951 to 1986 was 0.53 percent a year, compared to a recorded increase in real per capita GNP of 1.9 percent. The yearly differences, however, were substantial. Whereas the annual growth in the index was 2.01 percent for 1960-70, it was 0.14 percent for 1970-80 and -1.26 between 1980 and 1986. If they excluded estimates for resource depletion, the corresponding figures were 1.97, 0.66, and -0.84 percent.

The method used for the treatment of natural resources was first developed by El Serafy (1988) in a study for the World Bank. One of the difficulties is how to treat receipts from non-renewable resources in definitions of income. Leaving the resources (for example oil) in the ground forever does not benefit anybody. But how could their exploitation be made consistent with sustainable development? El Serafy argues that the revenue from the exploitation from a non-renewable resource should be separated into an income and a capital component. The income component is the portion of receipts that could be consumed annually in perpetuity, assuming that the remainder of the revenue was invested in renewable assets. The yield on the assets should be such that when the non-renewable resource is exhausted, the renewable asset would be yielding the same amount as the income component of the receipt (Daly and Cobb, 1989, p. 73). This method would require a different approach to national income accounting.

Repetto *et al.* (1989), working for the World Resources Institute, have recalculated the national accounts for Indonesia and Costa Rica using basically a very simple procedure in allowing for the depreciation of natural resources. For Indonesia, the researchers concentrated on three natural resources: oil, timber, and soils. In calculating the effect of tree cutting, they estimated the marketable value of timber cut as well as future timber revenues lost on clear-cutting the forest. Each year starts with an opening stock. The stock is added to through growth and reforestation, and estimates for harvesting, deforestation, logging, and fire damage are subtracted. The physical accounts are then put into monetary values through the use of imputed rents (stumpage values) for the standing forests and export prices for what is sold. The deduction of the depletion of the natural resources led to a decrease in the estimated growth rate in GNP for Indonesia from 7.1 to 4 percent between 1971 and 1984.

Smith (1992) constructed a set of similar accounts for the province of Alberta, taking into account the depletion of, and the additions to, the oil and gas reserves of Alberta. Like Repetto he found that growth rates of income and investment during the 1970s and 1980s differ significantly when oil and gas depletion and discoveries are factored into the provincial accounts. The 1970s did not experience the rapid growth in the provincial gross domestic product shown by the conventional accounts, nor did the 1980s experience as serious a slowdown.

GDP as a Measure of Well-Being

In the previous two sections of the chapter we looked at what GDP does and does not include, and what changes could be made to make GDP a better indicator of economic well-being. There have also been considerable efforts to develop more general indicators of well-being, led by the United Nations Development Program (UNDP), which proposed a **human development index** (UNDP 1990). This index is of considerable interest to Canada because in its first version Canadians came out on top. UNDP defined human development

> as a process of enlarging people's choices. In principle, these choices can be infinite and change over time. But at all levels of development, the three essential ones are for people to lead a long and healthy life, to acquire knowledge and to have access to resources needed for a decent standard of living. If these choices are not available many other opportunities remain inaccessible (UNDP, 1993, p. 104).

The index is an unweighted average of measures of longevity, education in terms of literacy and mean years of schooling, and real per capita GDP adjusted for differences in purchasing power between countries.[2]

Despite their shortcomings, GDP and its growth rate are probably the most common indicators of a country's economic well-being. During the Cold War, GDP and its growth rate became paramount in judging which economic system performed best: communism or capitalism. It became part of the struggle for dominance.[3] After the fall of the Soviet Union, the emphasis has shifted towards the performance of the Japanese economy compared to that of the United States, or the performance of the European economies compared to the North American economies. Politicians and parties in most countries are committed to economic progress, which is equated with economic growth as measured by the growth in GDP. Countries are ranked in terms of their per capita GDP. The success or failure of development programs is judged by their effect on per capita GDP.

Recently, the emphasis has also shifted from per capita GDP to the more elusive concept of competitiveness. If a country is competitive, it will presumably maintain or increase its rate of economic growth in the future. Competitiveness is now one of the primary objectives of government policy. Military strategies are replaced by competitive strategies. These two kinds of strategy have much in common. Lester

Thurow's recent book *Head to Head: The Coming Economic Battle Among Japan, Europe, and America* (Thurow 1992) and Michael Porter's *The Competitive Advantage of Nations* (Porter 1990), are both indicative of current thinking.

While most agree that GDP does not measure all aspects of human well-being, it is assumed that economic well-being and other aspects of well-being go hand in hand. Economic progress is assumed to be a good thing. But does it indeed make us happier? The evidence is contradictory. Richard Easterlin (1972) reviewed the evidence in the late sixties. On the basis of ten surveys taken in the United States between 1946 and 1966 and an additional 19 surveys in other countries, he found that without exception people in the highest income groups declared that they were happier on the average than did those in the lowest income group. On the other hand any correlation between income and happiness disappeared if the comparison was made between countries or over time. North Americans were no happier than Europeans, and people in rich countries no happier than people in poor countries. Similarly, even though Americans in 1970 had real per capita incomes 1.7 times higher than in 1947, there was no indication that they were happier in 1970. According to Easterlin, more money for the individual meant more individual happiness, but an increase in incomes for all did not increase the general level of happiness. However, more recent evidence from Canada (Bibby 1990, pp. 85-86) paints a different picture. In 1985, 90 percent of Canadians described themselves as "very happy" or "pretty happy," compared to 85 percent in 1960. Seventy-four percent said their present financial situation left them satisfied, compared to 63 percent in 1963. According to Bibby, Canadians also report higher levels of satisfaction with life than do people elsewhere.

The critics against growth argue that growth or progress is ultimately self-defeating. Fred Hirsch (1978), in his book *The Social Limits to Growth*, explored the links between the utility of one person with that of the utility of other individuals. He argued that as long as material privation is widespread, the conquest of material scarcity is the dominant goal of people. However, as average consumption rises, an increasing proportion of consumption takes on a social as well as an individual aspect. A person's utility depends not only on his or her own consumption, but on that of others as well. My utility from expenditure on education depends not only on the education level I will attain, but also on the education level of everybody else. My utility from a car and from a summer cottage depends not only on what I have, but also on how much everybody else has. Hirsch makes a distinction between **the material economy** and **the positional economy**. The positional economy relates to goods, services, and work positions that are scarce in some absolute or socially imposed sense, or subject to congestion or crowding through more extensive use. (Hirsch, 1978, p. 27).

The striving for positional goods is ultimately self-defeating:

> What the wealthy have today can no longer be delivered to the rest of us tomorrow; yet as we individually grow richer, that is what we expect. The dynamic interaction between material and positional sectors becomes malign. Instead of alleviating the unmet demands on the economic system, material growth at this point exacerbates them. The locus of instability is the divergence between what is possible for the individual and what is possible for all individuals. Increased material resources enlarge the demand for positional goods, a demand that can be satisfied for some only by frustrating demand by others. The intensified positional competition involves an increase in needs for the individual, in the sense that additional resources are required to achieve a given level of welfare. In the positional sector, individuals chase each other's tails. The race gets longer for the same prize. (Hirsch, 1978, p. 67).

In other words, if society has reached a certain level of material welfare, any further increase in general welfare does not seem to make us happier, unless you or I become better off and everybody else stays the same. In that sense everybody cannot become happier, and the quest for more material goods is ultimately self-defeating. "Affluence is obviously more agreeable when it is a minority condition."[4] Does that mean that economic growth should be abandoned as a goal to strive for? Arthur Lewis wrote in 1954:

The advantage of economic growth is not that wealth increases happiness, but that it increases the range of human choice... We certainly cannot say that an increase in wealth makes people happier. We cannot say, either, that an increase in wealth makes people less happy, and even if we could say this, it would not be a decisive argument against economic growth, since happiness is not the only good thing in life. We do not know what the purpose of life is, but if it were happiness, then evolution might just as well have stopped a long time ago, since there is no reason to believe that men are happier than pigs or than fishes. What distinguishes men from pigs is that men have greater control over their environment; not that they are more happy. And on this test economic growth is greatly to be desired. The case for economic growth is that it gives man greater control over his environment and thereby increases his freedom (Lewis, 1954, p. 420–21).[5]

This argument still holds for the majority of countries in the world. Even if affluence makes us unhappy, most people in poor countries would not mind sharing our brand of unhappiness. It appears that most ordinary people want more material goods, and the fact that the industrialized countries now want everybody to restrict their use of the cheap fossil fuels needed to produce these goods in order to curtail global warming is not well received by poor countries. To improve conditions for poor countries without economic growth would be politically impossible, for an increase in the welfare of some could not be achieved without a decrease in the welfare of others. With growth, some people's incomes can grow without the need for reducing the incomes of others. Growth also makes structural adjustments easier. For example, people are more likely to accept the closing of a factory if other sectors of the economy are growing.

However, in order to argue for a continuation of growth one would have to add a qualification. The growth we are talking about is not increases in per capita GDP as it is currently calculated. We must talk, rather, about sustainable income in the Hicksian sense or sustainable development in the Brundtland sense, making full allowance for any deterioration of the natural environment.

Canadian Economic Well-Being

From our earlier discussion, it is obvious that there is no single ideal measure of economic well-being and that the current national income accounts have serious shortcomings. With these qualifications in mind, we will look at a variety of measures of Canadian well-being. Figure 1.1 gives the growth rates of real GDP and GDP per capita. It is clear that the Canadian economy has grown rapidly since 1961 but that the rate of growth has slowed down in recent years. Between 1960 and 1970, real GDP grew by 65.34 percent, between 1970 and 1980 by 56.44 percent, and between 1980 and 1990 by 32.63 percent. Real GDP per capita showed a similar pattern. It grew by 38.77 percent, 36.98 percent, and 26.42 percent.

This slowdown in the rate of growth has been observed in most countries. Even though the rates do not appear to have changed much, the effects are substantial because of compounding. For example, a per capita income growing at 4 percent a year will double every 18 years. A per capita income growing at 2 percent will double in 35 years. The slowdown in growth rates can be attributed to a slowdown in productivity growth, but the reasons for the productivity slowdown are not clear.[6] This issue will be discussed further in the chapter on competitiveness.

How do our national income data compare to those of other countries? Table 1.1 ranks countries according to GNP per capita in U.S. dollars, GDP per capita with adjustments for different purchasing power among countries, and according to the UNDP Human Development Index. GDP is a more accurate measure of economic activity than of income or well-being. GDP is a measure of economic activity in the country, whereas GNP measures net income generated by our residents. In Canada, because of our indebtedness to foreigners, GDP is always greater than GNP. In 1960, GNP as a proportion of GDP was 98.4 percent; in 1970, 98.5 percent; in 1980, 97.47 percent; and in 1990, 96.4 percent. The results of comparisons using the different methods are considerably different. In 1990 Canada ranked eleventh in terms of GNP per capita but fourth in terms of GDP per capita adjusted for purchasing power (a change from 1987 when we ranked third). According to the

Human Development Index, we are in second place, having lost our first place to Japan because of Japan's rapidly growing per capita GDP. It is clear that, compared to most countries in the world, we are very well-off.

As pointed out above, GDP figures do not include the "underground economy" or non-market activities. Estimates of the size of the underground economy are particularly problematic. Mireille (1985), on the basis of increases in the use of cash (the underground economy tends to use cash), estimated the size of the Canadian underground economy to be 5 to 8 percent of GNP. A new study reported in *The Globe and Mail* (May 21, 1993), using the same methodology, estimated that the introduction of the GST in 1989 significantly increased the size of the underground economy, leading to an underestimation of GNP of 0.8 percent.

Statistics Canada has some estimates for the value of housework (Jackson 1992). They were derived from the 1986 General Social Survey on the daily activities of Canadians. The survey asked a sample of

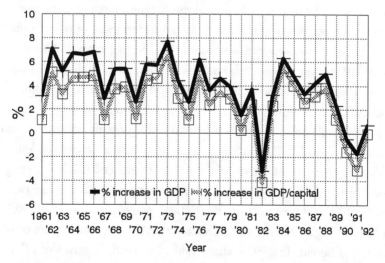

Figure 1.1
Canadian Growth Rates of GDP and GDP
per Capita, 1961-1992 (1986 prices)

Source: The Canadian Economic Observer, Historical Statistical Supplement, 1992-93, Tables 1.3 and 11.1.

9,946 people about the time they devoted to various activities on pre-assigned days of the week during November and December of 1986. There are three methods of putting a value on household work: **the opportunity-cost method, the market alternative-housekeeper cost method,** and **the market alternative or individual-function-cost method** (Eisner, 1988, p. 1673-674). The opportunity-cost method is based on the assumption that an hour allocated to household work takes away an hour of paid work. Therefore the method entails multiplying the time spent on housework by the average after-tax wages of those involved. The second method is based on the notion of replacement cost, where the time spent on household work is valued at the wage rate for domestic workers. The third method is a variant of the second. It decomposes household activities into cooking, cleaning, child care, and so on, and applies a different wage rate to each.

Statistics Canada provides parallel estimates for both the first and the third method. It refers to the first method as the opportunity-cost method and the third as the replacement-cost method. The value of household work in Canada for 1986, using the opportunity-cost method, was estimated at $159.4 billion (31.5 percent of GDP). The replacement-cost method gave higher estimates: $198.9 billion (39.3 percent) of GDP. This can be attributed to an average hourly replacement cost for household work of $9.61, compared with an opportunity cost of $7.71. If the value of household work were added to GDP, the average overall growth rate between 1981 and 1986 would decline by 0.5 percent.

There was also a decline in the relative importance of household work in the same period. Aggregate hours of household work relative to hours of paid work declined from 99.2 percent in 1981 to 97.7 percent in 1986 (Jackson, 1992, p. 3.13). Much of the change can be attributed to the increased employment rate of married women and to the general increase in economic activity. There are substantial provincial variations: the highest proportion of household work was in Newfoundland and the lowest in Alberta and the Northwest Territories. The estimates for Canada are consistent with those for other countries, where the estimates for the value of economic services produced by households is equal to about one-third of GNP (Eisner 1988).

TABLE 1.1

Ranking of Selected Countries by Three Measures
of Economic Well-Being, 1990

Country	Human Development Index	GNP/cap (U.S.$)	GDP/cap (PPP$[a])	GDP/cap growth (%) 1960-90 (PPP$[a])
Japan	1	25,840 (3)[b]	17,616 (6)[c]	552
Canada	2	20,380 (11)	19,232 (4)	148
Norway	3	22,830 (6)	16,028 (15)	194
Switzerland	4	32,250 (1)	20,874 (2)	124
Sweden	5	23,780 (5)	17,014 (8)	162
United States	6	21,810 (10)	21,449 (1)	115
Australia	7	16,560 (16)	16,051 (14)	123
France	8	19,590 (12)	17,407 (7)	226
Netherlands	9	17,570 (15)	15,695 (17)	181
United Kingdom	10	16,080 (17)	15,804 (16)	148
Iceland	11	22,090 (9)	16,496 (11)	208
Germany	12	22,360 (8)	18,213 (5)	202
Denmark	13	22,440 (7)	16,781 (9)	167
Finland	14	24,540 (4)	16,446 (12)	165
Austria	15	19,000 (13)	16,504 (10)	165
Belgium	16	17,580 (14)	16,381 (13)	164
New Zealand	17	12,570 (18)	13,481 (18)	134
Luxembourg	18	29,010 (2)	19,244 (3)	192

Source: Adapted from UNDP (1993), Table 31.
[a] Purchasing power parity
[b] Ranking for GNP/cap
[c] Ranking for GDP/cap

As noted above, the economic value of leisure has been included in many of the attempts to establish measures of economic well-being, the reason being that if the same level of GNP can be achieved with less work, there must have been an increase in economic well-being. Usher (1980) estimated that the annual average growth rate in the Canadian real GNP per capita between 1935 and 1974 was 3.34 percent. If the growth in leisure time was included, the rate increased to 3.88 percent.

The General Social Survey gives some interesting information on leisure time. In 1986, Canadians spent 7.5 hours a day (averaged over a whole week) on productive activity, which included paid work, education, and unpaid work (domestic chores, primary child care, and shopping) (Harvey et al. 1991). We spent 11 hours on sleeping, eating, and personal care and had 5.5 hours of free time.[7]

Table 1.2 shows how this compares to other countries. Canadians, in so far as these figures are comparable, spend a slightly less than average amount of time on productive activities and a slightly more than average amount on personal care and have a slightly more than average amount of free time. Does that mean that we are better or worse off than the other countries in the table? The fact that we spend a relatively small amount on productive activities but still have a higher per capita GDP than these countries would indicate we are better off.

Other commonly used indicators of well-being are life expectancy and infant mortality rates. Indeed, life expectancy is integrated into the United Nations Human Development Index. We tend to associate well-being with a long life, and economic affluence has been associated with a gradual increase in life expectancy. Usher (1980) imputed a value for improvement in life expectancy to his estimates for economic growth in Canada between 1935 and 1974. The estimate for average per capita growth if leisure and life expectancy were included increased from 3.34 to 4.38 percent. As can be seen in Table 1.3, we live longer than people in the United States but not as long as people in Sweden, Switzerland, and Japan.

Infant mortality rates are also used as indicators of well-being. Infant mortality rates drop rapidly when a country can afford adequate health care and nutrition for all of its citizens. Here again, we rate bet-

TABLE 1.2
Intercountry Comparison of Time Allocation

Country	Hours per Day Productive	Personal	Free
Australia	7.2	10.70	6.10
Canada	7.5	11.00	5.50
Finland	7.7	9.80	5.50
France	8.0	12.00	4.00
Japan	7.8	10.40	5.80
Average	7.6	10.78	5.38

Source: Harvey et al. (1991).

ter than the United States but worse than Japan and Sweden (see Table 1.3). It is likely that an affluent country with a relatively even income distribution such as Sweden will have lower infant mortality rates and higher life expectancy than a country like Canada where the gap between the rich and the poor is larger. We will look at our distribution of income in Chapter 6.

Do our national accounts indicate that our living is sustainable? Are we living beyond our means? There are three ways of looking at this issue: one is within a framework of future income, a second is in terms of our government deficits and the accumulation of debt; and a third is in terms of the environment. The sustainability of our environment is such a large topic that the discussion of it will be postponed to Chapters 3 and 4. The issue of whether or not we are generating sufficient investments in human, physical, and knowledge capital for our economy to continue to expand will be left to Chapter 7.

The federal government debt increased from approximately 11 percent of GDP in 1981 to 49 percent of GDP in 1991. In this, Canada is not alone (see Table 1.4). The United States has seen a similar debt explosion. Nevertheless, the rate of increase in our debt between

TABLE 1.3
Socio-Economic Indicators of Well-Being, Selected Countries, 1991

Country	Life Expectancy (years)	Infant Mortality per 1,000 population
Australia	77	8
Belgium	76	8
Canada	77	7
France	77	7
Germany	76	7
Italy	77	9
Japan	79	5
Mexico	70	39
Netherlands	77	7
New Zealand	75	10
Sweden	78	6
United Kingdom	76	8
Switzerland	78	7
United States	76	9

Source: Adapted from World Bank (1993).

1980 and 1986 was not surpassed by any other OECD country (Heil-broner and Bernstein, 1989, p. 124).

Will this debt cause a burden for our children or grandchildren? Have we mortgaged the future? There are several issues involved here. If the government went into debt in order to invest in productive facilities, the new income generated could more than cover the interest payments. We cannot tell if that is what happened because the government does not keep accounts in the same way as a business. Capital expenses are not written off gradually, but are entered as an expense in the same year as they occur. On the other hand, if a debt is incurred to finance current consumption, the debt has to be serviced by either raising taxes

TABLE 1.4

Net Public Debt as a Proportion of GDP Selected Countries, 1991

Country	Debt as a Percentage of GDP
Belgium	121.3
Canada	49.3
Denmark	27.7
France	27.1
Germany	23.1
Italy	102.7
Japan	5.9
Netherlands	55.9
United Kingdom	30.0
United States	34.0

Source: Adapted from OECD (1993).

or printing money (an option the provincial governments do not have). Servicing the part of the debt that is owed to Canadian residents is in theory not a problem since it involves raising money from one group of people in the country in order to pay another group of people: the bondholders (which are corporations, insurance companies, and private citizens).[8] However, the servicing of the foreign debt imposes a burden on current and future generations because money must leave the country. An increasing proportion of our debt is held by non-residents.

How did we get into this mess? Most of the problem dates back to the 1982-83 recession, when the deficit jumped from $1.2 billion in 1981 to $17.5 billion in 1982. The recession, combined with high inflation rates, led to inflated entitlements, high interest payments on public debt, and low tax revenues. Between 1981 and 1982 expenditures increased by 18 percent while revenues increased by only 6 percent. In the absence of any evidence that the federal government used the deficit to finance productive investments, we will have to argue that the debt is an indication that our current consumption is not sustainable. We have imposed a burden on future generations. Part of our high living standards has resulted from living beyond our means.[9]

Conclusions

In this chapter we have looked at various measures of economic well-being with an emphasis on the national accounts. We first examined what the national accounts measured, and the extent to which they gave an indication of well-being. We also looked at various attempts to improve the accounts by including natural resources, leisure, and household production and by excluding defensive goods such as police services and fire protection. The evidence indicates that our current methods of keeping the national accounts lead to an overstatement of improvements in well-being. We briefly discussed the United Nations Human Development Index and the extent to which there is a correlation between economic growth and happiness. We then turned to an evaluation of Canadian economic well-being. Compared to most countries we are doing very well; indeed, the United Nations Human Development Index puts us in second place behind Japan in terms of our human development, and we are among the top five in terms of real GDP per capita. However, the growth rate of our national debt indicates that our current standard of living is not sustainable. We did not discuss three very important features of well-being: the state of the environment, our income distribution, and our employment situation. The next chapters will deal with those topics.

TOPICS FOR DISCUSSION

1. How would you construct an index of economic well-being for a) students b) "yuppies"?

2. Do you see any evidence that material well-being is becoming less important for Canadians?

3. Ninety percent of Canadians described themselves as "very happy" or "pretty happy" in 1985, and 74 percent said they were satisfied with their current financial situation. Do you think you would get the same result if the same survey were done today?

RECOMMENDED READING

For an excellent study of the development of the idea that economic growth is desirable see *The Rise and Fall of Economic Growth* by H.W. Arndt (1978). Another classic is *Social Limits to Growth* by Fred Hirsch (1978). Both are suitable for undergraduates.

References

Auerbach, Alan J., Jagadeesh Gokhale, and Lawrence J. Kotlikoff. "Generational Accounting: A Meaningful Way to Evaluate Fiscal Policy." *The Journal of Economic Perspectives* 8 (Winter 1994): 73-95.

Arndt, H. W. *The Rise and Fall of Economic Growth*. Chicago: The University of Chicago Press, 1984.

Bibby, Reginald W. *Mosaic Madness: The Poverty and Potential of Life in Canada*. Toronto: Stoddart Publishing Company, 1990.

Canada. Department of the Secretary of State of Canada. *Profile of Higher Education in Canada*. [Ottawa]: Ministry of Supply and Services, 1992.

Canada. Ministry of Supply and Services. *Where Does Time Go?* [Ottawa]: 1991. Prepared by the Ministry of Supply and Services, Andrew Harvey.

Daly, Herman E., and John B. Cobb Jr. *For the Common Good: Redirecting the Economy toward Community, the Environment, and a Sustainable Future*. Boston: Beacon Press, 1989.

Denison, Edward. *Trends in American Economic Growth 1929-1982*. Washington D.C.: The Brookings Institute, 1985.

Easterlin, R.A. "Does Money Buy Happiness?" *The Public Interest* 30 (1973): 3-10.

Eisner, Robert. "Extended Accounts for National Income and Product." *Journal of Economic Literature* 25 (December 1988): 1611-85.

El Serafy, Salah, "The Proper Calculation of Income from Depletable Natural Resources." In *Environmental Resource Accounting* eds. Ernest Lutz and Salah El Serafy (1988):

Ethier, Mireille. "The Underground Economy. A Review of the Literature and New Estimates for Canada." In *Income Distribution*, Research Coordinator Francois Vaillancourt (1985): p. 77-111.

Fischer, Stanley. "Symposium on the Slowdown in Productivity Growth." *Journal of Economic Perspectives* 2 (Fall 1988): 3-9.

The Globe and Mail "Underground economy answer to high taxes." (Toronto), May 21, 1993.

Heilbroner, Robert and Peter Bernstein. *The Debt and the Deficit: False Alarms and Real Possibilities.* New York: W.W. Norton, 1989.

Hicks, John R. *Value and Capital*, 2nd ed. Oxford: Clarendon Press, 1948.

Hirsch, Fred. *Social Limits to Growth: A Twentieth Century Fund Study.* Cambridge: Harvard University Press, 1978.

Jackson, Chris. "The Value of Household Work in Canada, 1986." *The Canadian Economic Observer* (June 1992): 3.1-3.15.

Laidler, David research coordinator. In *Approaches to Economic Well-Being.* [Toronto]: The University of Toronto Press, 1985. Prepared for Royal Commission on the Economic Union and Development Prospects for Canada.

Lewis, W. A. *The Theory of Economic Growth.* London: Allen & Unwin, 1955.

Lutz, Ernst and Salah El Serafy eds. *Environmental and Resource Accounting and Their Relevance to the Measurement of Sustainable Income.* Washington D.C.: The World Bank, 1988.

Nordhaus, William D., and James Tobin. *Economic Growth.* New York: The National Bureau for Economic Research, 1972.

OECD. *Economic Outlook, December 1993* Paris: OECD, 1993.

Osberg, Lars. "The Measurement of Economic Well-Being." In *Approaches to Economic Well-Being*, ed. David Laidler (1985): 49-89.

Porter, Michael. *The Competitive Advantage of Nations.* New York: The Free Press, 1990.

Repetto, Robert. *Wasting Assets: Natural Resources in the National Income Accounts.* The World Resources Institute, 1989.

Smith, Roger S. "Income Growth, Government Spending, and Wasting Assets: Alberta's Oil and Gas." *Canadian Public Policy - Analyse de Politiques* 28 (December 1992): 387-413.

Thurow, Lester. *Head to Head: The Coming Economic Battle Among Japan, Europe and America.* New York: William Morrow & Co. Inc., 1992.

Usher, Dan. *The Measurement of Economic Growth.* New York: Columbia University Press, 1980.

Vaillancourt, Francois, Research Coordinator. *Income Distribution and Economic Security in Canada.* Toronto: The University of Toronto Press, 1985. Prepared Royal Commission on the Economic Union and Development Prospects for Canada.

United Nations Development Program. *Human Development Report 1990.* New York: Oxford University Press, 1990.

United Nations Development Program. *Human Development Report 1993.* New York: Oxford University Press, 1993.

World Bank. *The World Development Report, 1993.* Washington D.C.: The World Bank, 1992.

Zolotas, Xenophon. *Economic Growth and Declining Social Welfare.* Athens: Bank of Greece, 1981.

Endnotes

1   For a thorough discussion of what GNP measures, see Eisner (1988).

2   For a discussion of the index, see UNDP (1993), p. 104-14.

3   For an excellent survey of the importance of economic growth as a policy goal, see Arndt (1978).

4   Arndt (1984), p. 145. The quote is attributed to Anthony Crosland. Much of the criticism against economic growth voiced during the 1960s and 1970s was self-serving. It came across as an indictment by the economic elite of the discomforts that they claimed to suffer when a larger segment of the population acquired cars and had the opportunity to travel and spoil the countryside. Travel, until then, had been reserved for the privileged.

5   The quote is taken from Arndt (1984) p. 71.

6   For a survey of possible explanation, see Fischer *et al.* (1988).

7   The survey also indicates the difference between males and females. Males averaged 4.7 hours a day on paid work and 1.9 hours on unpaid work. Females averaged 2.5 hours on paid work and 4.1 hours on unpaid work. Employed women do 2.3 hours of housework a day; employed men do 1.7 hours. Television viewing takes up 40 percent of free time. Men watch 2.6 hours a day and women 2.1 hours.

8   This is somewhat simplistic. For further discussion of this point, see Chapter 9.

9   Economists in the United States have introduced the concept of **generational** accounting where it is estimated how much each generation can expect to pay now and later in taxes (Auerbach *et al.* 1994).

2

The Environmental Challenge and the Economics of the Environment

This chapter introduces the basic principles of environmental economics, which will assist you in understanding the following two chapters. In particular, it explains the concept of sustainable development, the theory behind market-based approaches to pollution control, and benefit-cost analysis.

So far in our examination of economic well-being in Canada, we have omitted the environment. Yet, the environment is an important component of well-being in several respects. First, the environment has a direct effect on the quality of our lives. Most of us like to be able to breathe clean air, drink clean water, and eat non-contaminated food. A lack of any of these is likely to affect our individual welfare in the sense that there will be repercussions on our health. We would also like to have an opportunity to enjoy an unspoilt environment if we so choose. Second, many Canadians earn a living from our natural resources, both from industries based on renewable resources (forestry, pulp and paper, fish, agriculture, and tourism) and from non-renewable resources such as oil, gas, and minerals. Frequently, the amenity value of the environment is in stark conflict with its resource value. The recent clashes between logging companies and environmentalists on the West Coast of Canada and the United States come to mind. Third, Canada has embraced the notion of sustainable development. Is our use of our resources sustainable, or are we compromising the future well-being of our children?

This chapter, which is the first of three to deal with different aspects of the environment, gives a brief review of environmental economics as a necessary background to the discussion in the following chapters. A survey of the environmental issues over the last few decades is followed by a discussion of sustainable development. The chapter then details two aspects of environmental economics: the rationale for using market-based approaches to pollution control and the use of cost-benefit analysis in decision making.

The Environmental Challenge and Sustainable Development

Concern about the global environment is not new. Paul Ehrlich's book *The Population Bomb*, first published in 1968, expresssed the prevalent concern in the 1960s about the dangers inherent in the population explosion. He predicted that between 1973 and 1983, 25 percent of the world's population would starve to death. The world would continue to be in a state of famine unless drastic measures were taken to limit population growth.[1] The rate of increase in food production, however, surpassed population growth in most parts of the world because of the improvements in agricultural technology that became known as the "Green Revolution." This involved the development of high-yielding forms of grains, specifically adapted to local conditions in the developing countries. Despite these developments, famine still persists, particularly in Africa, and even in rich countries some people do not get enough to eat. However the famine is caused by poverty and inadequate or insecure distribution networks rather than a shortage of food in the world as a whole. In 1972, the Club of Rome, in its report *The Limits to Growth* (Meadows *et al.* 1972), made dire predictions of an imminent shortage of non-renewable resources. Using simulations from a large computer model, the authors predicted that unless everybody started to economize on non-renewable resources, the world would run out of resources in the middle of the twenty-first century and have living standards far lower than the current ones. They even suggested that all economic growth had to be stopped immediately. Though the oil crisis of 1973 seemed to confirm the seriousness of the situation, in fact the crisis was political and was not caused by any real shortage of oil. Today, the danger of running out of non-renewable natural resources seems remote, even though some resources, such as conventional crude oil, will become scarce. What the earlier predictions of impending disaster did not take into account was the changes in technology referred to in Part I and the power of the price mechanism to encourage both conservation and substitution. When oil became expensive, people switched to smaller cars, installed more insulation in their homes, and in general wasted less energy.

Once again predictions of disaster are in vogue. There is increased concern about desertification, deforestation, the increase in the number of endangered species, the contamination of ground water by toxic substances, acid rain, global warming, and the thinning of the ozone layer. The emphasis is now on renewable resources in the wider sense, the threat is to the global environment as we know it. Some of the resources that have become the scarcest are unpolluted air, water, and soil. The difference between the situation today and that in the 1970s is probably that the dangers are now better documented and are therefore taken more seriously. The problems of the environment also appear to affect people more directly than they did earlier. In Canada we worry about the disposal of garbage and toxic wastes, the increased risk of skin cancer from the sun, the effects of food additives, and the disappearance of the codfish. In poor countries a lack of clean drinking water, a shortage of firewood for cooking, serious air pollution, and soil erosion create daily problems of survival for a large part of the population.

In 1983, environmental concerns led to the establishment by the United Nations General Assembly of the World Commission on Environment and Development (known as the Brundtland Commission after its chair, Gro Harlem Brundtland). In its report, *Our Common Future* (World Commission on Environment and Development 1987), the commission points out that development in both rich and poor countries is inseparable from the environment. Therefore all nations need to adopt a different approach to development; an approach that integrates production with the conservation and enhancement of natural resources and that links both to equitable access to resources and an adequate livelihood for all. The commissioners emphasize the concept of **sustainable development**, which they define as "development that meets the needs of the present without compromising the ability of future generations to meet their own needs" (World Commission on Environment and Development, 1987, p. 43). Unlike the report of the Club of Rome, *Our Common Future* does not rule out economic growth provided it is sustainable. It is only sustainable if it is environmentally sound.

Many governments, including ours, have adopted sustainable development as a policy without much debate about what it really means (Canada, 1990, p. 5). The World Bank in its *World Development Report 1992* embraces sustainability as a guide for all World Bank projects. There will also be a new commission on sustainable development operating under the auspices of the United Nations.

Sustainable development explicitly considers the interests of future generations.[2] Sustainability implies distributing rights and assets across generations in such a way that human well-being is sustained over time (Howarth and Norgaard 1992). It is argued that this means a shift from economic growth based on the depletion of non-renewable resources toward growth based on renewable resources. In particular, it is likely that the need for renewable resources of future generations will be just as great as ours. Therefore, it is our responsibility to use renewable natural resources in a manner that does not decrease their usefulness for future generations. This means that renewable resources have to be "harvested" on a sustained-yield basis. Examples of resources that have been mined rather than harvested sustainably are fish, rain forests, soils, whales, and elephants.

Goodland and Ledec (1987, p. 37) also argue that sustainable development implies non-renewable resources should be used in a way that does not prevent future generations from using them. Scrap metal should, for instance, be recycled rather than discarded. Non-renewable energy resources should be depleted slowly enough to ensure an orderly transition to renewable energy sources (for example solar, wood, and wind) when non-renewable resources become more expensive because of their scarcity.

Constanza (1991, p. 87) defines sustainable consumption to be the amount of consumption that can continue indefinitely without depleting the capital. Capital includes not only the traditional machinery and equipment, but also natural capital (soil, biomass, and mineral deposits). Every project should be scrutinized for its sustainability. For renewable resources the rate of harvest should not exceed regeneration at the optimal level of biomass, and rates of waste should not exceed the assimilative capacity of the environment. For non-renewable resources, the rate of depletion should be matched by the development of renewable substitutes.

The notion of sustainability as described above is not without its critics among mainstream economists. Solow (1993) argues that sustainability should not be interpreted on a resource-by-resource basis as an obligation to use every resource sustainably. Rather, sustainability is an obligation to preserve the capacity to be well-off through investments in general (in capital, knowledge, education, or renewable resources). Whether or not Solow is right depends on what assumptions are made about the complementarity or substitutability of resources and capital. Like most economists, Solow assumes that capital and resources are substitutable. (See the arguments by Daly and Cobb in the previous chapter). Solow (p. 185) also makes the valid point that "there is something inconsistent about people who profess to be terribly concerned about the welfare of future generations, but do not seem to be terribly concerned about the welfare of poor people today."

The Use of Market Incentives in Pollution Control

Environmental economics is a relatively new field within the economics discipline, a field that has grown out of the theory of public goods and externalities (spillover effects), both of which are examples of market failure.[3] Economists believe that environmental degradation results from a failure of markets and that therefore it can best be dealt with by measures that try to correct the deficiencies of the market.[4]

One of the basic tenets of neoclassical economics is that competitive markets guarantee the attainment of efficiency, a state in which the largest output can be achieved with the least use of resources and in which no one can be made better off without making somebody else worse off.

Efficiency can only be achieved if markets operate perfectly. Perfectly competitive markets require that producers and consumers be rational and have all the information necessary to make rational choices. Consumers consume only to maximize their own utility, and producers produce to maximize their profits. Consumers' utilities are independent of each other, and one producer's activity has no influence on another producer's productive capabilities either in a positive or negative way. No producer or consumer is big enough to have any command over the market price. If any of these conditions is absent, market failure will result. Examples of such market failures are the existence of public goods, the presence of monopolies, and externalities. Government has a duty to correct such a failure with taxes, subsidies, or regulations.[5]

Public goods have the characteristic that their use by one person does not diminish their use by other people. They provide benefits to more than one person simultaneously. Examples of public goods are defence, police protection, wilderness reserves, lighthouses, biodiversity, and scientific knowledge. My pleasure in the knowledge that there are large wilderness areas set aside in Canada is not diminished by the fact that other people have the same pleasure. No one can be excluded from the consumption of public goods, and for that reason public goods will not be provided for privately, through the market. Money could not be raised to finance them. If someone refused to pay for a public good, that person could still enjoy the good as long as some other people were prepared to pay. People would choose to act as *free riders* on the benevolence of other people. Therefore public goods must be provided by governments and financed out of taxes; otherwise they would not be provided at all.

The presence of externalities violates the assumption that one person's production or consumption does not affect another person's production or consumption. Both beneficial (positive externalities) and harmful (negative externalities) effects are pervasive in society. Examples of negative externalities are the smoking of cigarettes, the production and use of ozone-destroying chemicals, the dumping of sewage into rivers, and the use of highways at rush hour.[6] Positive externalities include such activities as inoculating your pet against rabies, planting a beautiful garden that gives pleasure to your neighbours as well as you, and conducting research which leads to the development of an AIDS vaccine. Even learning to read and write can be seen to have positive spillover effects since it is unlikely that a modern democratic society could function if most of its citizens didn't have basic literacy and numeracy.

The market failure associated with externalities could be corrected and resourcers allocated more efficiently if producers and consumers were made to take these side effects into consideration. The market by itself can only deal with the costs and benefits that accrue to the individual producer and consumer. Each producer balances marginal cost against marginal revenue in determining how much to produce. If marginal cost is less than marginal revenue, profit maximization dictates that more should be produced; if marginal cost is more than marginal revenue, less should be produced. But producers that create pollution also equate marginal costs with marginal revenue. The problem is that they do not include everything. They should take into account not only the marginal cost to their own firms, but also the costs that are imposed on the rest of society. Producers should equate marginal social cost with marginal social revenue (or benefit). This would result in an efficient use of resources, assuming that the producers operated under perfect competition. The market in equating marginal cost with marginal revenue overproduces the good, because in reality it operates in a situation where marginal social cost is greater than marginal social revenue. The market failure could be corrected if the government imposed a per unit tax on polluting producers, equivalent to the cost imposed on society. Similarly if the producer's activity had beneficial effects on society, the producer would produce a less than optimal level of output, since in this case marginal social revenue (benefit) would be higher than the firm's own marginal revenue. The producer should therefore be encouraged to produce more of the product by receiving a subsidy equivalent to the benefit the rest of society derives from his or her production. That is why most countries subsidize R&D.

In practice, the government agency responsible for controlling pollution has three options in dealing with polluting firms. It can institute a tax on pollution (an emissions fee). The tax would charge the polluters for the value of the clean air or water that they use free of charge. In theory, the optimum level of the tax would be where the marginal costs of reducing emissions equalled the marginal benefits to society of reducing emissions (see Figure 2.1). In practice, the government could meter emissions and bill the companies for the amount of pollutants they emitted, thus giving the firms an incentive to cut back. A second option would be for the government to sell or auction permits that would allow the firms to emit a specified quantity of pollutants. It can be shown that this option can produce the same result as the first. Either the authorities can set the price or the effluent charge and achieve a certain level of pollution abatement (the first option), or they can achieve the same level of abatement by issuing the requisite number of permits and allow the bidding among polluters to determine the market-clearing price of the permits (the second option).

The third option, which is most commonly chosen by governments, is to impose mandatory controls. It is politically popular because the message is obvious. Polluters know what is expected of them, and citizens know what is being done by the government. However, it can be easily shown that mandatory controls impose a substantial cost on society.[7] Regulations inflict high costs on some polluters and low costs on others. Blinder (1988, p. 41) quotes a study in St. Louis which found that the cost of cutting particulate emissions from its boiler was $4 a ton for a manufactuer of paper products but $600 a ton for a brewery. If the two firms were ordered to cut their emissions by an equal amount, the abatement cost for the paper plant would be low but for the brewery very large. Assume instead that an emissions tax of $100 a ton is imposed. The paper-products firm will cut back on pollution because it can save $100 in taxes at a cost of $4. Any firm whose abatement costs are less than $100 a ton will find it profitable to

Figure 2.1

Marginal Costs and Benefits of Emissions Reductions

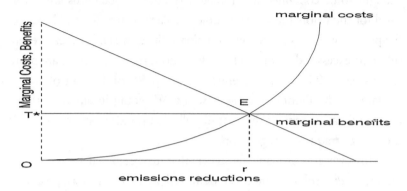

The graph recognizes that pollution clean-up will come at increasing costs (the marginal cost curve has a positive slope), and that additional benefits of clean-up will become gradually smaller (the marginal benefit curve has a negative slope). The optimum clean-up point is at E, where the marginal benefits of emissions reductions equals the marginal costs of reductions. This point also determines the optimum pollution tax OT*. If the tax is set at OT*, the optimum clean-up E will be achieved. At any clean-up less than or, the producer would lose money because the tax he or she had to pay would be greater than the cost of clean-up. Similarly, to the right of r, any further reductions would be too costly compared to the tax (the producer would rather pay the tax than reduce emissions further).

cut back on pollution. The brewery will not, so it will continue to pollute and pay the tax of $100 a ton.

Many environmentalists, however, do not like the idea that some firms will still be allowed to continue polluting. They argue that mandatory proportional reductions seem to be fairer. However, they provide no incentive to minimize the cost to society of environmental clean-up, nor any incentive to cut pollution beyond the legislated minimum. In the example of the two firms, a two-ton reduction in emissions shared equally between the two firms would cost society $604 a year. The same reduction of two tons would cost only $8 if the paper firm did all of the abatement.

There are many examples of market-based approaches. Chant, McFetridge, and Smith (1990, p. 78-79) report that many Canadian municipalities use effluent charges. The City of Winnipeg has had a system of sewer surcharges since 1958. France, Germany, and the

Netherlands have used effluent fees for water pollution for several decades.[8] In the United States there have been short trials of tradable emissions through the "bubble" policy. A group of polluters are thought to be contained in an imaginary bubble. Standards are developed for the whole imaginary bubble and each firm is allocated a target for pollution. Firms for whom emission reduction is not expensive can sell their excess reductions to firms for whom such reductions are more expensive. A 1983 study (Tietenberg, 1985, p. 85) of the control of particulates in the Baltimore area showed that trading in emission rights allowed firms to achieve the overall pollution standard at less than half the cost of traditional regulation.

However, it is probably fair to say that market-based approaches to pollution control have not yet delivered as much as was promised (Hahn 1989). The cost savings appear to be far lower than what would be possible in theory. The reason is that most jurisdictions have imposed charges or permit trading on an existing regulatory system. The charges tend to be phased in over time, and the trading of permits is usually optional.[9] Furthermore, efficiency is not the only relevant criterion for a government in the choice of an instrument. Other criteria are equity, political acceptability, the ease of monitoring, and enforcement. The combination of instruments used appears to be determined by political institutions, the nature of environmental problems, and the attitudes of interest groups. There is some evidence that environmental groups tend to prefer user charges while producer groups prefer regulation. Many environmental groups oppose some types of market approaches, such as the trading in pollution rights, because they feel that they give legitimacy to the act of polluting.

The control of cross-border pollution creates additional problems because nature does not respect international boundaries. When people in one country harm the environment, it may affect many other countries in different ways. Anything that affects the atmosphere and the oceans will directly affect the environment in all countries. The atmosphere and the oceans are true **common property resources**.[10] But since nobody owns them, nobody has an incentive to protect them. Some international pollution problems are more localized, for example, acid rain (which mainly affects northeastern North America and north-western Europe), and pollution in the large basins (the Great Lakes, the Mediterranean, and the Baltic Sea). Other environmental resources, such as elephants, can only be found in some countries, but their future may affect people in other countries in spiritual and emotional ways.

In the absence of a world government, no country can force another country to curtail pollution. Cross-border pollution has to be addressed through international agreements or treaties, but like all international treaties, those on the environment can be enforced only by the governments that are signatories to them. Examples are the Montreal Protocol on Ozone-Depleting Substances, the International Whaling Convention, the Basle Convention on the Transportation of Hazardous Waste, and the Convention of International Trade in Endangered Species. None of these conventions uses market-based approaches to pollution control or conservation. Many allow for trade sanctions as a potential weapon against non-complying countries.

Benefit-Cost Analysis

Another area of environmental economics that has attracted much attention is the use of benefit-cost analysis to evaluate environmental clean-up. This subject is at least as controversial as the use of market incentives in pollution control, for reasons that will become obvious. Benefit-cost analysis is an attempt to put monetary values on the environment. Discounted future costs and benefits are added and compared.[11] Environmental clean-up should only proceed if the benefits of cleaning up or maintaining the environment are greater than the costs of doing so. Criticism of the approach has focused on three issues: (1) the principle of using benefit-cost analysis in making decisions about the environment, (2) the methods used to evaluate benefits, and (3) the choice of a discount rate.

The first criticism on the matter of principle against the use of benefit-cost analysis in environmental matters is that the environment is so basic to human existence that it cannot and should not be dealt with in dollars and cents. There are many reasons why environmental problems are different from many other resource problems. First, the consequences of some environmental decisions are clearly *irreversible*. How can we assign a value to something that can be lost forever? Dirty water can be cleaned up, but an extinct species cannot be brought back again. Other examples of irreversible or nearly irreversible environmental effects are ground water contamination, soil erosion, the traditional knowledge of indigenous people if they adopt Western culture, and the destruction of slowly reproducing ecosystems such as coral reefs and certain type of forests. Second, we do not have enough knowledge of many ecosystems to be sure that the lack of action on some fronts will not lead to environmental catastrophes which would jeopardize the future of the human race. The difficulties of estimating the real as opposed to the monetary aspects of environmental changes are compounded by the fact that relatively gradual changes in resource use can produce discontinuous and catastrophic effects in multi-species ecosystems. An example is the collapse of the north Atlantic cod stocks. Third, many people believe that the environment has an intrinsic value that is separate from its value to human beings. They see human beings as part of the animal kingdom with no more rights than other animals. The amount of damage to the environment that we allow as a society involves ethical, cultural, and aesthetic questions that have to be settled on their intrinsic merits.

It is obvious that the use of benefit-cost analysis is open to valid criticism. However, most decisions that we make, including many involving human lives, are based on an implicit balancing of costs and benefits. Benefit-cost analysis may not be an ideal guide to environmental decisions, but it should be the starting point for intelligent discussion.

Though it is difficult to measure costs, the evaluation of benefits, such as having clean air or clean water, provides formidable challenges. There are two methods for evaluating benefits: **indirect market methods and direct questioning methods** (Cropper and Oates 1992). Indirect market methods try to infer from observation the value that people place on environmental goods. For example, a house in an area with severe air pollution would be less expensive than a similar house in an area with little air pollution. The difference in house prices would reflect the economic cost of air pollution.

Direct questioning methods of measuring environmental quality involve asking people directly how they would make trade-offs between environmental goods and other goods. There are situations where the lack of data make it impossible to estimate benefits by indirect market methods. For example, **existence values** (sometimes called non-use values) cannot be measured by observing markets. Goods with existence values are essentially public goods. Existence values are benefits received from the knowledge that a good exists. For example most people value the existence of rare animals, even though they are unlikely ever to see one. A study by Bowker and Stoll (1988) estimates that U.S. households are, on average, willing to pay $22 a year to preserve the whooping crane. Thus the value of the whooping crane is assumed to be equal to the sum of all households' willingness to pay. Similarly, direct questioning was used by the Resource Assessment Commission in Australia to decide whether to allow mining in Kakadu National Park in northern Australia (*The Economist*, August 17, 1991). Two thousand five hundred respondents (a fifth of whom lived in northern Australia) were asked how much they were willing to pay to protect the site. Half of the respondents were given information about the environmental damage that the mine would cause based on estimates by environmentalists; the information given to the other respondents was based on estimates by the mining company. Predictably, the mining company's estimates of environmental damage were lower than those of the environmentalists. The results of the survey showed that even if the damage was as low as the mining companies indicated, Australians were willing to pay U.S. $826 million a year to prevent mining, a sum exceeding the value of the minerals to be mined. The mining proposal was subsequently turned down.

Direct questioning techniques have encountered their fair share of criticism. First, the questions asked are hypothetical. People do not actually have to pay, and therefore may well overstate their willingness to pay if they think that will improve the likelihood of an environmental improvement. They may also understate their willingness if they think that will reduce their share of the cost of the project. Second, people may not know enough about the commodity to place a value on it. For example, do people know enough about biodiversity to make an informed judgement? The existence value may depend on the circumstances in which consumers are asked to give their evaluation. If the survey instrument is changed, it is possible that the answer will change as well. Third, people appear to be inconsistent, for they are usually much less willing to pay for an environmental improvement than accept compensation to forego the same improvement.[12] Fourth, the valuation would depend on income. A rich person is more likely to be willing to pay a high price for environmental clean-up than a poor person, even though the poor person could well value the environment more highly. A person with no money cannot pay anything. An additional criticism is that the calculation of existence value aims to employ formal economic methods to resolve matters of cultural symbolism and social ideology. The range of possible existence values may well be limitless (Rosenthal and Nelson 1992).

The third main criticism of benefit-cost analysis centers on the use of discounting and the choice of a discount rate. Economists generally assume that people value having a good today more highly than having the equivalent good next year. Savers require compensation for postponing consumption. The level of real interest rates reflects the time preference of society (the trade-off between the present and the future). High discount rates discourage projects with long-term benefits while promoting projects with long-term costs. The result is that benefits that will accrue to future generations are valued less highly than benefits accruing to the current generation.[13] We do indeed discriminate against our children in the sense that we put a higher value on our interests than on theirs. We do in effect assume that the present generation holds all the rights to decide how environmental resources will be used. The issue of a discount rate is particularly important in evaluating the costs and benefits of measures to halt global warming. The costs are incurred today, whereas the benefits will not be realized until the distant future. For example, if one uses a 1 percent discount rate, it would be worthwhile to spend $126 million today to avoid $1 billion worth of damages in 2200. Using a discount rate of 5 percent, one would only be justified in spending $32,000 (Schmalensee 1993).

For this reason, some environmental economists argue that the discount rate chosen for assessing environmental impact should be lower than for other projects. This does not sit well with some mainstream economists. The following is an excerpt from an article by the former chief economist of the World Bank, Lawrence Summers:

> The argument that a moral obligation to future generations demands special treatment of environmental investments is fatuous. We can help our descendants as much by improving infrastructure as by preserving rain forests, as much by educating children as by leaving oil in the ground, as much by enlarging our scientific knowledge as by reducing carbon dioxide in the air. However much, or little, current generations wish to weigh the interests of future generations, there is every reason to undertake investments that yield the highest returns.
>
> That means holding each investment, environmental and non-environmental, to a test of opportunity cost. Each project must have a higher return (taking account of both pecuniary and non-pecuniary benefits) than alternative uses of the funds.
>
> Once costs and benefits are properly measured, it cannot be in posterity's interest for us to undertake investments that yield less than the highest return. At the long-term horizons that figure in the environmental data, this really matters. A dollar invested at 10% will be worth six times as much a century from now as a dollar invested at 8% (*The Economist*, May 30, 1992).

This argument assumes (a) that we are able to put a true price on the environment, (b) that natural resources and capital are substitutes, and (c) that we have the knowledge to evaluate the consequences and assess the risks. None of these assumptions are necessarily true. The assumption that natural resources and capital are substitutable is dubious at best and is contrary to the concept of sustainability that was discussed above. (See also the discussion in the previous chapter.) Summers makes the additional point (not included in the quotation) that future generations will in all likelihood be richer than the current generation. Therefore it is not ethically justifiable to value their welfare at the same rate as ours. However, the assumption that living standards will always rise is not necessarily true. Living standards have continued to rise in industrialized countries, albeit more slowly than previously. This is not the case for many Third World countries nor for countries in eastern Europe. There is no guarantee that our living standards will continue to rise. For these reasons one could justify the use of a low discount rate for environmental projects.

Conclusions

This chapter examined in more detail the concept of sustainable development and surveyed the main approaches in environmental economics: pollution as a result of market failure, and the use of benefit-cost analysis in approaching environmental problems. Pollution as a market failure can be dealt with by regulation, taxation, or the use of tradable permits. Economists do not favour regulation unless the danger from pollution creates an immediate hazard. Emissions taxes or tradable permits (pollution rights) are seen as the least expensive alternative to regulation and have been tried on a small scale.

If one accepts the ethical principle behind the statement that we as humans have the right to decide the fate of all living organisms, benefit-cost analysis is a logical method of giving guidance as to whether an aspect or component of the environment should be saved. For example, should the preservation of wilderness take precedence over commercial development, be it a new mine, the damming of a river for hydro-electric power, or the clear-cutting of an ancient forest for lumber? We surveyed some of the difficulties in choosing a discount rate and in evaluating benefits.

TOPICS FOR DISCUSSION

1. At the present the public agenda seems to be dominated by unemployment rather than the environment, not only in Canada but also in other countries. Do you think that the environment should have a high priority in view of our many other serious problems?

2. Why do you think environmentalists and economists distrust each other? What do you think could be done to improve the situation?

3. To what extent do you think we should take the interests of future generations into account when we make decisions?

RECOMMENDED READING

The best introduction to to-day's environmental problems can be found in the Brundtland Report, *Our Common Future* (World Commission on Environment and Development 1987). Alan Blinder in *Hard Heads, Soft Hearts: Tough-Minded Economics for a Just Society* (1988) makes an impassioned plea for the use of economic principles in devising policies for environmental clean-up. For an equally impassioned book about the failure of economics to provide solutions to the world's environmental problems, see Daly and Cobb's *For the Common Good: Redirecting the Economy Toward Community, the Environment and a Sustainable Future* (1989). Herman Daly is an economist with the World Bank, and John Cobb is a theologian.

References

Blinder, Alan S. *Hard Heads, Soft Hearts: Tough-Minded Economics for a Just Society.* Reading: Addison Wesley, 1988.

Block, Walter ed. *Economics and the Environment: A Reconciliation.* Vancouver: The Fraser Institute, 1990.

Bowker, James and John R. Stoll. "Use of Dichotomous Choice Nonmarket Methods to Value the Whooping Crane Resource." *American Journal of Agricultural Economics* 70 (May 1988): 372-81.

Canada. Ministry of Supply and Services. *Canada's Green Plan for a Healthy Environment.* [Ottawa]: The Ministry of Supply and Services, 1990.

Chant, John F., Donald G. McFetridge, and Douglas A. Smith. "The Economics of the Conserver Society." In *Economics and the Environment*, Walter Block (1990): 1-95.

Constanza, Robert. "The Ecological Economics of Sustainability: Investing in Natural Capital." In *UNESCO* (1991): 83-90.

Cropper, Maureen L., Sema K. Ayded and Paul R. Portney. "Rates of Time Preference for Saving Lives." *The American Economic Review* 82 (May 1992): 469-72.

Cropper, Maureen L. and Wallace E. Oates. "Environmental Economics: A Survey." *Journal of Economic Literature* 30 (June 1992): 675-741.

Daly, Herman E. and John B. Cobb Jr. *For the Common Good: Redirecting the Economy toward Community, the Environment, and a Sustainable Future.* Boston: Beacon Press, 1989.

The Economist. "A price on the priceless." August 17, 1991.

Ehrlich, Paul. R. *The Population Bomb.* New York: Ballantine, 1971.

Goodland, R. and G. Ledec "Neoclassical Economics and Principles of Sustainable Development." *Ecological Modelling* (1987): 19-46.

Hahn, Robert W. "Economic Prescriptions for Environmental Problems: How the Patient Followed the Doctor's Orders." *The Journal of Economic Perspectives* 3 (Spring 1989): 95-115.

Hanemann, Michael W. "Willingness to Pay and Willingness to Accept: How Much Can They Differ." *The American Economic* Review 81 (June 1991): 635-47.

Howarth, Richard B. and Richard B. Norgaard. "Environmental Valuation under Sustainable Development." *The American Economic Review* 82 (May 1992): 473-77.

Meadows D. *The Limits to Growth.* New York: Universe Books, 1972.

Rosenthal, Donald H. and Robert H. Nelson. "Why Existence Value Should Not be Used in Cost-Benefit Analysis." *Journal of Policy Analysis and Management* 11 (Winter 1992): 116-22.

Schmalensee, Richard. "Symposium on Global Climate Change." *Journal of Economic Perspectives* 7 (Fall 1993): 3-10.

Solow, Robert M. "Sustainability: An Economist's Perspective." In *Economics of the Environment: Selected Readings*, eds. Robert Dorfman and Nancy S. Dorfman. New York: W.W. Norton & Company, 1993.

Tietenberg, Thomas H. *Emissions Trading: An Exercise in Reforming Pollution Policy.* Washington D.C.: Resources for the Future, 1985.

Unesco. *Environmentally Sustainable Economic Development.* Paris: Unesco, 1991.

World Bank. *The World Development Report,* 1992. New York: Oxford University Press, 1992.

World Commission on Environment and Development. *Our Common Future.* Oxford: Oxford University Press, 1987.

Endnotes

1   The prediction that population growth will outstrip the growth in food supply dates back to the Reverend Thomas Malthus (1798) who in his book, *An Essay on the Principle of Population as it Affects the Future Improvement of Society*, pointed out that population grows at a geometric rate while food supply grows at an arithmetic rate.

2   For a good summary of the arguments, see Goodland and Ledec (1987).

3   For a survey of environmental economics, see Cropper and Oates (1992).

4   Under certain conditions market failure can be corrected through bargaining between the parties involved (the Coase theorem).

5   The conservative backlash in the 1970s and 1980s gave regulation a bad name. Legislation was often in place to protect airlines and public utilities, which were thought to be natural monopolies, from "ruinous " competition. To protect the public from exploitation by the monopolies, there was regulation of rates and services. Article after article published during these decades showed that instead of protecting consumers against the excesses of natural monopolies, the regulators were often "captured" by the industry and acted in its interest to the detriment of the general public. Deregulation became the catchword of the day, particularly in transportation.

6   Each vehicle which enters the highway after the road has reached capacity makes other vehicles slow down. The result is a traffic jam.

7   Mandatory controls may be the only option if pollution is life-threatening and requires immediate action. An example would be the disposal of nuclear waste in public waterways.

8   See Cropper and Oates (1992), p. 692. However, the authors point out that the intent of the fees was not the regulation of discharges, but rather the raising of funds to finance water quality management. There is already in place an extensive command-and-control system.

9   In practice, the purpose of the two approaches seems to be different. Charges are used to improve environmental quality by raising revenue to finance environmental projects, while the trading of permits is used primarily to promote cost savings (Hahn 1989).

10 A common property resource is a resource which is owned by no one and which can be used by anyone.

11 The process of discounting involves the conversion of future dollars to current dollars. For example, a dollar earned today is worth $1.05 next year it if it is invested at an interest rate of 5 percent. Therefore a dollar earned next year is worth only $.95 ($1/1.05) today.

12 However, this is apparently not unique to direct questioning techniques. Monetary losses are valued more highly than monetary gains. Haneman (1991) argues that people respond to valuation questions with substitutes in mind. If a good has no substitute (for example the continued existence of Kakadu as a national park), the amount the respondent would be willing to pay at the limit would be his or her entire wealth, which is finite. The amount he or she would be willing to accept as compensation could be infinite. The person would feel so strongly that no compensation could make up the loss.

13 A recent study by Cropper et al. (1992) shows that if people have a choice in saving lives today and saving lives in twenty-five years, they would only choose a policy which saves lives later if four times as many lives are saved.

3

The Canadian Environment and Pollution

After studying this chapter you will be able to describe Canada's air- and water-pollution problems and the problem of waste disposal as well as discuss efficient policies for reducing them. You will also be able to assess the seriousness of the thinning of the ozone layer and global warming, and explain why action has been slow on the latter. You will also understand that air pollution both as a short-run and a long-run problem is related to energy use, in particular to the burning of fossil fuels.

The chapter will concentrate on pollution and its effect on the Canadian environment in the short term and in the long term. The question arises as to what indicators could be used to determine whether or not the environment is polluted. The United Nations Development Program includes among its environmental indicators the emissions of air pollutants per capita, municipal waste per capita, industrial waste per unit of GDP, waste paper recycled as a percentage of all paper consumed, spent nuclear fuel inventories, the percentage of the population served by sewage treatment plants, and the amount of hazardous and special wastes generated per square kilometre. We will examine a few equivalent indicators for Canada and offer an economic perspective on what we could do to improve the situation, using the

70

approach developed in the previous chapter. We will also look at the sustainability of our use of the environment by examining the long-term problems of the thinning of the ozone layer and of global warming resulting from the build-up of greenhouse gases in the atmosphere, both of which will require immediate action if we are to avoid environmental damage in the future.

Since today's environmental issues are increasingly complex, they require some understanding of the science involved. Environmental science spans many disciplines: chemistry, physics, biology, climatology, meteorology, oceanography, and geomorphology, to name a few. Mathematical modelling is used extensively in mapping the complex interplay of many of the forces involved in nature. Even so, many of the issues, particularly the global issues, are highly controversial.

Air Pollution

How clean is our air? Obviously, given our vast land mass, the answer depends very much on where we live in Canada. In general, urban areas are more susceptible to air pollution than are rural areas. Local air pollution depends on many factors, for example, prevailing winds, the presence or absence of heavy industry, and the physical characteristics of the area. The main air pollutants are sulphur dioxide, ground-level ozone, nitrogen oxide, and "suspended particulates." Table 3.1 shows that on a per capita basis, Canada and the United States have not done well at limiting air pollution.

Sulphur dioxide is a strong-smelling colourless gas. It is released into the atmosphere by the refining of oil and gas, the smelting of sulphur-rich ores, and thermal power plants. In the atmosphere sulphur dioxide combines with water droplets to form sulphuric acid. Exposure to sulphur dioxide can harm the respiratory system in humans. The average annual levels of sulphur dioxide in urban areas in Canada has decreased considerably over the last 15 years. Though the level fluctuates, the average level in the large urban areas is below the maximum acceptable level set by Environment Canada (Canada, 1991, p. 2-12).

Ozone is found not only in the stratosphere, where by acting as a

TABLE 3.1
Environmental Indicators from Selected OECD Countries

Country	CO_2 (tonnes per capita)	SO_2 (kg per capita)	NO_x (kg per capita)	% of Water Treated
Canada	4.8	146.4	74.9	66
Japan	2.2	6.8	9.6	39
West Germany	3.2	21.3	46.7	90
United Kingdom	2.9	63.1	44.0	84
United States	5.8	84.0	80.4	74
OECD countries	3.4	48.3	44.3	n/a

Source: Olewiler (1993), Tables 1 and 2.
Note: CO_2 figures are from 1989, whereas SO_2 and NO_x data are averages for the late eighties. Figures on waste-water treatment are also from the late eighties and are the percentages of the populations served by at least primary treatment plants.

shield against ultraviolet radiation, its effect is beneficial, but also at the ground-level, where it is harmful. Ground-level ozone, which is a major component of smog, builds up when there is sunshine, the air temperature is high, and the air contains volatile organic compounds (mainly hydrocarbons) and nitrogen oxides, often generated by heavy traffic. These compounds are transported over large rural areas beyond the cities. It is estimated that in the summer more than 50 percent of Canadians are exposed to high ozone levels. The problem is particularly severe in the Lower Fraser Valley, the Windsor-Quebec corridor, and around Saint John and Halifax (Canada, 1991, p. 12-18). High concentrations of ozone can harm children's lungs and also crop yields.

Nitrogen oxides are generated by motor vehicle traffic and by the burning of fuel in homes and industries. High concentrations affect people with asthma and bronchial problems. They can also have a detrimental effect on vegetation. The level of nitrogen oxides declined substantially in the late seventies, but since that time it has stabilized because of the increase in traffic (*ibid.*, p. 2-13). The concentration of "suspended particulates" has also decreased substantially. The sources of these particulates include mining, quarrying, pulp and paper operations, thermal power plants, motor vehicle emissions, and the burning of domestic solid fuels. The improvement is caused by improved pollution abatement in industry, the increased use of natural gas, and more frequent street cleaning.

One result of air pollution is acid rain. In the 1980s, acid rain became a symbol of environmental deterioration and a rallying cry in Canada, some U.S. states, and northern Europe. Normal rainfall is slightly acidic owing to the absorption of carbon dioxide and some other natural materials.[1] But in eastern Canada, rain has been far more acidic than normal because of airborne sulphur dioxide and nitrogen oxides that are picked up by the rain (Canada, 1991, p. 24.5), forming sulphuric and nitric acids. Acid rain (or acid snow or small, airborne dry acidic particles) influences a wide variety of ecological processes both on land and in water. There is evidence that declines and dieback of forests in Europe and North America can be attributed to acid rain, and the effect on lakes is well-known. The beauty of the clear, acidic lakes is caused by the lack of any type of aquatic life — that is, they are ecologically dead.

Considerable progress has already been made in reducing sulphur dioxide emissions (see above). However, the control of acid rain also required action in the United States, where at first there was little recognition that acid rain was a problem. But since the passage of the U.S. Clean Air Act in 1990, emission limits have been set for both sulphur dioxide and nitrogen oxides. Models show that further planned reductions in sulphur dioxide emissions will have a perceptible improvement on the incidence of acid rain. Emission controls appear to provide a much greater benefit to Ontario and Quebec than to the Atlantic region, where some areas are still expected to lose more than 10 percent of the species in 30 percent of the surface waters (*ibid.*, p. 24-19).

The improvement in air quality has taken place not only in Canada, but also in the United States and other industrialized countries.[2] The

Global Environmental Monitoring System (a United Nations program), which monitors air quality around the world, reports that some countries, such as Japan and Norway, have achieved spectacular improvements. In the developing countries, on the other hand, the air quality has deteriorated to such an extent that it is estimated that only 30 to 35 percent of the world's population lives in places where the air meets the guidelines recommended by the World Health Organization.

Most of the improvements in air quality in Canada have been achieved through direct regulation (command and control) and therefore at excessive cost (see Chapter 2). Many of the studies done in the United States on least-cost techniques (for example tradable emissions) found that regulation may cost up to 78 percent more than least-cost techniques. This is likely to be the case in Canada as well.[3] Much of the reduction in sulphur dioxide emissions have been due to Canada's Acid Rain Control Program, under which the seven provinces east of Saskatchewan agreed to reduce total emissions in eastern Canada to 2.3 million tonnes a year by 1994 (Canada, 1992, p. 4). Given that a cap on emissions has already been agreed to, the introduction of tradable permits is a possibility. (For a discussion of tradable permits, see Chapter 2.)

As air pollution is caused partly by motor vehicle traffic, cleaner air could also be achieved by (1) making more efficient engines, by (2) switching from gasoline to alternative fuels (for example electricity), and by (3) efficient road pricing. More efficient engines were developed in response to the high oil prices in the 1970s and are now used in all new cars. However, further efficiencies are possible. Electric cars have been developed but are not yet commercially viable.

The third solution, efficient road pricing, has not been tried in Canada. At present, drivers do not bear the full cost to society of air pollution, traffic congestion, and the wear and tear on roads. At rush hour, for example, a driver imposes a cost on all the other motorists because his or her presence makes them slow down; the cost of that wasted time can be estimated. For an efficient allocation of resources, all these costs should enter the motorist's calculations and be added to his or her private costs. This could be done by and would require the installation of meters and scanners on cars and roads and charging drivers directly for the distance they drive. The charges would be higher if they used the roads at rush hour. This technology already has been used in Singapore.

Water Pollution

In Canada water pollution is a serious problem that affects both surface water in lakes, rivers, and oceans; and ground water. Traditionally, most attention has been paid to water pollution in rivers and lakes, but recently pollution of the oceans (especially coastal waters and estuaries of great environmental sensitivity) by oil spills and the dumping of toxic wastes has also become an issue. Also of concern is the contamination of ground water, which has become an important source of drinking water. In fact, since 1960 the use of ground water as a proportion of total consumption has more than doubled, from 10 percent to 26 percent (Canada, 1991, p. 3-23). Ground water is being contaminated by agricultural pesticides in parts of British Columbia, Prince Edward Island, and southern Ontario. Ground water can also be contaminated by leaking storage tanks for petroleum products, by landfills, by the excessive use of fertilizers, and by feedlots for cattle. Once ground water contamination occurs, it is virtually impossible to eliminate.

The main source of water pollution is municipal sewage because so much of it is not properly treated. According to a 1989 survey covering 86 percent of the Canadian population, 30 percent had no treatment of any kind. Table 3.1 shows that we treat a smaller proportion of our sewage than Germany, the United States, and the United Kingdom. Montreal and Quebec City still dump some of their sewage untreated into the St. Lawrence, and Victoria and Halifax dump all of theirs straight into the ocean (*ibid.*, p. 13-13).

Other sources of surface water pollution are industry and agriculture. The mining industry can have detrimental effects on water quality by increasing the concentration of some heavy metals, particularly cadmium, as well as raising the acidity. The pulp and paper industry has received much adverse publicity because of the environmental effects of its effluent, which contains mercury and chlorinated organic chemicals such as dioxins and furans, by-products of the chlorine bleaching process.[4] Agriculture also has an adverse effect on surface water because run-off containing pesticides and chemical fertilizers finds its way into the water system.

Some pollutants are biodegradable. For example, much of the effluent from municipalities is consumed by bacteria. Like many other living organisms, these bacteria need oxygen to survive, and for that reason the breakdown of effluent by bacteria requires oxygen. The measure of the demand for oxygen placed on a stream by the effluent in it is called the biochemical oxygen demand. When the oxygen level of a water course falls, some fish will die and be replaced by other species that need less oxygen. But when the pollution reaches a certain level all organisms, including the aerobic bacteria, will die at which point the waterway becomes anaerobic. Then the effluent does not break down, and the water becomes a stinking mess. Other pollutants, notably nitrogen and phosphorus, stimulate the growth of some aquatic life such as algae and weeds and will have adverse effects on others.

Some pollutants never disappear because there are no natural processes that break them down, and unless the source is stopped, they will continue to accumulate. Examples are many inorganic chemicals (including dioxin, furans, and PCBs) and heavy metals (including cadmium, lead, and mercury). Some of these are highly toxic even in minute concentrations. For example, laboratory tests have shown that dioxin concentrations as low as 40 parts per quadrillion are lethal to rainbow trout. This is an amount equal to a thimbleful in 50,000 Olympic-sized swimming pools (*ibid.* p. 3-17). Similarly, one tablespoon of mercury in a body of water equal the size of a football field filled with water to a depth of 4.6 meters would be sufficient to make fish unsafe to eat. The dioxin and furans in the environment come from commercial chemicals (pesticides and wood preservatives containing chlorophenols), incineration of substances containing chlorine, pulp and paper mills that use chlorine for bleaching, and accidental spills and fires of PCBs that contain furan contaminants.[5]

Public concern has led to more stringent regulations for pulp mills. In British Columbia the forest industry must stop using chlorine by

2002. Ontario is requiring a reduction of 40 percent by 1996 and 70 percent by the year 2000 (*The Globe and Mail*, February 2, 1993). The cost to the industry may be as high as $1.2 billion.

The Generation and Disposal of Waste

The disposal of waste has become a problem for many Canadian municipalities. According to data presented in Canada's Green Plan (Canada, 1990, p. 58)[6], we generate more waste per capita per day than any other country listed. Most garbage ends up in landfill sites despite substantial efforts to encourage recycling, and there is little indication that the amount of garbage generated is diminishing. Indeed, a study for Ontario showed that the amount of waste produced increased by 25 percent per capita over the last decade. (Canada, 1991, p. 25-4). In 1990 it was estimated that by 1995 the existing land fills serving 71 percent of the Canadian population would be full (*ibid.* p. 25-11). It is more and more difficult to find suitable new sites, and even if such sites are found, opposition from local residents sometimes makes any new site political-ly unacceptable. Land fills are also becoming very expensive to operate, monitor, and care for after they are full. Most of the landfills now in use are no more than garbage dumps where the garbage is left on the ground to decompose until it is covered with new garbage. All landfills produce leachate, a combination of rain or ground water and waste products. If leachate reaches the ground water, it can poison the drinking water and affect the food chain. New landfill sites are lined with clay or other materials to collect the leachate, which can then be treated. Landfills also produce methane, a powerful greenhouse gas, from the breakdown of organic materials in the garbage. Indeed, 49 percent of all the methane produced in Canada comes from landfills.

An alternative to landfills is incineration, which is more common in Europe than in Canada. Japan, Sweden, and Switzerland incinerate over 50 percent of their garbage (OECD, 1991, p. 150). In many cases the energy is recovered and used for residential or commercial heating. Incineration does not completely eliminate landfills, because the process produces waste in the form of ash, which must be disposed of.

Incinerators must operate at very high temperatures or the burning of garbage can add toxic chemicals to the air, but modern incinerators appear to be successful in controlling toxic emissions.

Most of the waste is commercial waste, the largest category of which is wood. Thirty-five to 40 percent of garbage is residential waste. (Canada, 1991, p. 25-6) Judging from the more complete U.S. data, the largest category of waste is paper, followed by plastics, ferrous metals, and glass. It is estimated that over one-third of the total municipal solid waste is paper and cardboard. The largest amount of waste can be attributed to packaging, followed by non-durables (newspapers, books, magazines, tissue paper, office and commercial paper, clothing and footwear), garden wastes, durables (appliances, furniture, tires), and food. The Canadian situation is probably not much different (*ibid.* p. 25-8).

Because of the difficulties and expense of expanding landfill sites, many provinces and municipalities are committed to the four R's (reduce, reuse, recycle, and recover). The Canadian Council of Ministers of the Environment has set a nation wide goal of a 50 percent reduction in the per capita amount of garbage sent for disposal by the year 2000. So far recycling has only made a modest contribution to reducing the amount of garbage. The Ontario blue box program, which is the longest-running curbside program in Canada, after three years of operation had not managed to divert more than 3 to 4 percent of the garbage destined for landfills. In comparison, the Japanese recycle 40 percent of their solid waste; the remainder is incinerated and refabricated. Only 9 percent of all their waste ends up in landfills (Tietenberg, 1992, p. 190).

Recycling is usually done for two reasons: to save raw materials and to reduce the amount of garbage. If raw materials are scarce, recycling is efficient and market forces will in most cases make sure that it is done (see Chapter 4). But, if resources are not scarce, and if there are no externalities involved in extraction and refining, recycling does not make economic sense, because recycled metals are more expensive than metals made from virgin ore. Eventually, however, when resources become scarce, lower-grade ores, which are more expensive to refine, will be brought into production. With a denser population the disposal of waste will also become more expensive. A point will be reached where products made from recycled raw materials will cost less than products made from virgin materials. At that time, consumers will shift their purchases, and recycled materials will dominate the market. Aluminum is a case in point, for recycled aluminum is considerably cheaper to produce than aluminum from bauxite, because the refining process is extremely energy-intensive.[7] In other cases, recycling might not be the most efficient way of saving raw materials, particularly as some types of pollution generated in the manufacturing process could be higher with recycled materials than with virgin materials (Maclaren, 1991, p. 39).[8] Consumption of raw materials could also be reduced if their prices reflected the true social cost to society of their extraction and consumption (see Chapter 4). This could be done with consumption taxes.

Recycling for the purpose of decreasing garbage may or may not make economic sense. It is only efficient where (1) the cost of garbage disposal is relatively high, (2) collection costs are relatively low, and (3) there is a market for recycled products.[9] Because of the scarcity of available sites, the cost of disposal has probably increased considerably in many urban areas in Canada. On the other hand, it seems very difficult to find markets for recycled products. Although commodity prices are always volatile, it appears that prices for recycled materials fluctuate even more than those for raw materials, being subject to changes in consumer tastes as well as technology (*The Economist*, April 13, 1991). Ontario's recycling program has had difficulties in finding a market for newspapers, despite an attempt to create an artificial demand for recycled newsprint by legislating mandatory proportions of recycled materials in newspapers.[10] Plastics are difficult to recycle because of problems in removing impurities. Waste plastics tend to be contaminated with non-plastic substances (for example food or cleaning materials). In the case of metals, such impurities can be removed by high temperatures, but with plastics this is not possible as plastics are destroyed by high temperatures.

Many municipalities do not recover the full cost of collecting and disposing of waste, and some even allow private haulers to dispose of garbage for nothing. They could, however, reduce garbage by charging the households and businesses directly for the amount of waste they generate. Such a scheme can be found in New Jersey (Tietenberg,

1992, p. 206). To have garbage collected at the curb required a sticker. Each household was issued with 52 stickers at a price of $200 (previously the residents had been charged a flat annual fee for garbage collection), and additional stickers could be had for $1.65 each. The result was a reduction in garbage by 25 percent. It has been argued that those types of schemes could lead to an increase in illegal dumping, and that the highways would soon be littered with garbage bags or appliances. In New Jersey, however, dumping did not seem to be a problem.[11]

A third method of reducing waste would be to require manufacturers of appliances to take back the appliance at the end of its life or to require consumers to pay a deposit for disposal of the product. This would not necessarily be cost-effective. *The Economist* (April 13, 1991) reports that a study of a proposal to levy deposits on glass drink bottles in Australia found that the levy would cost industry and consumers between Australian$200 million and $350 million but would cut the cost of garbage collection by only $2 to $4 million and reduce the cost of waste disposal by only $26 million. Obviously a deposit scheme does not make economic sense under those conditions. The Canadian Soft Drink Association argues that in Canada soft drink deposits cost the consumer at least $700 a tonne of generated garbage, whereas curbside recycling costs less than $200 a tonne (*The Financial Post*, Friday, March 12, 1993).

Attempts are also under way to reduce packaging. The Canadian Council of Ministers of the Environment have adopted a National Packaging Protocol that aims to reduce the amount of packaging in use by 50 percent by the year 2000. How this would be achieved has not yet been spelt out (Canada 1991, p. 25–14).

Long-Term Pollution Problems: The Thinning of the Ozone Layer and Global Warming

The Thinning of the Ozone Layer

Ozone is one of the crucial components of the atmosphere, for it shields living organisms from the destructive effects of ultraviolet radiation from the sun. Ozone also helps to regulate the world's climate by re-emitting the absorbed ultraviolet radiation as heat. The concentration of ozone in the atmosphere varies both spatially and seasonally. Ozone is formed from the reaction of ultraviolet radiation with oxygen and is broken down by sunlight and various chemicals in the atmosphere. Normally, the destruction and formation balance each other.

The possibility of damage to the ozone layer was first recognized during the 1960s, when it was thought that water vapour from aircraft and rockets could cause ozone depletion (Government of Canada 1991, p. 23.5). Later it was also thought that chlorine emitted by the space shuttle might increase the rate of ozone depletion. It was not until the 1970s that chlorofluorocarbons (CFCs) and halons were recognized as the most serious threat to the ozone layer. Laboratory studies had shown that CFCs are very stable and for that reason they persist long enough to be transported to the stratosphere (the upper atmosphere); there the ultraviolet light decomposes the CFC molecules, releasing chlorine or bromine, which interact and destroy ozone. More recently concern has been expressed at the effect of bromine (*The Economist*, November 21, 1992). Bromine, which is closely related to chlorine, is a hundred times more efficient than chlorine at destroying ozone. Bromine is found in methyl bromide, which is one of the most common pesticides in the world.

CFCs are used primarily in refrigerators and air conditioners and in the production of rigid insulation foam and flexible foam for furniture. These uses account for approximately 80 percent of all the CFCs used in Canada (Canada, 1990, p. 114). CFCs are also used as a propellant in aerosols; as a component of the sterilant gas for cleaning hospital equipment, and as a solvent for cleaning computer circuit boards and other electronic components.

In the 1980s studies by Environment Canada of the stratosphere over Saskatchewan confirmed that ozone-depleting reactions were taking place. In 1985 it was found that springtime ozone values over Antarctica had declined by up to 50 percent since the late 1970s. This discovery came as a complete surprise since the best projections available had predicted that the depletion of the ozone layer would take place very slowly. In 1987, new data showed that 15 percent of the southern hemisphere was affected. A similar but less severe phenomenon has been discovered over the Arctic. Recently the loss of ozone concentration over the mid-latitudes of the northern hemisphere have been estimated at 4 to 5 percent every 10 years with rates the highest during the winter and early spring (Canada, 1991, p. 23.11).

The destruction of ozone leads to increased exposure to ultraviolet radiation. Some ultraviolet radiation is beneficial to humans because it stimulates the synthesis of vitamin D in the skin. Excessive exposure to ultraviolet radiation, however, increases the risk of skin cancer. Studies suggest that a 1 percent decrease in ozone results in a 3–6 percent increase in skin cancer (Canada, 1991, p. 23-12). Ultraviolet radiation can also increase the likelihood of cataracts, and there is evidence that it can cause skin allergies and suppress the immune system. The effect of increased radiation on animals and plants is poorly understood, but it is feared that it may affect the food chains of the southern oceans. The phytoplankton that live near the surface of the sea may be particularly vulnerable because their period of maximum growth coincides with the period when ozone depletion is at its highest. As the southern oceans account for up to 20 percent of the biological productivity of the seas, there is a potential for catastrophe.

In 1985, representatives of 20 countries signed the Vienna Convention on the Protection of the Ozone Layer. The convention called for cooperation in research and an exchange of information. The subsequent discovery of the depletion of ozone over the Antarctic in 1985 made it clear that more radical action was needed. The Montreal Protocol on Substances That Deplete the Ozone Layer was signed in September 1987. The 24 signatories, of which Canada was one, agreed to reduce their consumption, of CFCs and halons. CFC consumption would be reduced in 1989-90 to the 1986 level of consumption, in 1993-94 to 80 percent of the 1986 level, and in 1998-99 to 50 percent of the 1986 level. For halons, consumption would be frozen at 1986 levels in 1992. There was a provision for trade sanctions in case of non-compliance. The developing countries were allowed an easier timetable. The richer countries also agreed to contribute U.S. $160 million in a three-year period to 1994 to a central fund (the U.N.

Montreal Protocol Multilateral Fund) to assist developing countries in reducing their dependence on ozone-depleting substances.

The meeting in Montreal was followed by meetings in Helsinki and London, where the original agreement was refined and expanded to include carbon tetrachloride and methyl chloroform. Hydrochlorofluorocarbon (HCFC) was sanctioned as a temporary substitute for CFC, even though it also destroys ozone, albeit more slowly.

At a meeting in Copenhagen in November 1992 to review the progress of the Montreal Protocol, more restrictions were announced (*The Economist*, November 28, 1992). Rich countries now agreed to phase out CFCs by 1995. They also agreed to put HCFCs and methyl bromide on the list of chemicals that will ultimately be phased out completely.

At the end of 1991, world production of CFCs had declined by 40 percent since the inception of the protocol (*The Economist*, March 7, 1992). The phasing out of CFCs by 1995 means that users must either recycle the existing stock of CFCs or switch to substitute compounds. As yet little recycling is taking place. One of the main producers of CFCs, Dupont Canada, admitted that in 1991 it produced 8 million kilograms but received only 20,000 kilograms back for recycling (*The Globe and Mail*, April 7, 1992). For some uses of CFCs (in particular for foam in furniture and as a cleaning solvent), it is easy to find substitutes. But it has turned out to be far more difficult and expensive to find substitutes for the CFCs used in refrigerators. Most replacements are less efficient and have to be pumped at higher pressures. As a result they generate greater temperatures and require stronger hoses and compressors. They are not compatible with the materials used for seals and lubricants used in the refrigeration process.

Do the benefits of reducing ozone-destroying substances outweigh the cost? Using conventional benefit-cost analysis, Smith and Vodden (1989) estimate that for Canada they do. The estimated benefits in decreases in skin cancer and cataracts far outweigh the extra costs to industry, by approximately $3 billion.

Global Warming

The possibility of long-term environmental damage as a result of global warming has become one of the main topics in environmental discussions. The atmosphere is made up of nitrogen, oxygen, argon, water vapour, and the greenhouse gases: carbon dioxide, methane, nitrous oxides, ground-level ozone, and CFCs. The greenhouse gases, of which carbon dioxide is the most important, are essential in trapping outbound radiation from the earth and therefore in ensuring a livable climate (that is the greenhouse effect). Without the greenhouse effect the average surface temperature of the earth would drop to -18 degrees Celsius. An increase in greenhouse gases will result in higher global temperatures. Warmer temperatures will start to melt the polar icecaps, thereby raising the sea level, and threatening coastal settlements. A warmer climate may also be accompanied by more changeable weather, which may threaten agricultural production. The effect on forestry, particularly in northern regions, could be substantial. Some species of animals and plants may be unable to adapt to changing climates and may become extinct.

The causes of climatic change are not fully understood, but the concentration of greenhouse gases in the atmosphere is believed to be a critical factor. Over very long periods of time, natural changes in concentration occur that may explain long-term changes in climate. In the past 150 years, in the aftermath of the Industrial Revolution, greenhouse gas concentrations have increased dramatically. It is estimated that half the carbon dioxide added to the atmosphere throughout human history has been emitted in the past 30 years. The concentration of methane has doubled in the last hundred years. CFCs are doubling every 10 to 20 years (Canada, 1990, p. 97). Two-thirds of the build-up of greenhouse gases is due to carbon dioxide. The burning of fossil fuels adds 5.5 billion tons of carbon annually to the atmosphere, and deforestation an additional 3.5 billion tons. It is believed that half the emissions are absorbed by the oceans and that the other half remain in the atmosphere. It is estimated that to prevent further build-up, carbon emissions would have to be cut immediately by at least 60 percent (Cline, 1992, p. 10). The second most important source is methane, which accounts for one-quarter of the build-up. Methane comes from cattle, the cultivation of rice, the burning of biomass, coal mining, and natural gas flaring. It is believed that because methane does not last long, a cutback of emissions of only 10–20 percent would stabilize the concentrations of that gas.

Large-scale computer models have been used to estimate the effect on the world's climate of the build-up of greenhouse gases. These models, which are very complex, may require up to a thousand hours of computer time to carry out one simulation. The models divide the atmosphere into grids corresponding to the surface of the earth. The grids range in size from 200 by 200 kilometres to 500 by 500 kilometres. The atmosphere above each grid is divided into vertical layers, varying in number from two to 20. Taking into account climatic feedback processes, the models estimate the reaction of variables such as wind, temperature, ice, snow, clouds, and precipitation in response to the build-up of greenhouse gases.

The greatest difficulty in model building — and source of much controversy — is the estimation of feedback effects. One of the most important is the effect of the increase in water vapour that accompanies warming. Water vapour is in itself a powerful greenhouse gas that causes further warming. There are also difficulties modelling the effects of cloud feedbacks. Because clouds reflect solar radiation they have a cooling effect. But they also trap outgoing infrared radiation, and that has a warming effect. There are other uncertain feedbacks. For example, warmer temperatures may cause plants to emit more carbon dioxide through respiration. On the other hand, it is possible that higher concentrations of carbon dioxide would lead to greater rates of photosynthesis in plants and therefore to the removal of more carbon dioxide from the atmosphere. Another unknown is the effect of global warming on the Arctic. If the permafrost thawed, or if a large number of forests died because of warmer climates, large stores of carbon would be oxidized and released into the atmosphere, further aggravating the situation.

Because of these uncertainties, the estimates for global warming vary, depending on which assumptions are built into the climatic models. Most studies predict minor effects on climate in the next decade or so, with most adverse effects coming later. The majority scientific view according to the Intergovernmental Panel on Climate Change (1990) is that doubling of carbon dioxide in the atmosphere, which is likely to happen by the year 2025, will cause significant warming with a global mean increase of 2.5 degrees Celsius. The lower bound for the estimate is 1.5 degrees and the upper bound 4.5 degrees. But the temperature will not rise by the same amount in all places and in all seasons. There will be greater warming in the higher latitudes, and greater in winter than in summer. The models also agree that precipitation will increase, but not everywhere. In some places precipitation will actually decrease. There is also evidence that the variability of precipitation will increase.

Cline (1991, 1992) argues that the time span that has been studied is far too short. Most studies have concentrated on the effects of the doubling in the concentration of greenhouse gases that is likely to occur by 2025. However, global warming is likely to continue far beyond that particular year. Cline cites evidence to show that atmospheric concentration of carbon can be expected to increase sixfold by the year 2250. After that the increased mixing of carbon dioxide in the deep ocean layers would lead to a partial reversal of that trend (Cline, 1992, p. 20). A longer time horizon would therefore give considerably higher estimates for global warming.

Cline (1992) projects carbon concentrations and global warming for 2275. He estimates that carbon emissions may be about 10 times what they are at the present time, resulting in an atmospheric concentration of carbon dioxide eight times higher than the pre-industrial level. Global warming could then be expected to add 10 degrees Celsius to the average temperature rather than the 2.5 degrees by 2025. The lower bound is estimated to be 6 degrees and the upper bound as high as 18 degrees. Such a change would probably jeopardize the survival of a large proportion of the human race. Cline points out that the Intergovernmental Panel on Climate Change (IPCC) estimated that even if there were an aggressive program of policies to combat global warming, the warming would still level at 2.5 degrees by the year 2275. That does suggest, though, that the additional projected 7.5 degrees could be avoided. For each decade in which there is no action, the price is approximately 0.25 degrees Celsius (7.5 degrees Celsius of avoidable warming divided by 28 decades to the year 2275).

In principle there are three ways to deal with global warming (Nordhaus 1990). One is to learn to live with warmer climates, the second is to find a "technological fix," and the third is to prevent further increases in greenhouse gases. Technological solutions that could be explored include (1) seeding the oceans with iron filings, which would encourage the growth of certain carbon-eating organisms, (2) shooting particulate matter (for example "smart" mirrors) into the stratosphere to cool the earth, and (3) changing settlement and land use patterns in such a way that the earth's reflectivity increases. What sort of action is warranted depends on what the effects of climate change will be as well as the costs of doing something about it.

There are many uncertainties associated with estimating the ecological and economic effects of global warming. The ecological damage that would result is particularly difficult to estimate, and yet that might be the most critical effect. In particular, the destruction of forests and the increase in the rate of species loss is likely to be serious.[12] With a 2.5 degree increase in global temperatures, it is possible that the biomass of boreal forests would decline by 40 percent, temperate forests would increase by 1.3 percent, and tropical forests would grow by 12 percent, resulting in a net reduction of 3.7 percent. In Canada, the climate for boreal forests would be displaced northward by 800 kilometres. The southern limit would move north by 1100 kilometres. This means that the trees in the southern part of the boreal range will die of heat or lack of moisture and would be replaced by other types of trees. Today's forests would have to migrate north at rates of 100 to 200 kilometres per decade to survive. The current rate of migration is 20 to 50 kilometres per decade.

At present, human activity is reducing the number of species a thousand times faster than would occur naturally. With global warming the rate of species loss will increase. The loss in species would be due partly to the change in forests, but also to changes in rainfall, rising sea levels, and warmer temperatures in both air and water. For Canada it may be particularly serious in the Arctic.

Nordhaus (1991) plays down the economic effects of climate change by arguing that most economic activity does not depend on climate. Manufacturing, mining, research, and communications can be done almost anywhere. Agriculture is the most climate-sensitive activity, but it is no longer an important activity in rich countries. Other activities that will be affected by climate are construction and recreation. Costs will be incurred to contain higher water levels in low-lying areas. The design of houses will change because the weather will be warmer. More energy will be used for air conditioning and less for heating. Some recreational activities will be changed (there will be less snow skiing and more water skiing).

The most complete studies, so far, on the economic effects of global warming are for the economy of the United States. Nordhaus (1991) estimates that the economic effects for the United States of a doubling of carbon dioxide would be moderate: an annual cost to the economy of approximately 0.25 percent of GDP (see Table 3.2). For example, in the case of agriculture, Nordhaus assumes that the lower yields that result from warming will be offset by higher yields caused by the fertilization effects of higher concentrations of carbon dioxide. However, he does not include any estimates for the effect of global warming on water supplies, air pollution, human health, biodiversity, or the amenity values of everyday life. In fact, he quotes a study by the National Research Council in the United States which suggests that there are considerable amenity benefits from global warming.

The estimates by Cline (1992) are much higher (Table 3.2). A doubling of carbon dioxide would result in damage to the economy of between 1 and 2 percent of GDP. He argues that the long-term effects (long term = 300 years) could be as high as 6 percent of GDP. The reason for the large difference between Cline and Nordhaus is that Nordhaus restricts his analysis to economic activities directly affected by climate, whereas Cline takes a wider view and tries to estimate the influence of warming on air pollution, water supplies, and human life (see notes to Table 3.2).

A more recent study by Fankhauser (quoted in Nordhaus 1993), using a similar methodology to Nordhaus and Cline, estimates the damage to be 1.3 percent of GDP for the United States, 1.4 percent for

TABLE 3.2

Estimates of Annual Damage from Global Warming to the United States

Sector or Area	Billions ($1981) (Nordhaus)	Billions ($1990) (Cline)	
Agriculture	−10.6 to +9.7	−17.5	
Forest loss	Small + or -	−3.3	
Species loss	?	−4.0	−ds
Sea level rise: loss of land	−1.55	−5.8	
Sea level rise:			
Construction of dikes, etc.	−3.74	−1.2	
Electricity requirements	−1.65	−11.2	
Non-electric heating	+1.16	+1.3	
Human amenity	+	−Xa	
Human life	?	−5.8	
Human morbidity	?	−Xm	
Migration	No mention	− 0.5	
Hurricanes	No mention	− 0.8	
Construction	+	+/−Xc	
Leisure activities	?	−1.7	
Water supply	−	−7.0	
Urban infrastructure	No mention	−0.1	
Air pollution:			
Ground-level ozone	?	−3.5	
Other	?	−Xo	
Total	−6.23	−61.1−(Xa+Xm +Xo+ds+/−Xc)	
% of GDP	0.26	1 (+1)	

Source: Adapted from Table 6 in Nordhaus (1991), p. 932 and Table 2 in Cline (1992), p. 33.
Notes: A question mark indicates that the author is not certain whether the effect, if any, will be positive or negative. Cline puts in a minimum estimate for species loss (ds) of $4 billion but argues that the damage could just as likely be 10 times higher. He argues that the effect on construction (Xc) could go either way. In a warmer

climate construction costs might be less, on the other hand, in a wetter climate they might be higher. Human amenity (*Xa*) might be adversely affected, for hotter climates may be more uncomfortable. It is possible that the cost to amenity could amount to one-quarter of 1 percent of personal income ($10 billion).

In addition to the direct cost to human life from diseases affected by weather (for example heart attacks and asthma), which is estimated to $5.8 billion a year, there may be other effects caused by the spread of diseases normally found only in the tropics (*Xm*). These diseases could add ½ percent, or $3 billion, to medical cost. Global warming would also lead to more air pollution, partly through an increase in ground level ozone at a yearly cost of $3.5 billion, but also through an increase in acid rain. The economic cost could amount to $10 billion/year. If these unknowns are added to the damage of $61.1 billion, the total damage may amount to around $117 billion (2 percent of GDP).

OECD countries, and 1.5 percent for the world as a whole, assuming a three-degree increase in global temperatures. Most studies agree that the consequences for less developed countries would be more severe than for industrialized countries because the former are more dependent on natural resources.

There are no estimates of the cost of global warming to the Canadian economy. It is estimated that a doubling of carbon dioxide will only have a small net effect on our agricultural production, allowing for larger local variations, whereas the effect on the forestry sector could be much more severe (Canada, 1991, p. 22-17 to 22-19).

The evidence shows that global warming will cause irreversible damage both to the environment and the economy. What is unclear is the extent of the damage. It is conceivable that continued global warming could lead to an environmental catastrophe with incalculable economic consequences. Large amounts of carbon might be released from cold ocean sediments, thus accelerating global warming so that the west Antarctic ice sheet would disintegrate, causing the sea level to rise by five to six meters (Cline, 1992, p. 46). Moreover, the decrease in the salinity of the ocean resulting from the melting of the icecaps could change ocean currents and further destabilize the climates.

Barring catastrophic effects, it is fair to say that economists are far more sanguine than natural scientists about the consequences of global warming. In a survey of experts on global warming, Nordhaus (1994) found substantial differences in opinion between economists and natural scientists. The non-economists predicted larger adverse effects on world incomes and voiced deep concern about the adaptive capacity of natural ecosystems. The economists, on the other hand, were of the opinion that the only limits to growth in the long run were energy and brain power, neither of which was in short supply. They also felt that technology will develop that will help us to adjust to climatic change. As for the existence value of species, one of them said, "I don't care about ants except for drugs" (quoted by Nordhaus, 1994, p. 50).

How much would it cost to reduce the emissions of greenhouse gases? Again, the estimates vary. As the burning of fuel accounts for the largest proportion of carbon emissions, most of the studies concentrate on the cost of using less energy. Others estimate the cost of reducing CFC emissions and halting deforestation. Forests retain carbon while they are growing and release carbon when they are decaying. According to Nordhaus (1991), most studies suggest that a reduction up to 10 percent of greenhouse gases can be obtained at a modest cost. However, larger reductions can only be achieved at a high cost. A 50 percent reduction in emissions could cost $200 billion a year, which is equivalent to 1 percent of world output.

To hold carbon emissions at a level slightly below where they are now would require a reduction in general emissions of 70 percent, equivalent to a 35 percent reduction in energy use (Cline, 1992, p. 52).[13] A 1 percent cut in energy use reduces GDP in the United States by 0.06 percent. Therefore, a 35 percent reduction in energy use would reduce GDP by 2.1 percent, which is consistent with the results of many of the large sophisticated energy models.[14] Much depends, however, on substitutability. For example, the burning of natural gas releases only 56 percent as much carbon as does coal per unit of energy output. (Oil releases 75 percent.) (Cline, 1992, p. 52). Therefore, using natural gas rather than coal would reduce emissions considerably. No carbon at all is emitted by nuclear power, solar, hydro, and wind energy. These energy sources could be used for electricity but are more problematic for transportation, even though considerable efforts have gone into the development of electric cars (see Chapter 4). The use of non-carbon energy resources also reduces the emission of common air pollutants such as nitrogen oxides, sulphur oxides, and suspended particulates (dust and smoke) with concomitant beneficial effects on human health.

Engineering studies estimate that considerable energy savings could be obtained at little or no cost through the adoption of more efficient technologies. For example, the use of compact fluorescent bulbs rather than normal incandescent light bulbs could cut the energy used for lighting in the average household by half. Weather stripping, heat pumps, and solar heating could reduce the energy used for heating by one-half and the energy used for air conditioning by one-quarter (Cline, 1992, p. 63). Similar savings could be achieved in transportation in the use of lighter cars and more efficient engines. However, the elimination of these inefficiencies would be only a one-time gain and would still leave future emissions far above the present level.

The planting of trees has been promoted as a relatively inexpensive way of countering global warming because reforestation or a reduction in deforestation could temporarily lock up some of the carbon in the atmosphere.[15] There are also other benefits of increased forest cover: less soil erosion and increased water retention, resulting in less flooding and improved habitat for wildlife. However, once a forest has reached maturity, the carbon released into the atmosphere from the decaying trees balances the amount of carbon stored in young, growing trees.

Nordhaus estimates that benefits outweigh costs for a reduction in greenhouse gas emissions of up to 11 percent from the current level (2 percent from a reduction in carbon and 9 percent from a in reduction CFCs). Cline, on the other hand, provides a benefit-cost analysis of a policy to cut carbon emissions back to 4 billion tons of carbon a year from the current 6 billion, and to hold them at that level for three centuries. Assuming a median estimate for damage due to global warming, the benefits of curbing greenhouse emissions do not cover the costs. However, if people are risk-averse, which means attributing a higher probability to the high-damage case, then the benefits exceed the costs by a ratio of 1.3 to 1.

Since abatement is so expensive and the long-term implications of global warming have not been fully studied, Cline proposes a two-stage

strategy. In the first stage, the machinery would be set in place for dealing aggressively with global warming. However, only moderate measures would be applied pending scientific confirmation of the long-
term effects. Then, in the year 2000 there would be a full-scale review
of the scientific data to determine whether the problem was more or
less severe than previously thought. If it were less severe, the modest
measures already implemented could be dismantled. If the problems
were more severe, the whole policy could come into effect.

Another well-known environmental economist, David Pearce,
agrees with Cline that aggressive action is warranted because of the
combination of uncertainty, irreversibility, initial low control costs,
possible very high damage costs in the absence of action, and potential-
ly high benefits from control (Pearce, 1991, p. 939). There are others
who advocate a wait-and-see attitude.[16]

If carbon emissions have to be cut, most economists (including
Cline and Nordhaus) advocate a carbon tax. (For an analysis, see Figure
2.1, Chapter 2.) Most studies seem to suggest that a carbon tax of $100
per ton of carbon (equivalent to a 65 percent increase in the price of a
$20 barrel of oil) would appear to achieve stabilization of carbon at 1990
levels by 2000 or 2005 (Pearce, 1991, p. 945). The tax could be set on
the basis of the carbon content of fossil fuels: coal, for example, would
be taxed at a higher rate than natural gas. In order to be politically
acceptable such a tax would probably have to be fiscally neutral; that is,
the revenue raised from the tax would be used to finance reductions in
other taxes. One could then make the argument that it is possible that
carbon taxes would make us richer because the tax is more efficient than
other taxes. The tax would correct the distortion (the market failure)
arising from carbon emission. A carbon tax would also act as an incentive to adopt cleaner technology and conserve energy. And, unlike some
other measures, a tax could be modified in the light of new information.

A carbon tax would also have disadvantages.[17] Without precise
knowledge of the optimal level of the tax, the tax might not achieve the
desired emission reductions. Moreover, a carbon tax might fall disproportionately on low-income people, who spend a larger proportion of
their incomes on fuel than others. The effect on low-income earners

could of course be ameliorated through the tax system in much the same fashion as the Canadian tax system compensates low-income earners for the GST.

Two Canadian economists, Whalley and Wigle (as reported in Whalley 1991), show the effects on the world economy and on the regional economies of a carbon tax based on national production, a tax based on national consumption, and a global carbon tax where the revenue would be redistributed to countries on the basis of population. They also calculate the effects of per-person emission ceilings. They found that consumption taxes would be the least costly to the world economy (2.1 percent of world GDP), and per person emission ceilings would be the most costly. The developing countries would gain most from a redistributed global production tax. Oil exporters would gain from production taxes and lose substantially from consumption taxes.

Most of the OECD countries, with the notable exception of the United States, have committed themselves to targets for carbon emissions. Some of the targets, including the Canadian ones, specify stabilization of emissions at the 1990 level by the year 2000, and some go further (see Canada, 1991, p. 22-25). The signing of the Montreal Protocol created an impression that the way had been paved for a legally binding climate treaty in which the signatories would commit themselves to reductions. It was hoped that a climate convention would be signed at the United Nations Conference on Environment and Development in Rio de Janeiro in 1992. Though a Framework Convention on Climate Change was indeed signed, it contained neither targets nor timetables, mainly because the United States was not in favour of such strong measures. The United States claimed that global warming was as yet an unconfirmed hypothesis. President Bush is reported to have said, "Our lifestyle is not up for negotiation."[18] The developing countries also resisted cutbacks unless they were accompanied by more financial aid from the rich countries.[19] They argued that poor countries were responsible for only a fraction of the energy used in the world, and that the rich countries should take the responsibility for global warming and foot the bill for reductions in carbon emissions. Other countries not in favour of measures to reduce carbon emissions are the large energy producers, which stand to lose from any reduction in the demand for fossil fuels. Two-thirds of the world's coal deposits are shared among the United States, China, and the former Soviet Union; three-quarters of the oil reserves are in the OPEC countries; and three-quarters of natural gas sources are in the OPEC countries and the former Soviet Union.

The targets that many OECD countries have agreed on are inefficient in that they inflict the same reduction in emissions on both high-cost and low-cost producers. It is not clear, however, how an efficient global scheme could be devised. One possibility might be to allocate targets on the basis of population. In that case, the developed countries would already have used up their rights for emissions. On the other hand, if the targets are shared out on the basis of income it would leave every group of countries with some scope for emissions but would give most of the rights to the rich. One could argue that the more the initial allocation of targets coincides with some notion of fairness, the more essential it would be to allow for the trading of carbon emission rights.

The initial distribution of carbon emission rights would be as problematic as the initial distribution of targets. If, for example, rights to emit were sold at $25 a ton of carbon and if initial rights were given out on the basis of population, the rich countries would have to pay the poor countries a sum almost equal to the total of foreign aid in 1989 for the right to emit current levels of carbon (The World Bank, 1991, p. 166). Clearly some sort of payment is essential; otherwise a country that is likely to lose from a climate treaty will have no incentive to sign and a strong incentive to cheat. There is a mechanism for such payment in the Global Environmental Facility, which was set up in 1990 to pay for pilot projects that reduce global warming and conserve biodiversity.

Given the high costs of controlling global warming and the limited resources available, an argument can be made that other kinds of environmental damage deserve higher priority. More people could die from water pollution than from global warming. In some countries soil erosion leaves too many hungry, and the search for firewood for cooking and for new land for agriculture has led to massive deforestation, which in itself changes climate. Some argue that the highest priority should be to control population growth since it is unlikely that our current environment and living standards could support the projected world population of 8 billion by the year 2020.

Conclusions

In this chapter we looked at pollution as an important limitation on our well-being. Air quality in Canada appears to have improved but is still lagging behind that of some other countries. Air pollution, which is in our big cities, has in general improved owing to legislated emissions controls. However, ground-level ozone still appears to be a problem in many areas. Our water-quality problems are serious, particularly as they concern surface and ground water pollution. For example, some of our cities still dump raw sewage into waterways.

Canadian governments have been reluctant to use market-based approaches to pollution control. For example, Canadians do not usually pay directly for the water they use. It is possible that our hard-earned improvements in the level of pollution could have been achieved at substantially lower costs if fees or tradable permits had been used.

Waste disposal has become a serious problem in many urban areas. As a solution many municipalities have adopted costly recycling programs that have had litte success in reducing the amount of garbage. More cost-effective solutions might be offered by market-based approaches that would give people some incentive to minimize their waste.

We also analyzed two very serious long-term environmental problems resulting from increased air pollution. One was the destruction of the ozone layer caused by the build-up of chlorofluorocarbons in the atmosphere; the other was global warming caused by the build-up of greenhouse gases, the most important of which is carbon dioxide. The destruction of the ozone layer, which is the less controversial of the two, has prompted active intervention through the Montreal Protocol. Global warming is more contentious, even though the evidence is clear that warming is taking place. What is not agreed on is the likely damage from warming and the need for action, particularly as any action is likely to be very costly.

TOPICS FOR DISCUSSION

1. In your opinion, what is the most serious local environmental problem where you live? How are the politicians dealing with the problem? Have you any suggestions for improvement?

2. The Conference Board of Canada has suggested that Canada should consider introducing a carbon tax. Do you agree?

3. In 1994 Ontario Hydro was much criticized for a proposal to buy a tract of rain forest in Costa Rica to offset some damage created by the burning of fossil fuels in electricity generation. Do you agree with the proposal?

RECOMMENDED READING

Statistics Canada's occasional publication *Human Activity and the Environment* (cat. 11-509E) gives a good statistical summary of various environmental indicators. *The State of Canada's Environment* (Canada 1991) gives an encyclopedic overview of Canada's environmental problems. Comparative data can be found in the United Nations annual *Human Development Report* and the OECD's *State of the Environment Report*.

Cline (1992) provides a fairly readable summary of the causes and economic effects of global warming.

References

Cline, William R. "Scientific Basis for the Greenhouse Effect." *The Economic Journal* 101 (September 1991): 904-18.

Cline, William R. *Global Warming: The Economic Stakes*. Washington D.C.: Institute for International Economics, May 1992.

Doern, Bruce G. ed. *Getting It Green: Case Studies in Canadian Environmental Regulation*. Toronto: C.D. Howe Institute, 1990.

Dorfman, Robert and Nancy S. Dorfman eds. *Economics of the Environment: Selected Readings*. 3rd ed. New York: W.W. Norton & Co., 1993.

The Economist, "Costing the earth. A survey of the environment," Sept. 2, 1989; "How to throw things away," April 13, 1991; "CFCs Hole Stoppers," March 7, 1992; "A survey of the global environment," May 30, 1992; "Atmospheric interference," Nov. 21, 1992; "A quick fix on ozone," Nov 28, 1992; "Waste and the environment," May 29, 1993.

The Financial Post "Deposit or disposable? It's a can of worms," March 12, 1993.

The Globe and Mail. "Why effect of pulp mills on environment is complex," February 2, 1993; "Ontario toughening organochlorine rules," February 2, 1993.

Canada. *Economic Instruments for Environmental Protection. Discussion Paper.* [Ottawa]: Ministry of Supply and Services, 1992.

Canada. *Canada's Green Plan for a Healthy Environment.* [Ottawa]: Ministry of Supply and Services, 1990.

Canada. *The State of Canada's Environment.* [Ottawa]: Ministry of Supply and Services, 1991.

Intergovernmental Panel on Climate Change. *Potential Impacts of Climate Change: Report Prepared for IPCC by Working Group II.* New York: WMO and United Nations Environment Programme, June 1990.

Maclaren, Virginia M. "Waste Management: Current Crisis and Future Challenge." In *Resource Management,* ed. Bruce Mitchell (1991): 28-54.

Mitchell, Bruce. ed. *Resource Management and Development. Addressing Conflict and Uncertainty.* Toronto: Oxford University Press, 1991.

Nordhaus, William D. "Expert Opinion on Climate Change." *American Scientist* 82 (January-February 1994): 45-52.

Nordhaus, William D. "Reflections on the Economics of Climate Change." *Journal of Economic Perspectives* 7 (Fall 1993): 11-25.

Nordhaus, William D. "To Slow or not to Slow: The Economics of the Greenhouse Effect." *The Economic Journal* 101 (July 1991): 920-37.

OECD. *The State of the Environment.* Paris: OECD, 1991.

Olewiler, Nancy. "Environmental Quality and Policy in a Global Economy." In *Productivity, Growth and Canada's International Competitiveness,* eds. Thomas J. Courchene and Douglas D. Purvis. Kingston: John Deutsch Institute for the Study of Economic Policy, 1993: 351-405.

Pearce, David. "The Role of Carbon Taxes in Adjusting to Global Warming." *The Economic Journal* 101 (July 1991): 938-48.

Shaw, Jane and Richard L. Stroup. "Global Warming and Ozone Depletion." In *Economics and the Environment,* Walter Block. Vancouver: The Fraser Institute, 1990.

Smith, Douglas A. and Keith Vodden "Global Environmental Policy: The Case of Ozone Depletion." *Canadian Public Policy - Analyse de politiques* 25 (December 1989): 413-24.

Solow, Robert M. "The Economics of Resources or the Resources of Economics." *American Economic Review* 64 (May 1974): 1-14.

Tietenberg, Tom. *Environmental and Natural Resource Economics.* New York: Harper Collins Publishers Inc., 1992.

VanKooten, G.C., Louise M. Arthur and W.R. Wilson. "Global Warming: Sequestering Carbon in Canadian Forests. Some Economic Considerations." *Canadian Public Policy - Analyse de politiques* 28 (June 1992): 127-39.

Whalley, John. "The Interface between Environmental and Trade Policies." *The Economic Journal* 101 (March 1991): 180-89.

Weyant, John P. "Costs of Reducing Global Carbon Emissions." *Journal of Economic Perspectives* 7 (Fall 1993): 27-47.

Endnotes

1 Acidity is measured by the pH level, where pH level of 7 is neutral; anything less is acidic.

2 Tietenberg (1992), p. 405 provides a summary of the evidence.

3 For a few case studies of Canadian regulations, see Doern (1990).

4 The toxic effects of mercury depend on the type of mercury and on the character of water. Most dangerous is methyl mercury in combination with high organic loads.

   The effect of mercury poisoning was first seen in Japan where the so-called Minamata disease was found to be caused by mercury poisoning. Fifty-two people died and an additional 150 suffered brain and nerve damage (Tietenberg, 1992, p. 483). We had our own tragedy in Canada in the Ojibwa communities of Grassy Narrows and White Dog in northwestern Ontario. In 1970 it was discovered that the river which ran through the communities was polluted with mercury. The mercury came from a pulp and paper mill in Dryden which used a mercury cell in producing chlorine and which had discharged approximately 9-11 tons of mercury into the river. Many of the residents were found to have unacceptably high levels of mercury in their blood (Canada, 1991, p. 3-21).

5 Recent research appears to suggest that chlorine used in pulp mills may not be the culprit after all. The results of recent studies both in Canada and the United States suggest that another chemical may be responsible for the adverse effect of pulp mill effluents on fish. Which chemical of the 2000 or so chemicals in mill waste water is at fault is not clear (*The Globe and Mail*, February 2, 1993).

6 The countries listed were Canada, Australia, the United States, West Germany, Switzerland, Netherland, the United Kingdom, Japan, and Sweden.

7 Recycled glass is apparently cheaper to produce than glass from new materials. However, it is not clear if this still is true if the cost of collecting the glass is included in the price.

8 One example is the manufacture of high-grade paper from de-inked waste paper. In the process, three times more suspended solids are discharged compared to the manufacture from raw timber. On the other hand, one study quoted in Tietenberg (1992, p. 210) shows that the efficient private recycling ratio for making newsprint is 0.55. This is not the case if all the environmental costs were taken into account. Then, the optimum reuse ratio would be

9 According to *The Economist* (April 13, 1991), estimates from the United States show that an efficient curb-side collection scheme costs $70 per ton. The additional cost of sorting and cleaning waste brings the cost to $110 per ton. The market value of the scrap could be $30-$40 per ton. If landfill costs are in excess of $70-$80 per ton, recycling is worthwhile, otherwise not.

10 The municipality of Toronto requires newspapers to be sold in curbside boxes to contain a certain percentage of recycled materials.

11 Pay-to-throw schemes could also lead to the "Seattle stomp." Residents in Seattle proved to be good at fitting more garbage into a normal size container by compacting the garbage. (*The Economist*, May 29, 1993).

12 For a short survey of the literature see Cline (1991) p. 43-47 and for Canada *The State of Canada's Environment* (Canada, 1991, p. 22-17 to 22-23).

13 It is interesting to note that it would be impossible to limit emissions to 1991 levels by 2050 if China does not participate in the program. If carbon emissions in China grow at 4 percent per year, Chinese emissions alone would equal total world emissions today in 56 years (Weyant, 1993, p. 35).

14 For a survey, see Weyant (1993).

15 Van Kooten *et al.* (1992) shows that Canada functions as a "carbon sink" which means that our forests tie up more carbon than we generate in our activities. We could expand our forests to absorb an additional 9.6 percent carbon which would not be as cost-effective as increasing the fuel efficiency of cars.

16 See for example Shaw and Stroup (1989).

17 For a summary of the literature, see Pearce (1991).

18 The Clinton Administration reversed U.S. policy on this issue in April 1993, and it was expected at that time that the administration would press for the addition of a substantive protocol.

19 Some argue that the cost of curbing carbon emissions in many third world countries will not be very high, as it can be largely achieved through the elimination of costly subsidies. Electricity prices on average cover only one-third of the generating costs (*The Economist*, May 30, 1992).

4

Resources in
the Canadian Economy

This chapter will give you an appreciation of the importance of resources and resource extraction for Canadian economic well-being, and the principles involved in managing the resources in a sustainable fashion, with particular emphasis on renewable resources. You will be able to explain the causes of the failure of the fisheries on the East Coast, the controversy over clear-cutting on Vancouver Island, and the possibility of economical alternatives to the burning of fossil fuels for generating energy.

The livelihoods of Canadians are more dependent on natural resources, renewable and non-renewable, than those of people in most other industrialized countries. We are therefore very vulnerable if we lose our markets for these natural resources or if the resources decline in quantity or quality. In this chapter we will analyze the importance of resources in the Canadian economy. We will look briefly at the principles of managing non-renewable and renewable resources. We will discuss the global issue of biodiversity and the growing use of trade boycotts to force countries, including Canada, to improve their conservation efforts. We will then outline some economic principles for managing forests and fisheries. The last part of the chapter is an analysis of energy resources and their use in Canada, in the light of our discussion in the previous chapter of the effects of the burning of fossil fuels on air pollution and global warming. We will look at alternatives to fossil fuels: nuclear power and renewable energy sources such as hydro-electric power, solar power, and wind power.

Resources and the Canadian Economy

The production and export of renewable and non-renewable resources (staple products) have played a large part in the economic development of Canada. Most Canadians are familiar with the importance of the fur trade and the Hudson's Bay Company in the exploration and settlement of Canada.

The importance of staples in the development of Canada was described by the famous Canadian economic historian Harold Innis (1956) and further elaborated by Mel Watkins (1967). **The staples thesis**, as it came to be known, is basically a theory of export-led growth. When a new territory was settled, the immigrants, unable to produce all the goods necessary to maintain their traditional way of life, had to buy them from the mother country. Since these goods had to be paid for, the settlers were in constant search of goods that could be exported to earn the necessary income. Since the exports had to be transported over long distances, they had to fetch high prices to cover the high transportation costs. The earliest commodities to fit these requirements were cod, caught off the Grand Banks of Newfoundland, and fur, particularly beaver. When the fur trade collapsed, lumber became the dominant commodity, followed by gold, wheat, and minerals.

The staples thesis rests on the assumption that the export of staples is the leading sector in the economy and that development will take the form of diversification around the export base (see Watkins 1967). The extent of diversification depends on the linkages between the export product and other sectors of the economy. There are three types of linkage: backward, forward, and final-demand. A backward linkage occurs if there is investment in the domestic production of goods serving as inputs in the production of the export. For example, if the export is fish, a backward linkage would be the production of nets and boats. A forward linkage, by contrast, is the production of goods that use the export good as an input, such as the production of fish meal. A final-demand linkage is the production of consumer goods demanded by people who receive payments from the export industry in the form of wages, salaries, interest, rents, or dividends. The more numerous these linkages, the more beneficial is the effect of the export product on the economy as a whole.

According to Watkins, the success of a staple economy depends on its ability to shift resources from one staple product to another according to the dictates of the market. If this ability is lost, the economy would stagnate. The capacity of the staple thesis to explain Canadian economic growth, has been questioned, the chief criticism being that manufacturing provided more stimulus to growth than the theory allows.[1]

Today, the resource sector, which consists of forestry, agriculture, fishing, trapping, and the working of mines, quarries, and oil wells, accounts for less than 6 percent of GDP and total employment. That figure, however, understates the importance of resources in the economy in several ways. One is that it does not include the production of hydroelectricity, which is an important energy resource for Canada. A second reason is that the 6 percent does not include mining taxes and royalties paid on the extraction of oil and gas, and stumpage fees paid on the extraction of timber from crown land, even though these payments are part of the return to resource extraction. Third, some resources are the basis for an important processing sector. For example, forestry is the basis for the pulp and paper, newsprint, and wood-products industries. Indeed, manufacturing related to forestry is the largest employer in Canada.

The resource sector varies in its regional significance. Table 4.1 shows the percentage in provincial GDPs of selected resources. Saskatchewan and Alberta are far more dependent on resource extraction than the other provinces, Saskatchewan because of agriculture and Alberta because of oil and gas production.[2] It is interesting to note that direct earnings from fishing make up only a small fraction of gross domestic product in Newfoundland, and that even though agriculture accounts for a only a minute share of the provincial economy, Ontario is a more important agricultural producer than any of the Prairie provinces (see Table 4.2). By far the most logging, in terms of value, takes place in British Columbia, followed by Quebec and Ontario; and the most fishing

TABLE 4.1

Selected Resources as a Percentage of Provincial GDP, 1992

Region	Agriculture	Forestry	Fishing[a]	Mining	Total
Canada	1.83	0.49	0.14	3.30	5.78
Newfoundland	0.31	—	–0.74	2.73	3.78
Prince Edward Island	7.40	0.33	1.92	0.01	9.66
Nova Scotia	1.01	—	1.85	1.21	4.07
New Brunswick	1.22	1.83	0.49	1.46	5.00
Quebec	1.26	0.47	0.05	0.84	2.62
Ontario	1.08	0.19	0.01	0.89	2.17
Manitoba	5.18	—	0.10	1.66	6.94
Saskatchewan	10.78	—	0.04	10.16	20.98
Alberta	3.59	—	0.01	16.81	21.41
British Columbia	0.98	1.70	0.31	2.48	5.47
Yukon & the Northwest Territories	0.07	0.13	0.22	17.54	17.96

Source: Statistics Canada, Provincial Gross Domestic Product by Industry, 1984-1992 (15-203).

Note: GDP is gross domestic product at factor cost in current dollars Mining comprises mines, quarries, and oil wells.

[a] The closing of the cod fishery has affected the figures for 1992. The 1991 percentage figures for Newfoundland, Prince Edward Island, and Nova Scotia were 1.52, 2.21, and 2.23 respectively.

is done in Nova Scotia, followed by British Columbia and Newfoundland.

Fifty-two percent of our exports are raw materials or processed raw materials (see Table 4.3).[3] Therefore we still have some of the features of a staple economy, in that we are dependent on the health of our resource sector to pay our way in the world. We are the world's second-largest exporter of fish products, and we supply one-quarter of the world's

TABLE 4.2

Provincial Percentage Distribution of GDP in Selected Resources 1992

Region	Agriculture	Forestry	Fishing[a]	Mining	Total
Canada	100.00	100.00	100.00	100.00	100.00
Newfoundland	0.23	—	7.26[a]	1.11	0.88
Prince Edward Island	0.30	0.22	4.52	0	0.54
Nova Scotia	1.43	n/a	35.09	0.94	1.83
New Brunswick	1.33	7.44	7.15	0.89	1.72
Quebec	15.63	21.84	8.43	5.73	10.31
Ontario	23.28	14.89	4.19	10.53	14.80
Manitoba	9.99	—	2.47	1.77	4.24
Saskatchewan	17.82	—	0.83	9.28	11.01
Alberta	22.24	n.a.	0.77	57.52	40.10
British Columbia	6.73	43.85	28.46	9.47	11.90
Yukon & the Northwest Territories	0.02	0.14	0.83	2.76	1.62

Source: Statistics Canada. Provincial Gross Domestic Product by Industry, 1984–91 (15–203).

Note: GDP is gross domestic product at factor cost in current dollars. Mining comprises mines, quarries, and oil wells.

n.a. — not available for reasons of confidentiality.

[a] The Newfoundland share was 12.63 percent in 1991.

imports of softwood lumber. We are the largest uranium and zinc producer in the world, and are the second-largest in the production of nickel, asbestos, gypsum, potash, and titanium. We rank among the top five in gold, copper, lead, and some other metals (Canada, 1991, p. 11-6).

The prospects for some of our resource exports, however, are not good. We have lost our dominance in some resources to lower-cost producers, some of which are believed to be dumping ore on the world market to earn foreign exchange. We used to supply 80 percent of the

TABLE 4.3
Principal Merchandise Exports of Canada, 1991

Exports	Millions of dollars	Percentage of total
Live animals	1,399	0.79
Meat and fish	3,946	2.23
Cereals and preparations	4,038	2.28
Other food, feed, beverages and tobacco	4,212	2.38
Total food, feed, beverages and tobacco	12,196	6.89
Metal ores, contentrates, scrap	3,444	1.95
Other crude materials, inedible[a]	18,070	10.22
Total, crude materials, inedible[a]	21,515	12.17
Wood and paper	25,231	14.27
Textiles	1,011	0.57
Chemicals	9,025	5.11
Iron and steel	3,429	1.94
Non-ferrous metals	9,587	5.42
Other fabricated materials	8,495	4.81
Total, fabricated materials, inedible	56,778	32.12
Industrial machinery	5,681	3.21
Agricultural machinery and tractors	768	0.43
Transportation equipment	53,954	30.52
Other equipment and tools	9,921	5.61
Other end products	12,512	7.07

Total, end products	82,836	46.86
Special transactions	2,033	1.15
Total exports	176,757	100

Source: Statistics Canada. Summary of Canadian International Trade, December 1993 (cat. 650–001), Table X–3.
a This category includes crude petroleum (value $6,907 million), and natural gas ($5,801 million).

world's nickel, compared to 25 percent today. Renewable resources are also in difficulties. For example, the eastern cod fisheries have been closed for lack of fish. Environmentalists and loggers are at war in British Columbia, where the environmentalists want to stop further clear-cutting of virgin forests. Unless this issue is resolved, it is possible that Canadian lumber exports could be banned in parts of Europe. Similarly, future electricity exports from the James Bay project in northern Quebec to the United States were cancelled because of adverse publicity surrounding phase II of the James Bay development. Agricultural exports have suffered because of the overproduction on world markets caused by agricultural subsidies in Europe and the United States.

The Management of Non-Renewable Natural Resources

There are two problems in resource management: the problem of optimum exploitation, and the problem of pricing and the distribution of revenues earned from extraction. Optimum exploitation is an economic problem, but in the case of non-renewable resources it is also an ethical problem, for it involves deciding how much of the resource should be left for future generations to exploit and use. Mineral resources are not reproducible. They can be recycled, but their total stock can never be increased. Because of the second law of thermodynamics, recycling can never recover all the material, and therefore the stock is always decreasing if the mineral is being used. The

107

problem here is to decide how quickly the resource should be used.

A mineral deposit can be compared to any type of asset.[4] The value of a deposit stems from the discounted future income flows the owner expects to earn from its extraction and sale. The expected profit is then equal to the discounted income stream minus the discounted cost of extraction. A mineral deposit can increase in value if the price increases or the extraction cost decreases. In equilibrium, the value of a deposit must grow at a rate equal to the rate of interest (this is called the **Hotelling Rule** after Hotelling, 1931). If the value increases more slowly than the rate of interest, it does not pay the owner to hold on to the ore. If the owner expects the value of the deposit to increase by 5 percent a year, and the prevailing interest rate is 7 percent, the owner would be better off exploiting the resource quickly and investing the profit somewhere else at 7 percent. Thus, the higher the interest rates, the faster the ore will be exploited. On the other hand, if values were increasing quickly, it would pay the owners to delay production and thereby enjoy substantial capital gains. In theory, scarcity will finally force the market price so high that demand will fall to zero, and if markets operate perfectly, this will also be the time when the last tonne produced will be the last tonne left in the ground.

According to this analysis, a sequence of deposits and mines will be brought into operation, starting with high-grade deposits where the ore could be extracted at a relatively low cost. A high-cost mine and a low-cost mine cannot operate concurrently, because the value of the ore deposit cannot increase at the same rate for both, since the market price would be the same but costs would not. As time goes on, the "good" deposits will be exhausted and the higher-cost deposits will be brought into production. Recycled materials will also become an alternative to virgin ores, and substitute materials may be developed. For many resources it is possible that there is a "backstop" technology capable of producing at high cost, but from a resource base which is almost inexhaustable. Solar energy may be such a backstop technology. As there is no scarcity rent, the technology would come into production as soon as present energy prices had risen enough to cover the production cost of the new technology. The backstop technology provides a ceiling for the market price of energy.

The exploitation of non-renewable natural resources creates a quandary about the application of the criterion of sustainability. By definition the exploitation of these resources cannot be sustainable. Yet it is in nobody's interest to leave them in the ground forever. In this case, one could argue that sustainability would imply that if we use up something that is irreplaceable, then we should be thinking about providing future generations with a substitute of equal value.[5] Indeed, it can be demonstrated that if the pure return to non-renewable natural resources is invested, it will guarantee a constant capacity to consume in perpetuity for future generations (Hartwick 1978). The Alberta Heritage Trust Fund is an example of an attempt to do precisely that. The fund was created by the Alberta government in the seventies with the intention of setting aside some of the oil revenue to provide a basis for the Alberta economy when the oil runs out. But other examples are hard to find.

The problem of resource pricing and revenues has received much attention in Canada. The attention has often centred on the question of who is entitled to the economic rent generated by a resource. (Any excess profit earned in resource exploitation is scarcity rent.) How much of the rent should go to the landlord (the owner of the resource, which may be the federal or provincial government, or the individual) or the tenant (the corporation or the individual who has acquired the right to exploit the resource)? Because of disputes about oil and gas rents, relations between the Alberta government and the federal government were often acrimonious during the seventies and early eighties.

The Management of Renewable Resources and the Issue of Biodiversity

The successful management of renewable resources depends on the ability to determine and maintain the optimum resource stock. In theory, a renewable resource, properly managed, can be harvested in perpetuity; if it is not properly managed, it may become extinct. An example of a resource harvested to extinction is the passenger pigeon, and it seems likely that some African species, such as the black rhinoceros, will suffer the same fate.

Trees have become an issue in their own right, partly because they lock up carbon dioxide, but also because forests are home to most of the earth's species. For that reason, deforestation has been linked to the issue of biodiversity. A single hectare of a tropical rain forest may contain more than eight hundred species of woody plants, as many as exist in all North America. It is estimated that the tropical rain forests contain between 50 and 75 percent of all species, including 90 percent of all insects (*The Economist*, September 2, 1989).

Unlike the atmosphere, biological diversity is not global common property. Ecological habitats belong to individual countries that presumably have an interest in managing their resources well. However, the protection of biological diversity concerns all of us in different ways. First, the destruction of ecosystems and the extinction of species is irreversible, and many people value the existence of species, even though they may never see them. (In Chapter 2, we introduced the concept of **existence value**). Perhaps they feel that the natural ecosystems should be saved for future generations, or perhaps they feel an ethical responsibility to avoid the destruction of forms of life that have evolved over thousands of years. These types of externalities are not accounted for by the market. Second, there are economic and health benefits resulting from the use of plants and animals. It is estimated that five thousand plant and animal species are used in traditional and modern medicine in China, and two thousand in the Amazon Basin. Even in the United States a quarter of all prescriptions contain plant ingredients, and over three thousand antibiotics are derived from micro-organisms (Cline, 1992, p. 45). We do not know when a plant might become useful. For example, in the spring of 1992 the bark of the Pacific yew tree was discovered to be effective in the treatment of ovarian and breast cancer. Third, natural plant varieties are important in selective breeding. The reliance on one species in agriculture can have disastrous consequences if that particular species is wiped out by disease or drought. As a prevention wild crops are periodically bred back into cultivated ones to provide added resistance.

There are difficult issues here. Are some animals more important than others? If so, why? Why does the preservation of some animals receive a sympathetic hearing while the near extinction of others goes unnoticed? In 1991, after intense lobbying by environmental organizations, the U.S. government declared that 11.6 million acres of timberland in the Pacific Northwest should be protected from logging to preserve the habitat of the spotted owl (Cline, 1992, p. 45.). Would people be equally prepared to make sacrifices to preserve a rare earthworm? Should we preserve every species at any cost? Obviously that would be impossible. Polasky and Broadus, as reported in *The Economist* (June 3, 1992), argue that all species are not equally important to biodiversity. A criterion for preservation should be the evolutionary distance between species. Close relatives have many genes in common; therefore it may not be necessary to save all, only one. It could also be argued that if one were to take full account of the costs of preservation and if two species are equally important in genetic terms, it might be better to make the safe species safer, rather than the endangered species less endangered.

Since loss of biodiversity and the threat of extinction are local occurrences, a country that wants to protect a species or an ecological environment outside its own borders may not be able to do so. The most common way of making other countries take notice is to use trade or aid as a lever. For example under the Convention on International Trade in Endangered Species of Wild Fauna and Flora (CITES), all international trade in elephant products is forbidden. Austria and Holland have banned all imports of unsustainably produced tropical timber. Consumer boycotts in European countries have also been successful in limiting the trade in animal fur. The annual seal hunt off the Gulf of St. Lawrence was stopped after the market collapsed. Some Canadian lumber producers are threatened by a German consumer boycott. Several British firms cancelled their contracts with McMillan Bloedel in the spring of 1994 because of the adverse publicity surrounding clear-cutting in Clayoquot Sound on Vancouver Island.

The use of trade bans has come under the scrutiny of GATT after a complaint against the U.S. Marine Mammals Protection Act. The act states that imports of tuna from countries fishing in the eastern Pacific will not be allowed unless the countries have programs to prevent the accidental catching of dolphins, which are often caught in tuna nets, and unless the average number of dolphins caught is less than one and a quarter times the number caught by U.S. vessels. Under the act an embargo was imposed on tuna imports from Mexico, Venezuela, and Vanuatu (*The Economist*, May 30, 1992). Mexico complained to GATT, which ruled in Mexico's favour, arguing that, under the GATT non-discrimination clause, imported and domestic products should receive equal treatment regardless of the methods of production. Other cases are likely to follow because trade provisions are contained in several multilateral environmental agreements, including CITES, the Basle Convention, and the Montreal Protocol. GATT officials fear that at a time of slow growth and high unemployment there is a temptation to use the environment as an excuse to erect trade barriers.

In 1992 the United Nations Conference on the Environment and Development passed a biodiversity convention (The Convention on Protecting Species and Habitats), which the United States first refused to sign because of the provisions concerning biotechnology.[6] The convention was passed after prolonged discussions between rich and poor countries. The poor countries have the bulk of the world's biological diversity, whereas the rich countries have the capacity to use biodiversity through biotechnology. The rich countries obviously want access to the biodiversity of the poor countries as a basis for biotechnology, whereas the poor countries want the technology so that they can use their biodiversity. The convention makes a gesture towards recognizing the right of poor countries in a clause stating that biotechnologies developed from the resources of one country by a company from another country should be shared on a fair and equitable basis (that is, royalties should be paid) (*The Economist*, June 13, 1992).

The Management of Forests

The preservation of biodiversity was not an issue until recently in Canadian forestry management. Previously the emphasis was on the optimum harvesting of trees as a source of wood. Since trees mature slowly compared to plants, the amount of wood in a tree keeps accumulating up to a point. Therefore the management of forestry has concentrated on determining the best times to cut and replant in order to maximize the quantity of wood harvested. Today, however, efficient forestry management must take into account the functions of trees in the ecological system. Trees clean the air by absorbing carbon dioxide and other pollutants and by emitting oxygen. They counter the greenhouse effect by acting as carbon sinks. Forests harbour wildlife and plants that cannot exist without them, and they protect our waterways from soil erosion. Forests are also used for recreation. From society's viewpoint, all the beneficial functions of a forest have to be considered in decisions about harvesting and planting. One study has calculated that 41 percent of the value of the national forests in the United States is in recreation, and 12 percent in fish and wildlife, while the timber value was only 27 percent (*The Economist*, June 22, 1991).

In urban areas trees improve the air quality and also reduce energy costs by providing shade in summer and protection against cold winds in winter. A study of urban forests by the U.S. Forest Service estimates that the net benefit to Chicago and surrounding areas of planting 95,000 trees would be $38 million over 30 years, or $402 a tree (*The Globe and Mail*, April 16, 1994). The same study estimates that in 1991 alone the value of the removal by trees of the common air pollutants was $9.2 million.

From the viewpoint of a private owner of a stand of timber, when should a forest be cut? According to the foresters, cutting should be done when **the mean annual increment** is maximized. The mean annual increment is calculated by dividing the total volume of a stand at the end of each decade by the number of years the stand has been growing. From a business viewpoint that may not be economically efficient. The ideal time to harvest would be the time that maximizes the net present value of the wood. The net present value depends on the value of the timber, the discount rate, and the cost of planting and harvesting. It can be shown that profit maximization would dictate an earlier cutting of timber than the forester would suggest. On the other hand, if all the social costs and benefits of forests were included in the analysis, the forests would be left longer, and it is possible that some would not be cut at all. For example, it is possible that a cost-benefit analysis would show that virgin forests in British Columbia and Temagami in northern Ontario should not be cut. It is estimated that while the cutting of timber has increased fivefold in Canada since the 1920s, the recreational use of forests has increased a hundredfold (*The Economist*, June 22, 1991). This economic value of forests may in itself justify increased conservation.

In Canada, the annual harvest (the Annual Allowable Cut, or AAC) is based on mean annual increments as well as on the number and quality of species and their accessibility. Each province estimates its AAC, and private companies sign agreements for the right to cut certain areas. The right to harvest carries with it the responsibility to replant and in general to protect the forest. The annual area logged has increased from 700,000 hectares in the mid-seventies to one million hectares in 1988; little of this has been replanted (Canada, 1991, p. 10-11).

Most logging in Canada (89.6 percent) is done by the controversial clear-cutting method rather than by more selective cutting practices. The advocates of clear-cutting argue that it is an effective method of harvesting and renewing same-age stands of forest (where all the trees are the same age). Clear-cutting also provides lots of light, which is required by the new seedlings. In ancient forests, on the other hand, clear-cuts destroy the ecosystem, which may never regain its original character. Some animals, such as the woodland caribou and northern spotted owl, can live only in old-growth forests. And migratory birds that winter in tropical rain forests and breed in Canadian forests are also endangered by clear-cutting.

Some biologists argue that wildlife will do better if there are small clear-cuts linked by corridors of continuous growth, while others argue for logging in vast chunks, leaving large areas untouched and so provide an unbroken expanse of suitable habitat for animals (Canada, 1991, p. 10-13 to 10-14). There is also concern over the effect of the modern practice of stripping trees of their branches and leaves away from the logging site. This means that significantly fewer nutrients are returned to the forest floor, jeopardizing future forest growth.

In Sweden it has been shown that sustainable forestry can be made profitable. In that country, three-quarters of the forests are privately owned, compared to only 10 percent in Canada. Timber stocks have increased in Sweden, while Canadian statistics indicate that our current forestry use cannot be sustainable (Skogsindustrierna, 1993 and Canada, 1991, p. 10-15).[7] It is estimated that Swedish and Finnish tree farmers produce two or three times more wood per hectare of productive land than any province in eastern Canada (Canada, 1991, 10-16). According to the Swedish Pulp and Paper Association, sustainable forest management embodies the following principles (Skogsindustrierna, 1993, p. 15):

1. Forest land should not be regarded as a homogeneous unit; instead species of trees and forestry methods are chosen to suit the conditions on each site.

2. Important habitats are saved to protect biodiversity.

3. Low-productivity forest land (for example forests growing in dry areas, cold areas, or areas which are badly drained) is excluded from silviculture because it is often the home of many species of fauna and flora which would be adversely affected by cutting.

4. Forests near built-up and tourist areas are, because of their recreational value, tended by considerate methods such as selective cutting rather than clear-cutting.

5. Reserves should be set aside for protecting unique environments and sensitive flora and fauna. Many species depend on old growth forests.

In Canada the forestry industry currently generates one in fifteen jobs. The renewal of our forests and the transformation of forestry management to a sustainable basis is one of Canada's biggest challenges.

The Management of Fisheries

Fish are another important Canadian resource that has not been harvested sustainably. Indeed, the Newfoundland cod fisheries have been managed so badly that they were closed in 1992 in order to let the stock recuperate. The mismanagement of the resource has had devastating consequences for fishermen on the Atlantic coast, where almost one thousand communities depend on fishing for a living. Canada's position as a major fish exporter is clearly in jeopardy.

Fish are an example of a renewable, common-property resource, which is difficult to manage because it suffers from the "tragedy of the commons."[8] Because common-property resources cannot be controlled exclusively by a single agent, it is difficult to control access to them. When access is common and unlimited, there is no incentive to conserve. If I owned all the fish in the ocean, I would have an interest in managing the fish properly, since any benefit from the action would accrue to me or my children. But if there is no owner, the users of a resource consider only their own short-term interests, which are served by maximizing their own rate of use, before others take the catch. As a user I would have no guarantee that any unselfish action on my part would be matched by others. The fish that I don't catch in the interest of conservation would be caught by somebody else.

Suppose, however, that all the fish were owned by one person. How should that person manage the fish stock? The stability and growth of a fish population is illustrated in Figure 4.1. There is a relationship between the growth of a fish population and the size of the fish population. At point S4, the fish population is in its natural equilibrium, where births and in-migration of fish are equal to deaths and out-migration. If for any reason the population were to increase beyond this level (which is determined by the availability of food, water temperature,and so on), mortality rates would rise, and the population would revert to the equilibrium level (S4). Similarly, if the fish stock suddenly declined to S3, the births and growth in the population would rise and the population would increase to its equilibrium level. If, on the other hand, the addition to the stock were removed through fishing, the population could remain at S3. Fishing would be sustainable. S2 is known as **the maximum sustainable yield**, which is the size of the population that would yield the maximum fish catch. However, the maximum sustainable yield is not necessarily the most efficient yield for the person who owns the resource. From an asset viewpoint, the cost of harvesting as well as the rate of interest must be taken into account. A fisherman, like all other economic agents, would equate marginal revenue with marginal costs. It can be demonstrated that the higher the rate of interest and the higher the cost to the resource owner of maintaining any resource stock, the more intense will be the effort to harvest the resource. It can also be shown that, in some very special circumstances where the benefit of catching the last fish will exceed the cost of catching it, fishing will continue until the population is extinct.[9] Even if this extreme case is unlikely, in the real world, where there is no single owner of the fish stock,

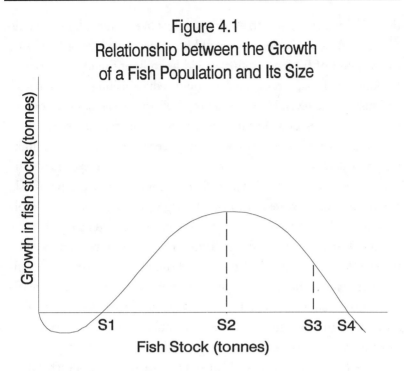

Figure 4.1
Relationship between the Growth
of a Fish Population and Its Size

Growth in fish stocks (tonnes)

S1   S2   S3   S4

Fish Stock (tonnes)

Source: Tietenberg (1984), p.189.

there will always be too much effort devoted to catching too few fish. Without regulation fisheries will be neither sustainable nor efficient. In summary, profitable fisheries always attract too much fishing, which will lead to the depletion of fish stocks and a low return.

What are the solutions? As most of the problems in the fisheries are caused by the unlimited access-common property features of the fisheries, one solution would be to introduce property rights. This sounds easy in theory but is more difficult in practice because fish do not stay in one place. In some areas and for some species, **aquaculture** is a solution. It works well with shellfish and salmon,but it does not appear to work well with other species such as codfish.

Another attempt at introducing property rights has been to extend each country's territorial limits to two hundred miles to give it more control over the fisheries (since most fishing is done in coastal waters), and to control fishing on the deep seas through international conventions. If a country is able to exercise control over fishing, how can it do so most effectively? One way would be to decrease fishing by raising the real cost of fishing; another would be to limit the catch. It can be demonstrated that a tax on effort could reduce fishing to an efficient and sustainable level. However, a tax on effort means that the government confiscates any surplus rent generated in the industry, which would hardly be a popular move. A more acceptable method for limiting the catch would be by quotas. An efficient quota system should entitle the holder to catch a specified weight of a certain type of fish, and if the holder chose not to use this right, it should be transferable to others. The total amount of quotas allocated should be equal to the efficient catch for the fishery. Transferability is important because then the right to fish would go to the fishermen who were most efficient. A transferable quota would have a price on the market. Inefficient fishermen would find it more worthwhile to sell their quota allocation than to fish. Efficient fishermen would have an incentive to buy more quota allocations because they could make more money.

The 1976 Law of the Sea Conference gave the right of each nation to establish a two hundred mile exclusive economic zone, Canada did so in 1977. The 1982 Law of the Sea Conference added the following principles:

1. Each nation should determine **the total allowable catch** (TAC) within its exclusive economic zone, using the best scientific evidence.

2. Each nation should determine its own harvesting capacity.

3. Each nation should conclude agreements with other states to allow them to establish quotas within the TAC after allowing its own residents first priority.

In the sixties and early seventies, Canadian fisheries control policy addressed mesh sizes and other limitations on fishing gear. The gear limitations proved to be inadequate for controlling the catches. The International Commission for the Northwest Atlantic Fisheries (ICNAF) started to implement TACs in 1970, and by 1974 virtually all stocks were protected by TACs. The early TACs were based on maximum sustainable yield criteria, but the stocks were so depleted that the allowable catches could not be reached and therefore there was no rebuilding of stocks. Further declines in stocks ensued. By 1975, Canada was advocating that TACs should be based on more conservative criteria. In 1977 the ICNAF adopted the concept of F 0.1, a biological criterion that corresponds to a level of fishing beyond which increases in total catch relative to increases in effort are marginal (Fisheries and Oceans, 1988, p. 261).[10]

Canada's declaration of an exclusive economic zone in 1977 served as a stimulus to the fisheries. Between 1974 and 1982 the number of licensed fishermen on the Atlantic coast grew by 45 percent, and freezing capacity more than doubled. On the Pacific coast, the number of licensed fishermen grew by 37 percent between 1977 and 1981.

After the declaration of the two-hundred-mile limit, some fish stocks on the Atlantic coast made a recovery. One that did not was the northern cod off Newfoundland. In recognition of the problem, the TACs for northern cod were marginally reduced every year after 1984 (Canada, 1991, p. 8-10). The success of this policy depended on equivalent reductions in catches by foreign fishing fleets, for part of the Grand Banks (the so-called nose-and-tail area) is outside the two-hundred-mile limit. Some foreign fleets did not comply. The Northern Cod Review Panel, established by the federal government in 1990, concluded that the stock was in decline, and recommended an immediate cut of 50 percent in TACs. That cut was not made and catches declined further in 1991. In early 1992 the situation was so bad that the cod fisheries were closed for two years to allow for the stock to recover; the closure has since been extended indefinitely. There is also concern that other groundfish such as haddock may meet a similar fate. If the fisheries are reopened, it is likely that the TACs will be kept far below the previous levels and that the number of people working in fishing will decline substantially.

Energy Use and Energy Resources

The management of energy resources is also difficult, partly because energy can be generated from either renewable or non-renewable sources, and partly because the use of some energy resources has adverse effects on the environment. It therefore becomes difficult to determine the optimum use and mix of different types of energy resources. At present most energy used in the world is from non-renewable sources. Non-renewable energy sources are different from other non-renewable resources because they cannot be recycled. Because of the second law of thermodynamics; the dissipated energy cannot be collected and resued. Consumption of the world's most commonly used non-renewable energy resources (oil, gas, coal) is the largest contributor to the greenhouse effect and indeed to air pollution in general. Scrubbers and other devices can get rid of sulphur and some other gases from emissions, but there is no technology to scrub carbon dioxide from the atmosphere. The principle of sustainable development would dictate an orderly transition to renewable energy sources such as solar power, wind energy, hydro, and energy from biomass.[11]

It is possible that, provided energy consumption were made to bear the full environmental cost, the market would ensure an orderly transition. In the previous discussion about mining, it was argued that the high-grade ore deposits would be used up first, to be followed by more and more expensive (low-grade) deposits. Finally, the cost of production or extraction will be so high that the demand will fall to zero, at which point the resource will be finished. At present, many of the renewable resources are not commercially viable; in the long run, however, as oil, gas, and coal become increasingly expensive because of their scarcity and the high environmental cost of burning them, there will be a price at which renewable energy resources will become widely used.[12] The world's reserve production ratio (total world reserves divided by current yearly world production) for oil is 43 years, for gas 58 years, and for coal 238 years (*The Economist*, August 31, 1991). These figures are not reliable estimates as they are based on the current rates of consumption and the current known reserves. Nevertheless they give an indication of the relative availability of these three fossil fuels. In the short run, if governments take the greenhouse effect seriously, they are likely to encourage a shift from high-carbon to low-carbon fossil fuels, that is, from coal and oil to natural gas.

Energy is needed for transportation, industry, and agriculture, for residential and commercial use, and as a feedstock for the chemical industry. Some is also lost in conversion and transmission. Table 4.4 shows the distribution of consumption among the various sectors.

TABLE 4.4

Energy Consumption by Economic Sector, North America
and the World

	North America (%)	World (%)
Transport	23	18
Industry and agriculture	22	31
Residential and commercial	21	22
*Non-energy	6	4
Energy conversion and losses	28	27
Total	100	100

Source: Chapman (1989), p. 21.
* Non-energy is the use of fossil fuels for purposes other than energy,
for example in making chemicals.

Energy consumption is difficult to predict because it depends on price, incomes, and other factors such as climate and industrial structure. The income elasticity of demand for energy in Canada is close to one, with some variation depending on the end use. This means that if prices do not change, energy demand will expand at the same rate as GDP. The income elasticity of demand for energy for residential purposes is estimated at 0.2–0.5 for industrial and 0.9–1.2 for commercial: for transportation it varies with the mode—(rail 0.3, marine 0.9, road 1.1, and air 3.7) (Berndt and Greenberg, 1989, p. 84-89).

There is some evidence that the income elasticity of demand for energy may actually decline as incomes rise beyond a certain level. As economies develop, their demand for energy in relation to their GDP tends to expand rapidly and then to peak. When countries become rich, they tend to close down their smokestack industries and adopt energy-efficient technology.

After the Second World War, the average expansion of world energy demand was 3–5 percent a year. After the high energy prices in the 1970s, energy demand decreased.[13] Since the mid-eighties, the yearly increase in energy demand has been around 2–3 percent (Chapman, 1989, p. 47).

The world is still dependent on petroleum for most of its energy. Forty percent of energy used in the world is from oil (*The Economist*, January 12, 1991). At current prices, oil is more attractive than other forms of energy. It is cleaner than coal and easier to transport than natural gas. Most oil (about 40 percent) comes from the Middle East, which also holds 65 percent of the total oil reserves (*ibid.*). Because of the world's dependence on oil and the volatile political situation in the Middle East, oil prices have fluctuated considerably, despite an attempt by OPEC, an oil cartel, to control output by production quotas. The first energy crisis in 1973 was caused by the Arab-Israeli War, and the second by the revolution in Iran in 1979. On both occasions, temporary shortages of oil, coupled with astute action by the oil cartel, led to huge increases in the price of oil (see Table 4.5). Each time the impact on the world economy

TABLE 4.5

World Prices and Reserves of Oil, 1938–87

Year	Production, Non-communist (billion barrels)	Reserves (billion barrels)	Price per barrel (1987 $US)
1938	2.2	33	11.0
1948–49	3.1	69	11.0
1970	14.6	521	3.5
1974	17.3	609	25.0
1981	16.2	593	43.0
1985	15.4	626	28.5
1987	16.2	817	17.3

Source: Adelman (1989), p.2.

was severe. It is perhaps surprising that the invasion of Kuwait in 1992 did not have the same effect. There are several possible explanations. First, the OPEC cartel is not as effective in controlling output as it was earlier, partly because Saudi Arabia is no longer willing to act as a swing producer, and partly because it has a smaller share of the oil market. Previously, if production was in danger of exceeding the quotas, Saudi Arabia would cut back its production. Second, prices are more responsive to market conditions than earlier because more oil is sold on the spot market or on futures markets. In the sixties and seventies most oil was sold through long-term contracts (*ibid.*).

In Canada, energy-related goods and services account for 7.1 percent of GDP, 11.8 percent of export income, and 3.7 percent of all jobs (Energy, Mines and Resources, 1988, p. 4). Canada uses 70 percent more energy in relation to GDP than the United States and four major European countries. We may indeed be profligate users of energy, but a climate that is colder than most does not help, nor does our large land mass, requiring large expenditures on transportation. Many of our main export industries are very energy-intensive (pulp and paper and primary metals). It is likely that underpriced energy has contributed to energy-intensive production and consumption.

Table 4.6 shows the composition of Canadian energy demand. Nineteen seventy-three was the year of the first energy crisis (note the price of oil from Table 4.5). Nineteen eighty-six is the most recent year for which data are available. As is obvious from the table, the distribution of energy demand between various sectors has not changed substantially, but there are substantial changes in the type of energy used. With the exception of transportation, energy use has shifted away from oil towards natural gas and electricity.

Canada is well endowed with energy resources.[14] Our reserves of crude oil are 731 million cubic metres, which with a current annual production of 95 cubic metres gives a reserve-to-production ratio of eight years. There is estimated to be a further ultimate potential of 1.2 billion cubic metres. In the frontier areas there are 454 million cubic metres with an ultimate potential of 4.1 billion. The Alberta Tar Sands are the world's largest known oil deposit: 270 billion cubic metres, only 10 bil-

TABLE 4.6

Energy Demand in Canada by Fuel Type and End-Use Sector,
1973 and 1986

Sector	Oil (%)	Gas (%)	Electric (%)	Coal (%)	Renewable (%)	Total (%)
1973						
Industrial	26.3	26.5	19.1	11.8	16.3	37.6
Transport	99.7	0	0	0	0	27.6
Residential	57.6	24.8	16.8	0.7	—	20.7
Commercial	37.2	34.3	28.3	0.2	—	14.1
Total	54.6	19.9	14.6	4.7	6.1	100.0
1986						
Industrial	13.2	31.3	26.7	10.0	18.7	37.3
Transport	98.8	1.1	0.2	—	—	27.7
Residential	19	31.9	24.5	0.2	6.3	21.8
Commercial	12.5	48.1	39.1	—	0.2	13.2
Total	40.0	28.4	20.1	3.5	8.0	100.0

Source: Berndt and Greenberg (1989), p. 76.

lion of which are thought to be recoverable, however. Conventional reserves of natural gas are 2.0 trillion cubic metres with a potential of an additional 1.4–2.5 trillion. Current production is 78 billion cubic metres a year. There are 665 billion in frontier areas with a potential of up to 7 trillion. Our coal reserves are equally impressive. We have reserves of 7 billion tonnes with a potential of 21 billion with a current production of 61 million. We also have recoverable uranium reserves with current production of 12,000 tonnes.

Given that we have a surplus of energy, can we close ourselves off from the rest of the world and keep our energy prices artificially low?[15] No, it would not be efficient for us to do so. The loss to Canadian energy producers would be larger than any gain to consumers. It would also be contrary to the free trade agreement with the United States, in which we have undertaken not to discriminate in prices between domestic consumers and consumers in the United States. Moreover, an artificially low price for energy would not take into account the environmental costs of using fossil fuels. It would send the wrong signal to the Canadian economy and discourage the development of alternative energy sources.

We will now examine some of the alternatives to fossil fuels: nuclear power, solar and wind power, and hydro-electricity.

The Rise and Fall of Nuclear Power

Until the early eighties, nuclear power was believed by many to offer a long-term solution to the world's energy problems. It is clean in the sense that it does not produce conventional air pollution, and it was cheap. Consequently, some countries embarked on huge nuclear programs; in France and Sweden for example, nuclear power was used to generate 72 percent and 52 percent respectively of all electricity generated in 1991 (see Table 4.7). About 17 percent of the world's electricity is generated with nuclear power.

In Canada, however, nuclear power supplies just over 16 percent of all our electricity; there are sixteen reactors in Ontario, one in Quebec, and one in New Brunswick. The Canadian reactors have a unique design that does not require enriched uranium but does need heavy water (deuterium). They go by the name of CANDU (Canadian Deuterium-Uranium). At present there are no plans to expand the generation of nuclear power in Canada or in most other countries. In fact, Sweden has begun decommissioning its nuclear reactors. Only Japan and South Korea still appear to be committed to nuclear power.

There are two problems with nuclear power that can explain its decline in popularity: safety of operation and the storage of radioactive waste. The production of electricity by nuclear reactors requires radioactive elements, which if they escape, will contaminate the air water, or soil. Contact with radioactive materials can lead to birth defects, various cancers, and, if the concentration is high enough,

TABLE 4.7

Percentage of Electricity Generated with Nuclear Power,
Selected Countries, 1991

Country	Percentage
France	72.7
Belgium	59.3
Sweden	51.6
Hungary	48.4
Republic of Korea	47.5
Switzerland	40.0
Taiwan	37.8
Spain	35.9
Bulgaria	34.0
Finland	33.3
Czechoslovakia	28.7
Germany	27.6
Japan	23.4
United States	21.7
United Kingdom	20.6
Argentina	19.1
Canada	16.4
Former USSR	12.6

Source: Ahearne (1993), p. 27.

death. The nuclear industry has tended to play down the risk of nuclear accidents, emphasizing the very high safety standards. The most serious accident that can happen is a meltdown of the core. This occurred at the Chernobyl nuclear plant in 1986 in the Ukraine. Though the official death toll was only 31, unofficial estimates put the real death toll near 7,000. Some Russian organizations claim that the accident may yet cause up to 300,000 deaths (*The Economist*, April

27, 1991). Safety fears obviously increase costs, as governments, in response to public demands, will require higher and more expensive safety standards. In addition, there is the problem of storing nuclear waste. In the first few centuries of storage, the dominant contributors to waste are strontium and cesium, which will become harmless in a thousand years. Other elements, however, remain dangerous for up to 240,000 years. It is difficult to see how anyone can guarantee safe storage for a hundred years, let alone a thousand years.

In estimating the costs of a nuclear plant, one must add the cost of capital, the cost of operating and maintaining the plant, the cost of fuel, and the cost of decommissioning a plant, which includes the cost of storing nuclear waste. All costs except the cost of capital are influenced by the regulatory policies of the government, which are subject to change. Capital costs account for more than 50 percent of the lifetime costs of a nuclear plant, compared to 25–35 percent for a coal-fired station and even less for gas-fired station (*The Economist*, November 21, 1992). Therefore the cost of nuclear power, compared to other sources of electricity, depends largely on interest rates. Given the high capital costs, nuclear power stations must produce power all the time to be economically viable. But they do not: the average lifetime load factors differ substantially (78.2 percent in Canada, 68 percent in Japan, and 60.5 percent in the United States), and in general the record is not very good (Ahearne, 1993, p. 28). The decommissioning costs, even if they are estimated to be high, do not weigh heavily in the calculations of the costs and benefits of nuclear power because of discounting. If a plant is to be decommissioned after 30 years, the costs involved, assuming they can be accurately estimated, become relatively small. Even so, nuclear power is no longer competitive with other forms of electricity generation. In the United States the average cost in constant dollars for a kilowatt of nuclear generating capacity rose from $817 in the early seventies to $3,100 in the late eighties (*ibid.*).

Renewable Energy Sources

The prospects for renewable energy sources are improving, and the commercial exploitation of solar energy is becoming a possibility. Of course direct solar energy has been used for heating for a very long time, at least in temperate climates, in the sense that people have always attempted to place their buildings and windows to catch as much light as possible in the winter and as little as possible in the summer. The most promising use of solar energy at the moment, however, is in the generation of electricity. Light can be made into electricity through the use of photovoltaic cells. Most of us are familiar with the use of these cells in solar-powered calculators. The photovoltaic technology is related to computer technology in the sense that photovoltaic semiconductors are similar to silicon chips (*The Economist*, May 19, 1990). Given the rapid advances in computer technology, it is likely that solar technology will also improve considerably. However, solar power suffers from one drawback: what do you do when there is no light? Some of the electricity generated would have to be stored. One possibility is hydro-storage, in which solar power is used to pump water uphill. When the sun is down, the water will flow down hill and generate electricity in the process.

Even though the price of solar-generated electricity has fallen by a factor of three since 1980, it is still more expensive than conventional electricity. For example, in the United States, electricity from coal costs 4–8 cents per kilowatt hour; from oil or natural gas, 5–10 cents; and from solar thermal plants 8–12 cents. Solar power from photovoltaic cells costs 25–30 cents to generate (*ibid.*). At present there are two main uses of solar-powered electricity: as a supplier of peak-load power and to supply power for areas where large networks of generating plants do not yet exist. As the technology improves and costs come down, it is likely that solar energy will become more important.

During the 1970s, wind power was seen as another substitute for fossil fuels. The technology was well known but had acquired a reputation of being unreliable. With the development of turning blades that produce more lift at low wind speeds and constant lift at high speeds, wind power has become more reliable. Better siting has also improved its efficiency. Recent figures from the United States show that the wind turbines produce power 90 percent of the time compared to the 1980s, when they generated power only 50 percent of the time (*The Economist*,

November 14, 1992). Improved reliability also cuts down the cost. Industry specialists expect the cost to come down to 4 cents per kilowatt, or less, at which point it could compete with conventionally generated electricity.[16]

A substantial amount of electricity is, of course, already generated from renewable energy (hydro-electricity) in Canada. Canada is the world's largest producer of hydro-electricity with four hundred hydro-electric stations with a combined capacity of 60,000 megawatts. There are several reasons why Canada has traditionally relied on water power. One is that hydro generation appears to cause less damage to the environment than the burning of fossil fuels or nuclear power — all that dams put into the air is water spray. A second reason is that Canada has many rivers that are suitable for power generation. A third is that even though hydro stations have very high capital cost, they have low maintenance costs. They can also be turned on and off to provide electricity for peak demand, which makes them financially very attractive. For all those reasons Canada is the world's largest producer of hydro-electricity with over four hundred hydro-electric stations with a combined capacity of 60,000 megawatts.

Some of the hydro-projects have required changing the flow of large rivers. Examples are the diversion of the Churchill River into the Nelson River basin in Manitoba, the diversion of three rivers into La Grande for the James Bay project in Quebec, and the diversion of three rivers into the Churchill River in Labrador. The volume of water diverted between river basins in Canada is larger than the combined volume in the United States and the former Soviet Union. The completion of the James Bay project in Quebec will flood an area as large as Lake Erie (Canada, 1991, p. 12–27). Other huge projects are being planned in Manitoba and British Columbia.

Almost one-third of the water in Canada's rivers drain into the James Bay. How these huge water systems diversions will affect the sensitive Arctic environment is not known. The National Energy Board, in giving approval to phase II of the James Bay project, admitted that it did not know whether or not the damming of the rivers would cause irreparable environmental damage (*The Globe and Mail*, September 28, 1990). The human costs in lost livelihoods and recreational values are also frequently neglected in cost-benefit calculations.[17] The Grand Chief of the Cree, Matthew Coon-Come in his testimony to the National Energy Board, argued that the James Bay II project

> will cause considerable erosion, alter the seasonal patterns and quantity of water flow in the concerned rivers and water basins, adversely affect the wildlife and marine resources of Hudson Bay and of James Bay, including marine mammals and fish, flood the nesting and feeding sites of waterfowl, including migratory birds, destroy the habitat of fur-bearing animals, change the migration routes and adversely affect caribou, destroy spawning areas of fish, deplete subsistence food resources upon which we depend, severely increase mercury contamination of fish, change the ecology of Hudson Bay and of James Bay, endanger a very fragile environment, threaten endangered species, cause substantial pollution, endanger the health, safety and welfare of the Native population and interfere with and cause extensive and irreparable damage, loss and prejudice to our livelihood, our way of life and our traditional use of the land and natural resources (quoted in McCutcheon, 1991, p. 153).

Because of the high cost of new power stations, be they thermal, nuclear, or hydro, many utilities have found that conservation is often cheaper. Amory Lovins argues that electricity use in the United States could be cut by 75 percent by employing the most efficient new lighting, appliances, and motors currently on the market (*The Economist*, August 31, 1991.). A Canadian study (*ibid.*), using 1984 prices (when a barrel of oil cost $22) found that it would cost only $13 to save the equivalent of a barrel of oil by cutting the average domestic energy use by 30 percent. Investing in conservation is also attractive because it can be done on a small scale.

One of the greatest difficulties in promoting sustainable energy is to find an alternative fuel for cars. Conventional motor vehicles are the third-largest producers of carbon emissions, after power stations and factories. Emissions from vehicles could be reduced by using less fuel or by using alternative fuels with a lower carbon content, for example methanol, or hydrogen, which has none. Methanol has been used for some time, but the use of hydrogen would require a new technology. Electric cars are currently being developed, spurred by legislation in California where 2 percent of all new cars must be free of all emissions by 1998, and 10 percent by 2003. This means that they must run on electricity. So far the electrical cars in existence are more expensive to run (operating costs include the cost of the battery and the cost of the electricity required to charge the battery) and are also more expensive to buy (*The Economist*, October 13, 1990). If the electricity used to charge the batteries is generated from fossil fuels, it is doubtful that a switch to electric cars would be an improvement except as a local solution to urban air pollution.

Conclusions

Natural resources still provide a living for many Canadians as well as earn a substantial amount of foreign exchange. However, the situation for many of our traditional export products is changing for the worse because of three factors. One is the loss of export markets to competitors whose production costs are lower. Another is our failure to harvest our resources sustainably, which threatens our future resource base. A third is the environmental movement, which has realized that consumer boycotts can be a powerful tool for forcing countries to abide by certain environmental standards.

The principle of sustainability dictates that governments should reinvest the rent earned on non-renewable resources for future generations. With the exception of oil and gas revenue in Alberta, this is not happening. Our fisheries suffer from the "tragedy of the commons" with the predictable result that the stock of fish has declined to a level where commercial exploitation is no longer possible. Our forests have been mined rather than managed, with little regard for their place in the ecosystem. Indeed, several economic studies show that their non-timber value is sometimes more important than their timber value. The net benefits to society of some of our large hydro-electric schemes have not been established. I also argued that despite our abundance of conventional energy resources, we should be careful to price them to reflect the full environmental cost of their use. We examined some alternative energy resources such as nuclear power, wind power, and solar power. Nuclear power, because of problems of safety and storage, has become too expensive. It is possible that wind and solar power will become commercially viable when the technology improves.

TOPICS FOR DISCUSSION

1. What would be the advantages and disadvantages of privatizing Canada's forestry resources?

2. If you were to speculate about the likely net benefits to Canada and Newfoundland of the Hibernia project, what would you conclude?

3. How would you determine whether fish farming would be a viable industry in Newfoundland?

RECOMMENDED READING

The classic article about common property resources is Hardin's 1960 article "The Tragedy of the Commons." For an interesting account of current debates over forest management, read *Paradise Won: The Struggle for South Moresby* by Elizabeth May (1990). There are a large number of economic studies dealing with the management of fisheries. One of the more recent is *Resource Prospects for Canada's Atlantic Fisheries*, 1989–93 (Department of Fisheries and Oceans 1988). For information about the James Bay project, Sean McCutcheon's *Electric Rivers: The Story of the James Bay* (McCutcheon 1991) is worth reading.

References

Adelman, M.A. "The Evolution of World Oil Markets." In *Petro Markets*, ed. Campbell G. Watkins (1989): 1-17.

Ahearne, John F. "The Future of Nuclear Power." *The American Scientist* 81 (January-February 1993): 24-36.

Anderson, F. J. *Natural Resources in Canada. Economic Theory and Policy*. Toronto: Methuen, 1985.

Berndt, Ernst R. and Paul E. Greenberg. "Canadian Energy Demand After the Oil Shocks." In *Petro Markets*, ed. Campbell G. Watkins (1989): 69-105.

Canada. *The State of Canada's Environment.* [Ottawa]: The Ministry of Supply and Services, 1991.

Canada. Energy, Mines and Resources. *Energy and Canadians into the 21st Century.* [Ottawa]: Ministry of Supply and Services, 1988.

Canada. Department of Fisheries and Oceans. *Resource Prospects for Canada's Atlantic Fisheries 1989-1993.* [Ottawa]: Ministry of Supply and Services, 1988.

Chapman, J.D. *Geography and Energy. Commercial Energy Systems and National Policies.* New York: Longman Scientific and Technical, 1989.

Cline, William R. *Global Warming: The Economic Stakes.* Washington D.C.: Institute for International Economics, May 1992.

The Economist. "Waiting for the sunrise," May 19, 1990; "The Future of forests," June 22, 1991; "Energy and the environment. A power for good, a power for ill," August 31, 1991; "The car that drinks cocktails," September 28, 1991; "The quixotic technology," November 14, 1992; "The beautiful and the dammed," March 28, 1992; "A survey of the global environment," May 30, 1992; "So much to save," June 13, 1992; "Nuclear power–losing its charm," November 21, 1992.

The Globe and Mail "NEB Okays Hydro-Quebec exports." (Toronto), September 28, 1990; "Potential Cash Value of Urban Greenery," April 16, 1993.

Hardin, Garrett. "The Tragedy of the Commons." *Science* 162 (1968): 1243-48.

Hartwick, John M. "Substitution among Exhaustible Resources and Intergenerational Equity." *Review of Economic Studies* 45 (June 1978): 347-543.

Innis, H.A. *The Fur Trade in Canada: An Introduction to Canadian Economic History.* Toronto: University of Toronto Press, 1956.

May, Elizabeth. *Paradise Won: The Struggle for South Moresby.* Toronto: McClelland and Stewart, 1990.

McCutcheon, Sean. *Electric Rivers. The Story of the James Bay Project.* Montreal: Black Rose Books, 1991.

Skogsindustrierna. *Forestry for the Future.* Stockholm, 1993.

Solow, Robert M. "The Economics of Resources or the Resources of Economics." *American Economic Review* 64 (May 1974): 1-14.

Tietenberg, Tom. *Environmental and Natural Resource Economics.* New York: Harper-Collins Publishers Inc., 1984, 1992.

Watkins, G. Campbell. ed. *Petro Markets: Probing the Economics of Continental Energy.* Vancouver: The Fraser Institute, 1989.

Watkins, M.H. "A Staple Theory of Economic Growth." In *Approaches to Canadian Economic History,* eds. W.T. Easterbrooke and M.H. Watkins. Toronto: McClelland & Stewart, 1967: 49-74.

Endnotes

1 For a discussion and survey of the arguments, see Anderson (1985).

2 As mentioned, the figures are of course misleading as they do not include industries dependent on the resource sector (for example fish processing, pulp and paper making, or iron and steel production). The ranking might change sub-

stantially if a different definition of the resource sector were used.

3   The figure is the sum of exports of live animals, food, feed, beverages and tobacco, total crude materials, and total fabricated materials.

4   This section is based on Solow (1974).

5   Solow (1991). See also the discussion of the treatment of natural resource in the national income accounts in Chapter 3.

6   The Clinton administration signed the Convention in Spring 1993.

7   It is estimated that only 80 percent of the cutover forests are regenerating naturally or artificially (ibid.)

8   The expression was coined by Hardin (1968).

9   See for example Tietenberg (1992) p. 303-316.

10 More precisely it is the level of fishing mortality where the marginal yield (catch per recruit = young fish first exposed to harvesting) due to a small increase in fishing activity is 10 percent of the marginal yield per recruit when the same stock is very slightly exploited.

11 See the discussion on sustainability in Chapter 2.

12 The situation is of course not as likely to resolve itself smoothly as the theory implies. Any growth in future energy demand will come largely from the less developed counties, mainly because of population growth. The average energy use in third world countries is the equivalent of 1-2 barrels of oil per year, compared to the average North American use of 40 barrels per year (*The Economist*, August 31, 1991). Energy is income elastic, therefore economic growth in less developed countries will expand the use of energy considerably. China is the location of one-third of the world's known coal resources and would quite likely be reluctant to institute any pricing policy which would discourage the use of coal.

13 The short-run price elasticity of demand is 0.3 to 0.6. The long run elasticity is higher, because in the long run consumers have a range of options to economize on energy (smaller cars, more efficient engines, better insulation in houses, etc.)

14 This section is based on Energy, Mines and Resources (1988), p. 20.

15 The National Energy Program which was brought in by the Trudeau government in 1980 is an example of an attempt to hold Canadian energy prices at artificially low levels.

16 Use of wind power has generated considerable opposition in Wales where people are upset about the visual impact on the landscape by a large number of modern wind mills.

17 *The Economist* (March 28, 1992) reports that a study by Robert Stavins for an environmental lobby group about the effects of a proposed dam on the Tuolumne River in California showed that the annual social costs from losses of fishing and white-water rafting would amount to $214 million while the benefits in terms of hydro-electric power and recreation would be worth $26 million less.

5

Employment

Most people in Canada would rate unemployment as the most serious economic and social problem of the 1990s. After completing the chapter you will be able to describe who is unemployed and what type of jobs are held by the people who are working. You will be familiar with the main theories of unemployment and be able to offer some explanation of why unemployment has increased.

The quantity and quality of work of work are an integral part of economic well-being. At the time of writing, Canada has just come out of a recession with an unemployment rate of 10.6 percent, having lost an unprecedented number of manufacturing jobs. Over the years the unemployment rate has gradually increased, a feature we have in common with other industrialized countries. High unemployment have been justified and legitimized by some economists and politicians, who have argued that a substantial element of unemployment is voluntary and that people choose to be unemployed. They argue that, first, measured unemployment is an artifact in the sense that the measurement process classifies as unemployed people who are not really available for work.[1] Second, it is an institutional artifact resulting from a system of social insurance and social assistance that encourages job searches to be prolonged. Third, it is an artifact of the language in that the term in everyday usage has a negative connotation of forced idleness (Piore, 1987, p. 1834). It is claimed that a moderate amount of unemployment in fact benefits the economy by promoting efficiency and by increasing the possibility of achieving a better match between the supply of labour and the demand for labour.

If one believes that unemployment is an artifact, the lowering of the unemployment rate should not be the goal of policy makers — it is more important to come to grips with inflation and to promote long-term growth. This belief was integrated in **neo-conservatism** as practised by the Reagan administration in the United States, the Thatcher government in the United Kingdom, and the Conservatives under Brian Mulroney in Canada. Zero inflation was adopted as the main goal for macroeconomic policies.

In this chapter we will review the literature on the concept of unemployment. The degree to which unemployment is voluntary or involuntary is disputed to the extent that there are no generally accepted definitions of the terms. Much of the debate is ideology in the guise of economic theory. It comes down to a basic disagreement between conservative economists (the **new classicals**) and liberal economists (the **new Keynesians**) about how the markets work. The new classicals believe that markets behave as if they were perfectly competitive, and therefore any interference will detract from efficiency. Any surplus or shortage will result in an immediate price adjustment that will clear the market. The new Keynesians believe that because of imperfect competition, unions, minimum wage laws, and long-term contracts, the markets do not work perfectly. For this reason markets do not necessarily clear, and shortages and surpluses may persist for some time.

After a short survey of economic theory, we will examine Canada's employment record and changes in the nature of work. We will look at what we know about the people who are unemployed and examine why our unemployment rate is so high.

Modern Theories of Inflation and Unemployment: Cyclical Unemployment

In theory, labour is like any commodity in that the price and the quantity supplied and demanded are determined by the intersection of the demand and supply curves for labour. The price of labour is the real wage, and the equilibrium quantity is the level of employment. If the quantity supplied is greater than the quantity demanded at the going wage, unemployment will result. However, even if the quantity supplied is equal to the quantity demanded, there will be some unemployment because it will take time for unemployed workers to be matched with the vacant positions.[2]

Economists before Keynes believed that prolonged unemployment was not possible because a fall in real wages would clear any excess supply of labour. The Great Depression, however, showed that long-term unemployment was indeed possible and that labour markets did not clear automatically. Keynes (1936), in his *General Theory of Employment, Interest and Money*, demonstrated that if money wages were sticky and failed to fall in response to an excess supply of labour, the unemployment could persist because the economy could still be in equilibrium in the sense that the aggregate supply of goods and services was equal to the aggregate demand for goods and services. But there was a way out. The government could use fiscal policy and increase aggregate demand to a level corresponding to full employment by either increasing government expenditures on goods and services or encouraging consumption expenditures through a cut in taxes. Either would involve a budget deficit. The government could also encourage investment through monetary policy, by lowering interest rates, but that was thought to be less effective. If the government tried to stimulate the economy beyond the full-employment level of output, the result would be inflation. Inflation and unemployment could not occur simultaneously.

Later it was demonstrated by A.W. Phillips (1958) in an empirical study of money wages and unemployment in postwar Britain that a situation of either unemployment or inflation was unlikely. A graph showing the relationship between unemployment and inflation as measured by increases in money wages (the Phillips curve) was smooth rather than abrupt.[3] Low unemployment corresponded to relatively high inflation, high unemployment to low inflation. There appeared to be a trade-off between inflation and unemployment. Fuller employment could be purchased only with an increase in inflation, and a reduction in inflation only with an increase in unemployment. The reason could be that real wages adjust only gradually to the equilibrium level. If there is a substantial shortage of labour in the market, there will be upward pressure on money wages, and the real wage will rise. Similarly, if there is unemployment, real wages will have to drop to clear the market. If money wages do not move down, unemployment may persist for some time. The Phillips curve appears to have given an accurate description of the trade-off between inflation and unemployment in the 1960s (see Figure 5.1).

The formulation of the Phillips curve was attached by Friedman (1968) and Phelps (1968), who argued that it must break down in the long run.[4] There cannot be a stable relationship between inflation and unemployment. Employment, and therefore unemployment, does not

Figure 5.1

The Canadian Phillips Curve 1961 - 1971

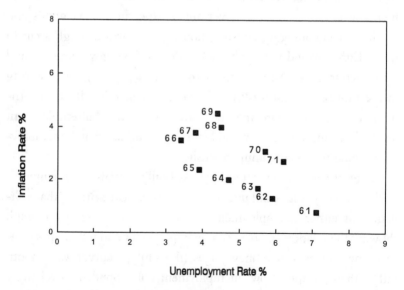

Source: The Canadian Economic Observer, Historical Statistical Supplement, 1992-93, Tables 2.6 and 3.2.

138

depend on money wages but on real wages. When workers accept employment, they consider not only the money wage, but also their own expectation of the future inflation rate, that is, their estimate of what the *real* wage is likely to be. The change in money wages used in the Phillips curve has to be corrected for inflationary expectations. Indeed, Friedman and Phelps were right. Any attempt during the 1970s to forecast wage inflation from the data in the original Phillips curve failed (see Figure 5.2). The Phillips curve shifted each time inflationary expectations changed. Attention in the literature now turned to the formation of inflationary expectations.

Assume that people form their inflationary expectations on the basis of their previous experience of inflation. It can then be demonstrated that inflation is unchanging only when the current unemployment rate coincides with the long-term equilibrium rate, where total labour demand equals total labour supply. Any attempt to reduce unemployment below that rate by using expansionary policies will cause inflation to accelerate. The unemployment rate corresponding to a stable inflation rate was called the **natural** unemployment rate by Friedman (1968). It is now referred to as **the non-accelerating inflation rate of unemployment (NAIRU)**. In the long run there is no trade-off between inflation and unemployment. The long-run Phillips curve is vertical at NAIRU, since NAIRU is consistent with any stable inflation rate. Suppose that a government attempts to get the unemployment rate down from the NAIRU rate of 8 percent by stimulating the economy through an expansive monetary policy (see Figure 5.3). We are assuming that the inflation rate is only 2 percent (point A); both wages and prices are increasing by the same amount. Lower interest rates will stimulate aggregate demand. The increase in aggregate demand will increase the inflation rate to 5 percent. Firms will have higher profits because prices are rising faster than wages (5 percent compared to 2 percent) and will therefore expand production and hire more labour, resulting in a lower unemployment rate of 6 percent (point B). Given the tightness of the labour market, money wages will increase by 5 percent as workers attempt to catch up with inflation. Higher wages will lower profitability, and business will be no better off than it was initially. The

Figure 5.2

The Canadian Phillips Curve 1971 - 1992

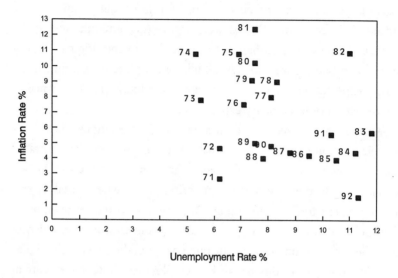

Source: The Canadian Economic Observer, Historical Statistical
Supplement, 1992-93, Tables 2.6 and 3.2.

original incentive for business to increase output and employ more workers will disappear. Employment will return to its natural level of 8 percent but at a higher rate of inflation (point C, corresponding to a different, and higher short-run Phillips curve). If the government continues with its expansionary policy, the inflationary spiral will continue and the economy will move to D with an inflation rate of 7 percent.

If the government wants to lower the inflation rate, it will have to lower aggregate demand by pursuing a restrictive monetary or fiscal policy. A decrease in aggregate demand will lower the inflation rate and raise unemployment because wage increases will be larger than price increases, and will reduce business profits. The unemployment rate will return to its previous level when workers have adjusted their wage demands to the new lower inflation rate. The cost in terms of the necessary temporary increase in unemployment (or necessary reduction in

Figure 5.3
The Long-Run Phillips Curve

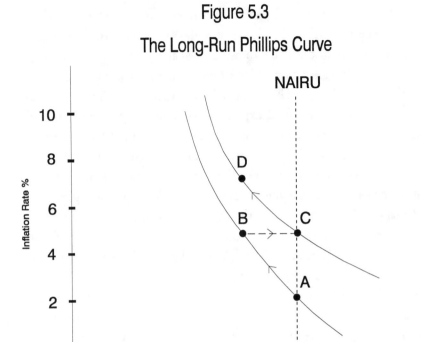

real GDP) can be calculated; it is known as the **sacrifice ratio**. A typical estimate for the sacrifice ratio in terms of the fall in real GDP is five: for every 1 percent that inflation is made to fall, GDP will fall by 5 percent in a year. This is equivalent to a sacrifice ratio for unemployment of 2½ percent (a 1 percent fall in the inflation rate requires an increase in the unemployment rate of 2.5 percent).[5]

The theory assumes that there are automatic mechanisms which ensure that the economy will move towards the NAIRU rate of unemployment. If unemployment is below the NAIRU rate, workers will bargain for higher wages, and higher wages will lead to a decline in the number of jobs. If the actual rate is higher than NAIRU, then the possibility of layoffs will moderate wage demands and therefore increase the demand for labour. Periods where the actual rate deviates from NAIRU follow the fluctuations in the economy (the business cycle).

The assumption that people base their expectations on previous experience was attacked by Sargent and Wallace (1975), who argued that people are just as likely to use all available current information in forming their expectations of the future; indeed, it would be rational for them to do so. This approach to expectations formation has become known as **rational expectations**. The assumption of rational expectations, combined with an assumption made by the new classical economists of immediate adjustments in labour markets (no long-term contracts), destroys the notion of even a short-term trade-off between inflation and unemployment. If policy makers pursue aggregate-demand policies that are restrictive enough to achieve zero inflation and at the same time announce that they are pursuing a policy of zero inflation, and if they are believed, zero inflation will be achieved without any sacrifice, that is, without any temporary increase in unemployment. Therefore costless zero inflation can be achieved provided there are no long-term wage contracts, that people form rational (forward) expectations, and that the government has credibility with the public. It is unlikely that these three conditions will be fulfilled.[6]

The theory of the business cycle has also seen radical changes. Earlier it was thought that business cycles were caused primarily by fluctuations in inventories or in investments in general. Keynes himself thought that business cycles were caused by the volatility of investments, which in turn was caused by the extreme volatility of entrepreneurial expectations of future sales and profits. Recently, the emphasis in theory has shifted to the effect of shocks to the economic system. These can take the form of shocks induced by government policy or shocks affecting the supply of goods and services. One example of a supply-side shock is the increase in oil prices during the 1970s. Supply-side changes could also be induced by real economic factors such as technological change.

There is evidence in the United States that most fluctuations in economic activity have been induced by government policy. Republicans tend to deflate the economy, and Democrats tend to inflate the economy. The economy under every Republican administration between 1953 and 1984 experienced a fall of GDP in the second year of a four-year presidential term, whereas during every Democratic administration there was fast growth in the second year (Sachs and Larrain, 1993, p. 530). In Canada, it seems likely that our recessions in 1981–82 and 1990–92 were induced by restrictive monetary policies (see Chapter 9).

The new classical economists argue that business cycles are not caused by policy-induced shocks but rather by technical shocks operating in a perfectly competitive economy in which wages and prices adjust instantaneously (the so-called **real business cycle theory**). Cycles can be caused by technical improvements or deteriorating technologies. Fluctuating technologies lead to fluctuating prices and therefore to incentives for individuals to change their labour supply and consumption. Any unemployment that happens during a recession is purely voluntary in the sense that workers withhold their services deliberately. When the real wage is high, households work many hours, wheras when it is low they withhold their labour. If workers do not accept a new job immediately after they have been laid off or have quit, it must mean that their unemployment is voluntary.

There is little empirical evidence for this theory. Most economists would have difficulty agreeing that some changes in technology lead to deterioration in productive efficiency. Most would also argue that changes in employment do not reflect changes in the amount people want to work. For most people, unemployment means a lower living standard and psychological distress, neither of which is desirable. In particular, the high unemployment in recessions suggests that the labour market does not clear through falling wages, and that unemployment is not voluntary. If people chose not to work during recessions, they would not call themselves unemployed. In reply, the new classical economists point out that individuals may choose to call themselves unemployed in order to collect unemployment insurance, or they may say they would be willing to work if they were offered the wages they had received previously. (Mankiw, 1992, p. 385).

Keynes emphasized rigid money wages in explaining why unemployment could occur and persist. The new Keynesians have attempted to formulate more rigorous theories based on the occurrence of either sticky wages or sticky prices as an explanation for fluctuations in unemployment. The following comment is by the Nobel Prize winner in Economics, James Tobin:

> Wages and prices rise more readily than they fall. Consider government-supported floors on farm prices, minimum wages and asymmetrical indexation. Consider the inexorable ascent of costs of health care, undisciplined by market forces when payments are by third party insurers, governmental or private. Consider the limited sensitivity to excess capacity of "administered" industrial prices and the stubbornness of negotiated wages in the face of unemployment. When government interventions are responsible for these biases, they are obvious though politically elusive targets of legislative reform. When governments grant private agents and groups — trade unions or trade associations — immunities from competition, the public has at the very least the right to insist that the privileges are not exercised in ways that inflict inflation or unemployment on the whole society. For example, if indexing is permitted at all it should be symmetrical. In most countries, collective bargaining procedures are sanctioned, protected and regulated by legislation. A general problem is that no one represents workers laid off or never hired. All too often the wages of senior employed workers take precedence over the number of jobs (Tobin, 1987, p. 24).

Clearly, union contracts, which in general cover one to three years, reduce the general responsiveness of wages to economic conditions. The wages of unionized labour are not set by supply and demand, but by collective bargaining. Even if workers have rational expectations, they cannot foresee random shocks to the economy. Furthermore, unions may be successful in raising wages to monopoly levels. Unions usually negotiate on behalf of their own workers (the insiders) with little regard for non-unionized or unemployed labour (outsiders). Unions clearly strengthen the hand of employed workers rather than unemployed workers and may therefore prevent unemployed workers from having a downward effect on money wages (**the**

insider–outsider theory). Wages could therefore remain above market-clearing levels. The real wage at any time may or may not be the market-clearing wage. Unemployment resulting from wage rigidity is sometimes called **wait unemployment**. The speed at which real wages will adjust and therefore the extent of wait unemployment depends on the extent of unionization in the economy, the time of contract negotiations (do they all happen at the same time?), the length of the contract, and the features of the contract, such as indexation or a provision for reopening the contract if conditions change.[7] There is some evidence from the United States to support the hypothesis that increased unionization leads to increased unemployment. Summers (1986) compared unemployment rates in different states to the degree of unionization. Using data from 1985, he found that an increase of 10 percent in the proportion of the unionized labour force led to an increase in unemployment of 1.2 percent.

The **efficiency wage theory** attempts to explain sticky real wages with reference to the effect of high wages on the effort and productivity of individual workers.[8] It is assumed that people can and will vary their work effort while they are employed. Occasionally they will shirk; if you are caught shirking you will be fired. The cost of being fired is the wages you were receiving minus the wages you would be paid in a new job. Therefore shirking becomes more expensive the more you are paid compared to workers in other industries in similar jobs. By paying above-market wages, the firm reduces the incentive to shirk, and therefore productivity will improve. High wages could attract better workers and reduce labour turnover, which would also enhance productivity. For all those reasons firms might not reduce wages in the face of persistent unemployment.

The other new Keynesian explanation for persistent unemployment is the presence of price rigidities. There is evidence that prices may not change rapidly in response to changes in demand or supply and may therefore contribute to rigidities in real wages. Price changes can be costly. Prices will have to be changed on price lists, in catalogues, and on restaurant menus, and vending machines have to be recalibrated. All the costs of making price changes are called **menu** costs. If these costs are large, producers may be reluctant to change their prices. Mankiw (1985) and others found that even when the costs are small, they can cause significant rigidities in nominal prices.

Determinants of NAIRU

According to theory, the unemployment rate cannot be forced below NAIRU by monetary and fiscal policies. Any attempt to do so would permanently increase the inflation rate. The NAIRU rate is the equilibrium rate in the labour market, where the long-run supply of labour equals the long-run demand for labour. The fact that unemployment still exists at this rate indicates that, even though the total number of jobs equals the total number of job seekers, there is not necessarily a match. New workers are constantly entering the labour force, while other workers are laid off or quit their jobs to look for other jobs. Newly created jobs do not necessarily require the same skills as the jobs that have disappeared, nor are they necessarily in the same place. We refer to the former type of unemployment as **frictional** and the latter type as **structural**.

The NAIRU rate can be quite high. Why? One reason could be that different sectors of the economy grow at different rates. There will always be expanding and contracting sectors, and the workers in the contracting sectors will not necessarily be assimilated into the expanding sectors. The process can, however, be speeded up by retraining programs and job mobility schemes. Lilien (1982) found that structural factors accounted for most of the changes in the unemployment rate in the United States during the 1970s. We will examine the evidence for Canada below.

Another factor that appears to increase NAIRU is unemployment insurance because it makes it less expensive for people to stay unemployed. Workers are supposed to keep track of the so called **replacement ratio**, which is the ratio of their disposable income while unemployed to the disposable income while employed. The higher the replacement ratio, the higher the unemployment rate. However, the link between the replacement ratio and the unemployment rate is not strongly supported by empirical evidence (Sachs and Larrain, 1993, p. 499-500). What appears to be more important than the replacement ratio is the duration of unemployment benefits. It appears that many unemployed workers remain unemployed until their unemployment insurance runs out and then immediately accept a job. Evidence from the United States suggests that a one-week increase in the duration of benefits increases the average length of unemployment by 0.16–0.2 weeks (*ibid.*). The absence of benefits appears to increase the search effort of unemployed workers.[9]

Recently, the whole notion of NAIRU or a "natural" unemployment rate has been attacked. It has been suggested that the NAIRU is affected by the cyclical unemployment rate. Shocks to the actual rate of unemployment lead to changes in NAIRU. There may be **hysteresis** in the economy. Hysteresis refers to a situation when a variable that has been subjected to an external force does not return to its initial value when the external force has disappeared. Assume, for example, that unemployment has increased because of high interest rates. If interest rates come down, unemployment may not return to its original level. Unemployed workers may lose some of their job skills after remaining out of work for a long time. They may be discriminated against by employers, who often look at the employment record of a prospective employee. They will also lose their union protection. They are now outsiders to the process, and if the insiders (the employed, unionized workers) pay no attention to their plight, the insiders may negotiate real wages for themselves that make it impossible for outsiders ever to become employed. There is some evidence that hysteresis may be a problem in some European countries (Blanchard and Summers 1986).

Canadian Unemployment

According to the definition adopted by the International Labour Office in Geneva, the unemployed are the pool of people above a specified age who are without work, are available for work, and are seeking work during the reference period (Sachs and Larrain, 1993, p. 490). All three conditions have to be fulfilled for a person to be considered unemployed. To be seeking work, a person must take some action to look for a job, such as registering with an employment agency, sending out résumés, or placing advertisements in the papers. The labour force consists of the persons who are employed and those who are unemployed. The unemployment rate is the number of unemployed as a proportion of the total labour force. Persons who are not working and who are not looking for work are not in the labour force and therefore do not count.

The unemployment rate in Canada is calculated from monthly labour force surveys of 56,000 households representing residents of Canada over 15 years of age, except for persons living in the Northwest Territories and the Yukon, persons living on Indian reserves, people who are institutionalized, and members of the armed forces. The labour force is composed of that proportion of the population 15 years or over who, during the sampling week, (a) did any work at all; (b) had work, but could not work that week because of illness or disability, personal or family responsibilities, bad weather, strike or a lock-out, vacation or other reasons; (c) were without work, had actively looked for work in the past four weeks, and were available for work; or (d) had not actively looked for work in the previous four weeks, but had a new job that would begin in four weeks or less from the reference week, and were available for work.

People in categories (a) and (b) are counted as employed, and those in categories (c) and (d) as unemployed.

Figure 5.4 shows the Canadian unemployment rate from 1960 to 1992.[10] It is clear from the graph that unemployment has gradually moved upward since the 1950s. In the 1940s, the average unemployment rate was approximately 2 percent, in the fifties it was 4 percent, in the sixties, 5 percent; in the seventies, 6.7 percent; and in the eighties 9.5 percent. Other countries have also experienced increases in the unemployment rate. Figure 5.5 shows the unemployment rates in some of the OECD countries.[11] The two years selected for comparison are not necessarily representative. Nineteen eighty-one was the year of the severe recession of 1981–82, and in 1992, the countries were either in a recession or just coming out. The Canadian unemployment rate is usually higher than that of most other industrialized countries, and since

Figure 5.4
The Canadian Unemployment Rate
1961 - 1992

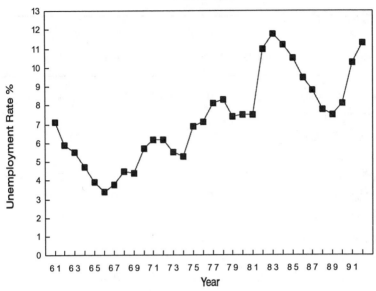

Source: The Canadian Economic Observer, Historical Statistical
Supplement, 1992-93, Table 2.6.

1982 it has been considerably higher than that of the United States.
We will return to that issue below.

In 1992 unemployment was slightly higher for males than females
and was higher for younger people than for older people (see Table 5.1).
The current situation is unusual in that the female unemployment rate
has traditionally been higher than the male rate, possibly because of the
dramatic increase in the participation rate of women. In 1960, the participation rate was 28 percent; in 1970, 38 percent; in 1980, 50 percent;
and in 1992, 58 percent. [12] The participation rate is still increasing, and
compared to other countries, it is relatively low. (Sweden had a participation rate of 78 percent in 1980). The reason for the current lower
unemployment rate for women may be the faster growth of part-time
work compared to full-time (see below). Traditionally, women are more
likely than men to accept part-time work. The recent high unemployment rate for young people is particularly disturbing.

TABLE 5.1

Canadian Unemployment and Participation Rates by Age and Sex,
1989, 1992

	1989			1992		
	Males	Females	Both	Males	Females	Both
Unemploym.rate	7.3%	7.9%	7.5%	12.0%	10.4%	11.3%
Unemploym. rate ages 15-24 years	12.4	10.1	11.3	20.2	15.2	17.8
Unemploym.rate >25 years	6.1	7.3	6.6	10.4	9.3	9.9
Participation rate	76.7	57.9	67.0	73.8	57.6	65.5
Participation rate ages 15-24 years	73.0	67.7	70.2	67.0	63.1	65.1
Participation rate >25 years	77.1	55.8	66.3	75.4	56.5	65.6

Note: The participation rate is the number of individuals in the labour force as a proportion of the total number of individuals.
Source: The Canadian Economic Observer

The unemployment rate also varies with the level of education (see Table 5.2). You are more likely to be unemployed if you do not have a high school diploma. Indeed, unemployment in this category has increased substantially compared to the other categories. The lowest unemployment rate is to be found among university graduates.

Not only has the unemployment rate been rising, but so too has the average length of unemployment. Older workers in particular have remained out of work for longer. The proportion of the unemployed who were out of work for six months or more was 15.3 percent in 1980–81, 24.7 percent in 1984–87, and 20.2 percent in 1988–89.[13]

Corak (1991), looking at unemployment over time, found that the total burden of unemployment is very concentrated. The small

TABLE 5.2

Unemployment Rate in Relation to the National Average by Level
of Education, 1975, 1981, and 1989

	1975	1981	1989
National unemployment rate	6.9%	7.5%	7.5%
Relative unemployment rate	(percentage points)		
0–8 years' education	1.3	1.3	3.6
High school diploma	1.1	1.1	1.4
Some post–secondary	–0.5	–0.5	–0.2
Post–secondary certificate or diploma	–2.6	–2.5	–2.3
University degree	–3.9	–4.5	–3.8

Note: The relative unemployment rate is the difference between the
unemployment rate for the category and the national rate.
Source: Gera and McMullen (1991), Table 1.5 p. 8.

proportion of the labour force that spends more than six months
unemployed accounts for a disproportionate share of the total time
spent unemployed. In 1980 only 3.3 percent of the total labour force
remained unemployed for more than six months, but it accounted for
42.5 percent of the total time spent unemployed. In 1987, 4.2 percent
of the labour force accounted for 54 percent of the total time of
unemployment. Summers and Clark (1979) also found that in the
United States the high unemployment rate could be explained by a
relatively small number of workers who are out of work a long time.

Canadian unemployment insurance statistics show that most of the
unemployed have been unemployed before. For example, in 1989, 80
percent of the claims made by men were made by persons that had had
another claim since 1971; 48 percent were made by persons who had
had at least five claims. The corresponding figures for women were 78
percent and 30 percent (Corak 1992).

Figure 5.5
Unemployment Rates, Selected OECD
Countries, 1981, 1992

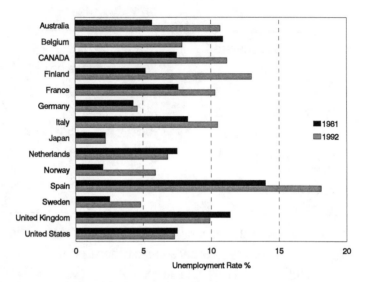

Source: OECD, Main Economic Indicators, 1983 and 1993,
p. 16, 22.

More than 50 percent of the unemployed are out of worked because they lost their jobs, approximately 20 percent quit voluntarily, fewer than 5 percent have just entered the labour market, and the remaining 25 percent have re-entered the labour force in search of a job.[14] The proportion of job losers among the unemployed increases during a recession.

Canada has always had substantial disparities in unemployment rates between the provinces. Since the 1960s the lowest rates have been in Ontario and the Prairie provinces, and the highest rates in the Maritimes. The disparities appear to have increased, which in Newfoundland's case is due to the sorry state of the fishing industry.

We will now examine changes in Canadian employment for clues as to why our unemployment rate is so high.

Canadian Employment

Employment in Canada, as in most other countries, has gone through some fundamental changes in terms of the industries where most workers are employed, the type of jobs, and the skills required. Table 5.3 shows that employment has expanded much faster in the service sector than in the goods sector. Almost all the new job creation during the 1980s took place in the service sector, which now employs 70 percent of Canadian workers. We will follow the example of the Economic Council of Canada (1990) in dividing the sector into dynamic services, traditional services, and non-market services (see Table 5.3). Dynamic services have to do with distribution (transport, communications, utilities, and wholesale trade) and commerce (finance, insurance, real estate, and business services). They are traded internationally and are high-value-added industries. Traditional services consist of retail and personal services. They are mostly based locally and have to a large extent been insulated from globalization and changes in technology. Non-market services consist of health and social services, education, and public administration. Though they do not operate in a competitive environment, they are very important for the competitiveness of other sectors in the economy for two reasons. First, they are an important input into business activities since they provide infrastructure, health, and education. Second, their financing affects the public finances and therefore the general fiscal climate.

Like the manufacturing sector, the service sector has been subject to rapid technological change, in particular the development, application, and diffusion of interconnected computer and telecommunications technologies capable of processing and transmitting huge amounts of information (Economic Council of Canada, 1990, p. 2). Indeed, these changes have made it increasingly difficult to separate goods from services. Goods production has taken on service elements in that most of the job growth in goods production has been in the white-collar occupations that provide services such as administration, R&D, and data collection and processing. It is also common to integrate training and maintenance contracts into equipment sales.

TABLE 5.3
Percentage of Total Employment and Annual Growth by Industry, Canada,1967–1988

Industry	1967	1988	1967–88
Goods sector	40.6	29.1	3.4
Primary industries	10.3	6.0	–0.1
Manufacturing	23.9	17.2	0.9
Construction	6.5	5.9	2.1
Service sector	59.4	70.9	3.4
Dynamic services	19.7	23.0	3.2
Transportation, communications, utilities	9.0	7.4	1.5
Finance, insurance,real estate	4.3	5.9	4.1
Business services	1.9	5.1	7.3
Traditional services	21.7	25.7	3.3
Retail trade	12.1	13.1	2.8
Personal services	9.6	12.6	3.8
Non–market services	18.0	22.2	3.5
Health and social services	6.2	8.9	4.3
Education	5.8	6.6	3.2
Public administration	6.0	6.7	3.0
Both sectors	100.0	100.0	2.5

Source: Economic Council of Canada (1990), Table 1, p. 5.

There are several explanations that could be offered for the increased importance of service employment in the economy. One is that when the economy is growing, the demand for services may expand faster than the demand for goods. However, estimates of income elasticities show that this is not the case. Both the income elasticity for goods and that for services appear to be close to one with no significant difference in size (Economic Council of Canada, 1991, p. 32). Another possible explanation is that there are substantial differences in labour productivity between the service industries and manufacturing. If labour productivity is very low in the service sector compared to the goods sector, any expansion in the service sector would require large increases in the number of people employed in the industry. The Economic Council of Canada (1991, p. 33) found that productivity growth in the traditional and non-market services is much lower (0.7 and –0.2 percent) than in manufacturing (1.8 percent). The dynamic services sector had productivity improvements of 2 percent. However, the expected link between low productivity and employment growth was not strong.

A third explanation for the growth of the service sector could be a change in business practices. Previously all manufacturing firms produced their own services; now they purchase those from other firms. The evidence, though, shows that while contracting out has increased, it cannot account for more than a small proportion of the total shift to services (*ibid.*, p. 35). The Economic Council of Canada found the most evidence for a fourth explanation: increased demand for services as an input into production. The goods and services sectors are closely linked and dependent on each other. Expansion of the goods sector requires the purchase of more services as an input, and expansion of the service sector requires the purchase of more manufactured goods (for example, computers). However, the Council found that growth in manufacturing has a larger effect on the growth in services than growth in services has on manufacturing. When incomes grow in the economy, the demand for both goods and services will increase proportionately, given an equal income elasticity of demand. But because of the stronger linkage from manufacturing to services, there is a constant bias in favour of the service sector, that is, the service sector will expand faster.

Not only have the industries where people will work changed, but the type of job has changed as well. There has been an increase in part-time employment (jobs with fewer than 30 working hours a week) from 4 percent of all jobs in 1953 to over 15 percent in the early nineties (ECC, 1990, p. 11). (A quarter of all part-time employees, though, would rather have full-time work.) Most part-time work is found in the traditional service sector. Part-time workers are more likely to be employed by small firms, to be non-unionized, and to earn less per hour than full-time workers. The traditional service sector has also been characterized by an increase in short-term work (jobs lasting less than six months). Self-employment has grown in importance, accounting for 10 percent of the job growth in the 1980s. This category consists mainly of small operations such as newsstands, one-truck movers, hot dog stands, etc., with earnings lower than average. Work for temporary help agencies tripled in the 1980s, again with wages well below those for full-time workers. These four forms of non-standard employment accounted for approximately 50 percent of all new jobs created between 1981 and 1986 and for 30 percent of total employment.

Skill requirements are also changing. The Economic Council of Canada estimated that in 1986, 52.4 percent of employment was in occupations primarily concerned with the creation and use of data: 63 percent in the service sector and 27 percent in the goods sector. Even in the goods sector, information-based jobs accounted for 57 percent of all new jobs between 1971 and 1986. Jobs involving routine data handling do not require high skill levels, while jobs that involve the development and interpretation of information do. Managerial, administrative, professional, and technical occupations accounted for 77 percent of employment growth from 1981 to 1986, and their share of total employment increased from 19 to 26 percent (Economic Council of Canada, 1990, p. 14). The distribution of skills is more polarized in the service sector than in the goods sector: very high-level skills are found in financial business and non-market services and low skill levels in traditional services. The goods sector tends to employ people with intermediate skills. The shift in employment towards the service sector has therefore contributed to a widening of the gap between skills required in employment with gains in highly skilled occupations, a decline in the share of middle-level skilled jobs, and a stable proportion of low-skill jobs. Not surprisingly this has resulted in an increased polarization of earnings (*ibid.*), lending support to Reich's (1991) hypothesis about the effects of globalization on employment. Reich claims that the new global economy will be characterized by three types of employees: symbolic analysts, routine producers, and in-person servers (see Introduction). The symbolic analysts will do very well, but the routine workers will lag further and further behind because of competition from cheap labour in poor countries.

The structural shift towards a demand for services has been seen by some as a favourable development for the slow-growing high- unemployment regions of Canada. It is argued that the reliance on telecommunications and computer services in the dynamic service sector makes it possible for firms in this sector to locate anywhere. Unfortunately this does not seem to be the case. Dynamic services tend to locate in and around large cities, which offer highly skilled labour and complementary activities such as office functions, financial institutions, and good transportation networks. It appears that the rapid growth in the dynamic service sector increases the disparities among regions as well as between urban and rural areas within regions (The Economic Council of Canada 1990).

Why Has the Unemployment Rate Increased?

The Canadian unemployment rate been rising since the mid-sixties. Most estimates for NAIRU give a rate around 5 percent in the 1960s and 7 percent in the 1970s and the early 1980s. After that the estimates differ because of difficulties caused by disagreements about separating structural from cyclical unemployment. Gera and McMullen (1991, p. 12) argue that the rate increased to 9.7 percent during the 1981–82 recession, and then decreased to 7.7 percent in 1987. As the estimates show, the rate has not remained constant but has risen in line with the general level of unemployment. Burns (1991) found that structural changes, such as improvements in unemployment insurance benefits and increases in minimum wages and taxes, could explain the increases in the unemployment rate to the mid-seventies. Since then the influence of these factors has declined. The requirements for unemployment insurance have been tightened and the minimum wage in real terms has declined. On the other hand, unemployment caused by mismatches between labour demand and labour supply appear to have increased, owing to the disruptive effects of rapidly changing energy and commodity prices. This appears to have been particularly true for the Atlantic provinces, where unemployment also increased because of spillovers of Ontario high wages to low-productivity labour.

There have been several other attempts to explain the increase in the Canadian unemployment rate by reference to structural change. Lilien (1982) found that nearly all unemployment in the United States could be explained by differential growth rates among industries. A worker being laid off in a declining or slow-growing industry would in all likelihood have to look for a job in a fast-growing industry. It is probable that the unfamiliarity of the laid-off workers and the growing firms with each other could lengthen the job search. There could also be mismatches. Samson (1985) and Charette and Kaufman (1984) provided evidence in support of Lilien's hypothesis for Canada. These studies, however, have been criticized on the grounds that differential growth rates are caused by fluctuations in aggregate demand, and therefore much of what the authors name structural unemployment is in fact cyclical unemployment. In a survey of the literature, Kaliski (1987) points out that it appears that Canadian workers often change industry and occupation, but not locations, a finding that partly contradicts the structural-change hypothesis and also the hypothesis of occupational mismatch. He points out that the lack of geographic mobility appears to be a problem.

Gera, Rahman, and Arcand (1991) also emphasized the importance of structural mismatches as a cause of the rising unemployment rates, particularly considering that the number of unfilled jobs has not decreased at the same rate as the rise in the unemployment rate. They examined three reasons for the structural imbalance. The first is the increasing regional disparities in economic performance; that is, jobs are not necessarily in the same place as the highest unemployment. The second reason is the rise in the proportion of long-term unemployed (see above). There may be a group of workers whose characteristics are no longer in demand. The high unemployment rate among people who have not finished high school would support this hypothesis. The third reason is the unbalanced growth across sectors, which could also lead to mismatches. The workers laid off from the declining sectors in the economy are not necessarily hired in the expanding sectors. They found most support for the second explanation: the increase in the long-term unemployed. They argue that the long-term unemployed tend to look for jobs less intensely than other unemployed workers. They also point out that employers often discriminate against the long-term unemployed. These findings presumably lend support to the hypothesis of hysteresis.

Gera and Grenier (1991, 1994) found some support for efficiency wages as an explanation for why the unemployment rate remained high in the eighties. Wages ranged from 33 percent above the Canadian average in the tobacco industries to 32 percent below the average in health and welfare services. They also found that employment growth in high-wage industries had twice as much influence on unemployment rates as employment growth in low-wage industries. They argue that one of the reasons why unemployment in Canada was so persistent in the 1980s was that the high-wage sector was slow to recover from the recession in the early eighties. It is possible that workers laid off in high-paying sectors prefer to wait for another high-paying job rather than accept a low-paying job. This type of unemployment is sometimes called **transitional unemployment** (Summers, 1986, p. 315). Workers who have lost well-paid jobs may find it difficult to accept their fate and prefer to be unemployed than to acknowledge the permanence of their loss by accepting a poorly paid job, especially since status in our society is affected by the type of job one holds. It is also possible that they feel that by accepting low-paying jobs they might disqualify themselves in the eyes of potential high-wage employers for better jobs.

Even though there is disagreement about the extent to which differential industrial growth rates can explain the persistence of high unemployment in the eighties, the enormous restructuring in the world economy must have had an effect on the speed of adjustment in the labour market. Both Canada and other countries have had increases in the incidence of long-term unemployment. The changing nature of employment referred to above has severe implications for the workers laid off in the last two recessions. Frequently, they lost high-paying, intermediate-skilled manufacturing jobs when factories either closed their operations in Canada or significantly reduced their labour force in an attempt to become competitive. Conditions in the agricultural and resource sectors also deteriorated. The jobs created during the recoveries were in the service sector and required either advanced skills that the laid-off workers did not possess or very low skills in the traditional service sector; in the latter case the workers may have been reluctant to accept these jobs because of the low pay. (Note, here the lower unemployment among university graduates.) Furthermore, the growth in service jobs was concentrated in large urban areas, while job losses in the goods sector frequently occurred outside these areas. All of these factors contributed to mismatches between the available jobs and the workers who were unemployed.

Many studies have analyzed the effect of the liberalization of unemployment insurance in 1971 on the Canadian unemployment rate. In 1971 the period of work necessary to qualify for benefits was shortened from 30 to eight weeks and the maximum duration of benefits was lengthened to 44 weeks with longer periods in regions with high unemployment. The national extended-benefit provision provided four additional weeks of benefits if the national unemployment rate was greater than 4 percent and eight additional weeks if it was more than 5 percent. Regional extended benefits, which varied according to the differential between regional and national unemployment rates, provided six additional weeks if the regional unemployment was one to two percentage points greater than the national, and up to 18 weeks if the regional rate was three percentage points higher. The benefit rate was also increased from 43 to 66.6 percent of previous earnings. In 1977, the national extended period was dropped, and the rules for the regional benefits were revised. Further revisions in 1979 lowered the benefit rate to 60 percent and raised the requirements for new entrants. Most researchers estimate that the 1971 changes led to an increase in the unemployment rate of .5 – 1.5 percent.[15]

The evidence is contradictory as to whether unemployment insurance can explain the persistence of high unemployment through the eighties. What is particularly puzzling to researchers is the divergence between Canadian and U.S. unemployment rates after 1982. The rates were similar until that time. Since then unemployment has been at least three percentage points higher in Canada than in the United States. Two possible explanations include an increased divergence between the institutional and regulatory frameworks of the two countries and differences in their monetary and fiscal policies. The institutional differences include such things as increased unionization, higher minimum wages, and more generous unemployment insurance in Canada; and deregulation in the United States, which could have enhanced flexibility in labour markets. The United States experienced a decrease in unionization from 31.5 percent of the labour force in the fifties to 22 percent of the labour force in the early eighties. Canada had the same rate of unionization in the fifties but that increased to 39 percent in the early eighties. Unionization contributes to wage rigidity and might therefore increase unemployment.

Ashenfelter and Card (1986) and Gunderson and Meltz (1987) found little evidence that the increase in labour market rigidities in Canada (or decrease in the United States) could explain the diverging unemployment rates. They point out that the differences between the two countries were more pronounced during the seventies than during the eighties, when the rates started to diverge. On the other hand, Grubel and Bonnici (1986) and Daly and MacCharles (1986) argue that the high unemployment in Canada after the 1981-82 recession was caused by real wages that were too high for the markets to clear. The expected effect on unemployment was masked by the natural resource boom in the seventies. When the boom came to an end, workers could no longer be employed at the high wages.

Gunderson and Meltz (1987) attributed the different rates to lower aggregate demand in Canada caused by the very restrictive monetary policies. Ashenfelter and Card (1986), on the other hand, found that the divergence could not be explained by differences in output or aggregate demand. McCallum (1987) attributed the rise in the unemployment rate before 1983 to monetary restrictions in both Canada and the United States. He cannot account for the persistence of high unemployment after 1983.

Keil and Symons (1990) showed that the gap in the unemployment rates between the two countries in the eighties was caused by the 1971 changes in unemployment insurance and that the negative effects on unemployment were masked by high prices for raw materials in the 1970s. The large increase in unemployment in 1981–82 was attributed to the extremely tight monetary policy and was made worse by a fall in export prices. Milbourne, Purvis, and Scoones (1991) showed that the 1977 revisions to the unemployment insurance rules made the benefits more dependent on the previous unemployment rates and substantially lengthened the period for which unemployment could be claimed. The new rules therefore created an incentive in the system for prolonging the periods of unemployment. Unemployment in effect fed on itself. Their model explains the slow recovery of the unemployment rate after 1983.

Card and Riddell (1993), using individual data from a survey of family heads in Canada and the United States in 1979–80 and 1986–87, found that the employment rates were quite similar in the two countries and became more similar during the late 1980s. The differences in unemployment rates could be explained by their finding that in Canada people who are not working are more likely to be classified as unemployed, while in the United States they are more likely to be outside the labour force. They attributed part of this difference to the more generous unemployment insurance in Canada. For example, the relative increases in the number of Canadian men and women reporting 10–12 weeks of employment and the relative increases in unemployment by these workers accounted for 13 percent of the relative rise of female unemployment and 22 percent of male unemployment. However, differences in unemployment insurance could not explain most of the increase in the differences in unemployment rates.

Conclusions

In this chapter we surveyed recent developments in the theory of inflation and unemployment. There is agreement among economists that there is a short-term trade-off between inflation and unemployment; in the long term the trade-off disappears. Fiscal and monetary policies cannot force the unemployment rate below the level that is determined by supply and demand in the labour markets (the natural rate of unemployment or NAIRU: the non-accelerating inflation rate of unemployment). Any attempt to do so would lead to a permanent increase in the inflation rate. Similarly, any attempt to lower the inflation rate when the labour markets are in equilibrium will lead to a temporary increase in unemployment (the sacrifice ratio). The more slowly the labour markets adjust to lower inflation, the more severe the necessary unemployment. The speed at which labour markets will adjust depends on institutional factors such as the degree of unionization in an economy, minimum wage laws, and the nature of labour contracts.

NAIRU cannot be affected by monetary and fiscal policies. It is determined by structural and institutional factors in the economy. Unemployment insurance is one reason why NAIRU can be quite high. Another reason could be that unions keep wages too high for full employment. Structural changes in the economy could also lead to mismatches between the available jobs and the available workers.

Recently, the whole concept of NAIRU has come under attack in the face of European evidence that NAIRU appears to be affected by cyclical factors, and not to be immune from them, as conventional theory suggests. The new theory has become known as the hysteresis theory because it states that variables do not necessarily return to their previous equilibrium values. Workers who have been laid off for a while may no longer be employable, in the sense that they lose their job skills; they no longer fit in.

The Canadian unemployment rate has increased over the last few decades, suggesting that NAIRU has also increased. The persistence of high unemployment in both incidence and duration in the eighties is particularly puzzling. Our situation has deteriorated substantially compared with that in the United States. So far, the results of the empirical studies are contradictory: some lay the blame on the generosity of our unemployment insurance system and others on restrictive monetary policies (see also Chapter 9).

We also found evidence in our survey that not only has unemployment increased, but also that employment has become less secure in the sense that self-employment, and short-term and part-time work have expanded in relation to traditional full-time work. The labour market has also become more segmented between the skill levels required and therefore the salaries earned. Unemployment tends to be high for workers with few skills, in particular those who lack a high-school education. There is evidence of increased geographical polarization in the labour market between good, high-paying jobs and insecure, low-paying jobs, in that the good jobs are found in large urban areas. All of these factors point towards serious challenges for various levels of government to deal with the increasing unemployment and low wages of a large segment of the Canadian population. We will look at the whole issue of poverty and income distribution in the next chapter.

TOPICS FOR DISCUSSION

1. Do you think the changing nature of employment is consistent with Reich's hypothesis of the segmentation of the labour market into "symbolic analysts, in-person servers, and routine production workers," which was discussed in the introductory chapter.

2. According to the new classical economists, some of the unemployed are willingly unemployed. Do you agree?

3. Recent empirical studies cannot explain the large difference in unemployment rates between Canada and the United States. What factors do you think could explain the difference?

RECOMMENDED READING

Robert Campbell, in *The Full-Employment Objective in Canada, 1945–85*, gives an historical account of full employment as a goal for economic policies. The best-known study of the changing nature of employment in Canada is the Economic Council study *Good Jobs, Bad Jobs, Employment in the Service Economy* (1990). For an impassioned plea for policies to create employment, read Alan Blinder's book *Hard Heads, Soft Hearts: Tough-Minded Economics for a Just Society*.

References

Ashenfelter, O. and D. Card. "Why Have Unemployment Rates in Canada and the United States Diverged?" *Economica* 53 (supplement) (1986): S171-96.

Beach, C.M. and S. F. Kaliski. "The Impact of the 1979 Unemployment Insurance Amendments." *Canadian Public Policy* 9 (1983): 356-67.

Blanchard, Oliver J. and Lawrence H. Summers. "Hysteresis and the European Unemployment Problem." In *Understanding Unemployment*, Lawerence H. Summers (1990): 227-86.

Burn, Andrew. "The Natural Rate of Unemployment: Canada and the Provinces," In *Canadian Unemployment*, ed. Surendra Gera (1991): 39–53.

Blinder, Alan S. *Hard Heads, Soft Hearts: Tough-Minded Economics for a Just Society.* Reading, Mass.: Addison-Wesley Publishing Co. Inc., 1987.

Canada. Economic Council of Canada. *Employment in the Service Economy. A Research Report Prepared for the Economic Council of Canada.* [Ottawa]: Ministry of Supply and Services, 1991.

Campbell, Robert M. *The Full Employment Objective in Canada, 1945-85: A Study Prepared for the Economic Council of Canada.* [Ottawa]: Ministry of Supply and Services, 1991.

Canada. Economic Council of Canada. *Employment in the Service Economy. A Research Report Prepared for the Economic Council of Canada.* [Ottawa]: Ministry of Supply and Services, 1991.

Canada. Economic Council of Canada. *Good Jobs, Bad Jobs: Employment in the Service Economy.* [Ottawa]: Ministry of Supply and Services, 1990.

Canadian Economic Observer. Various issues.

Card, David and Richard Freeman eds. *Small Differences that Matter: Labour Markets and Income Maintenance in Canada and the United States.* Chicago: The University of Chicago Press, 1993.

Card, David and Craig W. Riddell. "A Comparative Analysis of Unemployment in Canada and the United States." In *Small Differences that Matter*, David Card and Craig W. Riddell (1993): 149-89.

Charette, M. F., R. P. Henry, and B. Kaufmann. "The Evolution of Canadian Industrial Structure: An International Perspective." In *Canadian Industry in Transition*, Research Coordinator D. G. McFetridge (1986): 61-135.

Clark, Kim B. and Lawrence H. Summers. "Labour Market Dynamics and Unemployment: A Reconsideration." In *Understanding Unemployment*, Lawerence H. Summers (1990): 3-48.

Corak, Miles. "Canadian Unemployment in Retrospect." In *Canadian Unemployment*, ed. Surendra Gera (1991): 65-79.

Corak, Miles. "Repeat Users of the Unemployment Insurance Program." *Canadian Economic Observer* (January 1992).

Daly, D. J. and D. C. MacCharles. *Focus: On Real Wage Unemployment.* Vancouver: The Fraser Institute, 1986.

Friedman, Milton. "The Role of Monetary Policy." *American Economic Review* 58 (March 1968): 1-17.

Gera, Surendra ed. *Canadian Unemployment: Lessons from the 80s and Challenges for the 90s.* [Ottawa]: The Economic Council of Canada and Ministry of Supply and Services, 1991.

Gera, Surendra and Grenier, Gilles. "Interindustry Wage Differentials in Canada: Evidence and Implications." In *Canadian Unemployment,* ed. Surendra Gera (1991): 129-41.

Gera, Surendra and Gilles Greniers. "Interindustry Wage Differentials and Efficiency Wages: Some Canadian Evidence." *Canadian Journal of Economics* 27 (February 1994): 81-101.

Gera, Surendra and Kathry McMullen. "Unemployment in Canada: Issues, Findings, and Implications." In *Canadian Unemployment,* ed. Surendra Gera (1991): 1-21.

Gera, Surendra and Syed Sajjadur Rahman. "Sectoral Labour Mobility, Unemployment and Labour Market Adjustment in Canada: Evidence from the 1980s." In *Canadian Unemployment,* Surendra Gera (1991): 117-28.

Gera, Surendra, Syed Sajjadur Rahman, and Jean-Louis Arcand. "Unemployment and Job Vacancies: Matching People and Jobs." In *Canadian Unemployment* (1991): 53-65.

Grubel, Herbert G. and Joseph Bonnici. *Focus: Why Is Canada's Unemployment Rate so High?* Vancouver: The Fraser Institute, 1986.

Gunderson, Morley and Noah M. Meltz. "Labour-Market Rigidities and Unemployment." In *Unemployment,* Gunderson et al. (1987): 164-76.

Gunderson, Morley, Noah M. Meltz, and Sylvia Ostry eds. *Unemployment: International Perspectives.* Toronto: The Centre for Industrial Relations and University of Toronto Press, 1987.

Kaliski, S.F. "Presidential Address: Accounting for Unemployment— A Labour Market Perspective." *Canadian Journal of Economics* 20 (November 1987): 665-94.

Keil, M.W. and J.S.V. Symons. "An Analysis of Unemployment." *Canadian Public Policy* 16 (March 1990): 1-17.

Lilien, David M. "Sectoral Shifts and Cyclical Unemployment." *Journal of Political Economy* 90 (August 1982): 777-93.

Mankiw, N. Gregory. "Small Menu Costs and Large Business Cycles: A Macroeconomic Model." *Quarterly Journal of Economics* 100 (May 1985): 529-38.

Mankiw, N. Gregory. *Macroeconomics.* New York: Worth Publishers, 1992.

McCallum, John. "Unemployment in Canada and the United States." *Canadian Journal of Economics* 20 (November 1987): 802-23.

McFetridge, D.G., Research Coordinator. *Canadian Industry in Transition.* Toronto: University of Toronto Press, 1986. Prepared for the Royal Commission on the Economic Union and Development Prospects for Canada, Study No. 2.

Milbourne, Ross D., Douglas D. Purvis, and David Scoones. "Unemployment Insurance and Unemployment Dynamics." *Canadian Journal of Economics.* 24 (November 1991): 804-27.

Nakamura, Alice and Masao Nakamura "A Survey of Research on the Work Behaviour of Canadian Women." In *Work and Pay*, Research Coordinator Craig W. Riddell (1986): 171-219.

OECD. *Main Economic Indicators*. Paris: OECD various years.

Phelps, Edmund S. "Money-Wage Dynamics and Labour Market Equilibrium." *Journal of Political Economy* 76 (July-August 1968): 687-711.

Phillips, A.W. "The Relation Between Unemployment and the Rate of Change of Money Wages in the United Kingdom, 1861-1957." *Economica* 25 (November 1958).

Piore, Michael J. "Historical Perspectives and the Interpretation of Unemployment." *Journal of Economic Literature* 25 (December 1987): 1834-851.

Riddell, W. Craig, Research Coordinator. *Work and Pay: The Canadian Labour Market*. Toronto: University of Toronto Press, 1986. Prepared for The Royal Commission of the Economic Union and Development Prospects for Canada.

Sachs, Jeffrey D. and Felipe B. Larrain. *Macroeconomics In The Global Economy*. Englewood Cliffs: Prentice Hall, 1993.

Samson, L. "A Study of the Impact of Sectoral Shifts on Aggregate Unemployment in Canada." *The Canadian Journal of Economics* 18 (1985): 518-30.

Sargent, Thomas and Neil Wallace. "Rational Expectations: The Optimal Monetary Instrument and the Optimal Money Supply Rule." *Journal of Political Economy* 83 (April 1975): 241-54.

Summers, Lawrence H. "Why is the Unemployment Rate So Very High Near Full Employment." In his *Understanding Unemployment*, (1990): 286-328.

Summers, Lawrence H. *Understanding Unemployment*. Cambridge, Mass.: The MIT Press, 1990.

Tobin, James. "Macroeconomic Diagnosis and Prescription." In *Unemployment*, Gunderson *et al.* (1987): 12-41.

Woodbury, Stephen A. and Robert G. Spiegelman. "Bonuses to Workers and Employers to Reduce Unemployment: Randomized Trials in Illinois." *American Economic Review* 77 (September 1987): 513-30.

Yellen, Janet. "Efficiency Wage Models of Unemployment." *American Economic Review. Papers and Proceedings* 74 (May 1984): 200-05.

Endnotes

1   For an historical discussion of the interpretation of unemployment, see Piore (1987). Campbell (1991) gives an interesting account of the full employment as a goal for Canadian economic policy after the Second World War.

2   Friedman (1968) coined the term the natural unemployment rate for the rate that exists at the intersection of the long run labour demand and supply curves. Friedman argued that the unemployment rate can never be zero because of the structural characteristics of the labour markets. Some people will always be

167

between jobs. There are also likely to be some mismatches between skills available and skills demanded as well as regional imbalances.

3   If unemployment and inflation could not occur at the same time, the graph would be L-shaped.

4   The following account of recent developments in macroeconomic theory is based on Mankiw (1990) and Sachs and Larrain (1993). For a very readable account of the developments of theory and policy in the United States, see Blinder (1987).

5   From Okun's law. Okun's law states that a change in the GDP of one percent leads to a half percent change in the unemployment rate.

6   In this context one should note the vigour with which the Bank of Canada pushed its policy of zero inflation. For all intensive purposes, we probably reached zero inflation in 1992. It is difficult to argue that it was costless.

7   An economy where all negotiations take place centrally at the same time will have less rigidity than an economy where contract negotiations take place all the time by a multitude of unions. Similarly, the longer are the labour contracts, the more rigid the wages.

8   See for example Yellen (1984).

9   There is additional evidence from the United States of the importance of economic incentives in job search. The State of Illinois in 1985 offered randomly selected unemployed a bonus of $500 if they found employment within 11 weeks. The duration of unemployment for the ones who were offered the incentive was 17.3 weeks compared to an average duration of 18.3 weeks for the ones who were not (Woodbury and Spiegelman, 1987).

10 This part draws extensively on the material in Gera and McMullen (1991).

11 One has to exercise caution in comparing unemployment rates. Notwithstanding the ILO definition, countries do use different criteria to define the labour force with respect to age limits, how frequently the person looks for work, the statistical treatment of people temporarily laid off and with regard to people looking for a job for the first time. There are also differences in how information is collected. Some use sample surveys of households, some use unemployment insurance data, or statistics from employment offices. (Sachs and Larrain, 1993, p. 491).

12 For a discussion of the reasons behind the increased participation rates, see Nakamura and Nakamura (1986).

13 These figures do not include those workers who became discouraged during their job search and dropped out of the labour force, only to reenter it at a later date.

14 These estimates are derived from Gera and McMullen (1991), Table 1-6 p. 9.

15 See for example Beach and Kaliski (1983).

6

Distribution of Income
in Canada

The purpose of this chapter is to give you an understanding of the link between economic well-being and distribution of income with particular focus on poverty. You will be able to discuss the various ways of defining poverty and describe who is poor in Canada. You will also be able to discuss the merits of some income redistribution policies, such as employment equity and the requirement for people on welfare to work.

There appears to be a direct link between economic and physical well-being. Countries that maintain a reasonable degree of income equality tend to have healthier populations than countries that don't (Keating and Mustard 1993). But income distribution is also important because it indicates how well society treats its less fortunate members. I will argue that a good and just society that contributes to our well-being is a society where people are treated fairly from a social, economic, and political perspective. We will look at the notion of a fair distribution of income and examine whether or not there is agreement about what it is. This will be followed by a discussion of how income distribution is measured and how our distribution of income compares to that of other countries. We will then turn our attention to poverty and the controversial issue of how poverty is defined. The incidence of

169

poverty in Canada will be analyzed, with particular attention given to the high incidence of female poverty and its likely causes, and also to poverty among Canada's aboriginal peoples. Finally, we will examine the efficacy of some suggested solutions to long-term poverty, such as training and "workfare" (work for welfare).

What Is a Fair Income Distribution?

The concepts of efficiency and productivity have great prominence in economics as a measure of how the economy is working (see Chapter 1). An efficient economy maximizes output given the available resources. If the economy works efficiently, no one can be made better off without making somebody else worse off. Efficiency is consistent with any distribution of income, and economists are reluctant to declare one income distribution better than another because the choice depends on value judgements. It is usually argued that the electorate should decide what is fair and just.

Theoretically, it is possible to arrive at a perfect income distribution if one operates from the premise that a perfect income distribution would maximize utility for society as a whole, and where utility for society as a whole is the sum of the utilities of all individuals. If, for example, individual A derives less pleasure from money than individual B at the margin, because A is rich compared to B, society's total utility would increase if $100 were taken from A and given to B.[1] Total utility would be maximized if the marginal utility of the last dollar's worth of income were equal for all individuals. This would not necessarily entail an absolutely equal distribution of income. People are different. Individual A may enjoy the pleasures of life that income can buy far more than individual B. Therefore total utility might increase if money were taken from B and given to A instead. In order to distribute income to maximize utility, we would have to be able to measure the utilities of individuals, a clearly impossible task.[2]

The philosopher John Rawls (1971) has influenced economic thinking about what is a just distribution of income.[3] He argues that progress should be judged for its effect on the least well-off members of our soci-

170

ety. Being well-off is judged in relation to the resources that are at hand to generate utility for the individual rather than in relation to utility itself (utility is after all not measurable). Rawls argues that in any society the economic and social rewards are set by "rules of the game." The level of justice should be judged by comparing the rules as they exist with the rules that would be set if people did not know their future circumstances. If we did not know whether we were going to be poor or rich, we would be more likely to devise favourable rules for the poor than if we knew that we would be protected from economic misfortune. According to Rawls (1982, p. 161), a just society should be organized around two principles: 1. Everyone has an equal right to the most extensive scheme of basic liberties compatible with a similar scheme of liberties for all; 2. In order to be just, any social and economic inequalities must benefit the least advantaged members of society most, and these inequalities must be part of offices and positions open to everyone. What Rawls is saying is that economic well-being increases only if the incomes of the poor increase.

Measurements of the Distribution of Income in Canada and Abroad

The most common measure of income distribution is the **size distribution** of income. In contrast to the **functional distribution**, which measures how much income goes to labour and how much to capital, the size distribution measures the share of income each income class receives. The size distribution is achieved by ranking all incomes in ascending order and dividing the population into five equal groups (**quintiles**). The percentage of total income earned by each group is then calculated. In 1992, the lowest quintile calculated for families by Statistics Canada earned 6.3 percent of total income, the second-lowest 12.2 percent , the third-lowest 17.8 percent, the second-highest 24.0 percent and the highest 39.7 percent. In other words, in 1992 the top 20 percent of families took home nearly 40 percent of total income. (If the distribution of income were perfectly equal, each quintile would earn an equal share — 20 percent — of the total.) Statistics Canada also gives information on the upper limits of income quintiles (see Table

6.1). If your family income in 1992 was less than $25,373, your family belonged to the poorest 20 percent of Canadian families. If your family income exceeded $75,428, you belonged to the top 20 percent.

The size distribution of income is usually illustrated diagrammatically by a **Lorenz curve**. The Lorenz curve plots the cumulative distribution on a graph, with the proportions of the population on the horizontal axis and income shares on the vertical axis (see Figure 6.1). If the income distribution were absolutely equal, the Lorenz curve would fall along the diagonal, since each quintile would receive 20 percent. If the income distribution were absolutely unequal, all incomes would accrue to the top income class (nobody received any income except Mary, who received the whole GDP), and the Lorenz curve would follow the horizontal axis to the 100 percent point and then take off vertically; it would have the shape of an inverted L.

Figure 6.1
The Lorenz Curve for Canadian Families, 1992

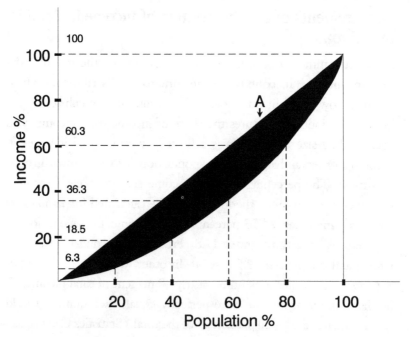

Source: Calculated from Table 6.1.

Sometimes the information from the size distribution and the corresponding Lorenz curve is collapsed into one number called the **Gini coefficient**. The Gini coefficient is a measure of the distance of the Lorenz curve from the diagonal. More precisely, it is a measure of the proportion the area A takes up of the total area under the diagonal. Corresponding to the extreme positions of the Lorenz curve, an absolutely equal income distribution would imply a Gini coefficient of zero, whereas an absolutely unequal distribution would have a coefficient of one. Therefore, the closer the Gini coefficient is to zero, the more equal is the income distribution. Some measures of income distribution are the **coefficient of variation**, which measures the variance of incomes around the mean; **Theil's index of inequality**, and **Atkinson's measure**. The latter two are far more complex than the Gini coefficient in both theory and design.[4] All four measures are biased in different ways in their weighting of different income groups. The Gini coefficient is sensitive to changes of equality around the median, whereas the Theil index and the coefficient of variation are sensitive to changes at the top part of the income distribution. The Atkinson measure is sensitive to changes in the lowest part. It is therefore possible that in a comparison of two income distributions for the purpose of deciding which is the most equal, the conclusion will depend on what measure has been chosen.

Table 6.1 gives the size distribution of income for families and unattached individuals and the upper limits for each quintile for 1992. The source of this information is an annual survey of consumer finances. According to Statistics Canada, a family is a group of individuals sharing a common dwelling unit and related by blood, marriage, or adoption. All relatives living together at the time of the survey are considered to be a family. An unattached individual, on the other hand, is a person living alone or in a household where he or she is not related to the other household members. Income consists of income from gross wages and salaries, net income from self-employment, investment allowances, child tax credit, unemployment insurance, workers' compensation, training allowances, pensions to the blind and disabled, pensions and miscellaneous income (for example scholarships or alimony). Capital gains or losses, gambling gains or losses, and income in

TABLE 6.1

Size Distribution of Income and Upper Limits of Quintiles, 1992

| | Quintiles | | | | |
	1st	2nd	3rd	4th	5th
Percentage Shares					
Families	6.3	12.2	17.8	24.0	39.7
Unattached individuals	5.5	10.5	15.4	24.4	44.2
Families and unattached individuals	4.6	10.3	16.7	24.8	43.6
Upper limits ($)					
Families	25,373	39,964	55,336	75,428	—
Unattached individuals	10,252	14,565	22,580	35,000	—
Families and unattached individuals	16,295	29,313	44,896	65,949	—

Source: Income Distribution by Size in Canada, 1992 (cat. 13–207).

kind, such as free meals or accommodation, are excluded. Most of the income received by persons in the lowest quintile comes from transfer payments, whereas those in the upper quintiles derive most income from wages and salaries.

The size distribution of income has changed very little over the last decades. Evidence indicates that it has become slightly more equal. For example, the share of the lowest quintile for families and unattached individuals was 4.4 percent in 1951, 4.2 percent in 1961, 3.6 percent in 1971, 4.6 percent in 1981, and 4.6 percent in 1991.[5] It is surprising that the distribution has not become much more equal in view of the large increase in transfers since 1950. How can this stability be explained? The measured income distribution can be affected by changes in how the data are collected, changes in the composition of the population (for example in the relative number of young and old, or in family com-

TABLE 6.2

Income Shares by Quintiles and Gini Coefficients, 1981, 1991

Families and Unattached Individuals.

	1st	2nd	3rd	4th	5th	Gini Co-efficient
			Quintile Shares (percentages)			
Income before transfers						
1981	1.4	9.6	17.8	26.4	44.9	0.439
1991	0.9	7.6	16.3	26.3	48.9	0.488
Total money income						
1981	4.6	10.9	17.6	25.2	41.8	0.377
1991	4.7	10.3	16.6	24.7	43.8	0.396
Income after tax						
1981	5.3	11.8	18.0	24.9	40.0	0.351
1991	5.6	11.5	17.3	24.6	41.1	0.358

Source: Vaillancourt (1985), p. 11, and Statistics Canada, Income After Tax Distribution by Size in Canada, 1991 (cat. 13–210).

position), and changes in labour force participation, earnings differentials, and transfer payments. Vaillancourt (1985), in reviewing the existing studies of the Canadian income distribution to 1981, argues that changes in data collection methods are unlikely to explain the stability of the distribution and changes in the demographic composition of the population appear to cancel out any changes in the labour force participation rates. Transfers, on the other hand, clearly have had an effect. A different picture emerges when we look at figures that exclude transfer payments. Table 6.2, shows as we would expect, that income before transfers is far more unequally distributed than income after transfers.

Note also that the pre-transfer income distribution has become significantly worse, presumably indicating the increasing disparities in earnings referred to in the previous chapter, and the disproportionately high unemployment among low-income people. Transfers appear to have a larger effect on the income distribution than taxes. We can conclude, therefore, that the income distribution would have worsened considerably had it not been for the tax and transfer system.

International comparisons are fraught with difficulties. Neither the statistical surveys nor the definitions of income and family units may be comparable. Recently, however, data from the Luxembourg income study have become available for analysis. This study was begun in 1983 under the auspices of the government of Luxembourg. The purpose was to collect comparable data sets on measures of income and economic well-being from different industrialized countries. Table 6.3 shows Gini coefficients for the countries surveyed for the period 1979–83 for disposable family income and disposable family income adjusted for family size. The table shows that, among the countries surveyed, disposable income is most unequal in the United States, followed by Australia, Canada, and the Netherlands in that order. Canada is more unequal than the average. The most equal income distributions are in Sweden and Norway. These rankings are not substantially changed if the Theil or Atkinson measures are used in place of the Gini coefficient (Smeeding 1991). The country rankings are a reflection of the proportion of GDP that these countries spend on redistributive measures. There is also some evidence that the countries with a more equal income distribution tend to have more equal distributions of wages and earnings (*ibid.*).

Poverty: Definition, Measurement, and Incidence

There is no agreement on how to define poverty and therefore on who is poor and how many people are poor and in need of help. Obviously it is easy to recognize when people are actually starving, but poverty can also be relative in an affluent society where through no fault of your own, you are deprived of many of the amenities most people take for granted. If you have basic shelter and enough food on the table to

TABLE 6.3
Coefficients for Gini Selected Countries, Disposable Family Incomes, 1979–83

	DI[a]	ADI[a]
Australia	0.314 (2)	0.292 (2)
Canada	0.306 (3)	0.290 (4)
Germany	0.280 (8)	0.249 (8)
Israel	0.292 (6)	0.276 (5)
Netherlands	0.303 (4)	0.291 (3)
Norway	0.255 (10)	0.222 (9)
Sweden	0.264 (9)	0.197 (10)
Switzerland	0.292 (6)	0.275 (6)
United Kingdom	0.303 (4)	0.275 (6)
United States	0.330 (1)	0.315 (1)
Simple average	0.294	0.268

Source: Smeeding (1991), p. 45.
[a] DI is disposable personal income; ADI is disposable personal income adjusted for family size. The figures in parentheses are rankings.

feed your family, are you poor? There is a vast literature addressing this issue. We will only examine the main streams.[6]

Most studies aim to identify poverty at the household level, on the assumption that the poverty of one member of a household is not independent of that of other members.[7] All members of a household usually share their incomes as well as some of the household work. There are three different methods in the literature for defining a poverty line used to classify a household as poor or not poor: the **income method,** the **consumption method,** and the **welfare method.** At first glance the income method seems the most obvious, since income is what determines our living standard, but this method has its weaknesses. For example most students at universities have very low incomes — many at poverty levels. Are they poor? Most people would say no, because over a lifetime their incomes are likely to be quite high. Clearly, lifetime income should be considered. Others argue that income may not be a suitable measure because your income might be due to your choice in life. For example, you might choose to work part-time rather than full-time because you value leisure very highly. Perhaps you would rather forego having a car or a house to spend a large part of your time reading, playing golf, or working in your garden. Therefore, the income measure used should be the total amount of money you *could* earn if you devoted all your available time to paid labour. Others point out, however, that most poor people do not have a choice between income and leisure. The difficulties of arriving at an income concept based on lifetime earnings or potential earnings are immense. For this reason, most researchers use annual cash income.

The next difficulty is to determine if the poverty line should be absolute or relative. An absolute poverty line tries to determine the minimum income necessary to meet a person's basic needs (food, clothing, and shelter). A relative poverty line, on the other hand, defines poverty as a state of relative rather than absolute deprivation. If your resources fall substantially short of those of the average person or family in your community, then you are poor. Relative poverty lines are usually set at a percentage of mean or median income in society, or less commonly, they define the lowest decile or quintile of the income distribution to be poor. Note here the different implications for anti-poverty policies of the two different approaches. A reduction in absolute poverty requires that the incomes of the poor increase, whereas a reduction in relative poverty requires a more even income distribution. An increase in the income of the poor does not necessarily entail a decrease in relative poverty since everybody's income might increase by the same proportion. In theory, relative poverty could not be eliminated unless incomes were equalized![8]

Other poverty lines are based on the cost of consuming some specific goods. In a way, they do not differ substantially from the concept of an absolute poverty line discussed above. Absolute poverty is usually calculated by estimating the minimum income necessary to meet basic needs. Again, we run into difficulties in deciding what are basic needs. Are basic needs the things that are physiologically necessary for survival, or are they the things that are bought by the average consumer in the same society? After all, people are social beings, and in North America survival is not usually regarded as the main purpose of life. Consumption-based poverty lines also run into difficulties since there are legitimate differences in household needs because of differences in health, age, and so on.

Ideally a poverty line should be based on welfare, and we should study distribution of welfare rather than the distribution of income. Such a poverty line, however, suffers from the difficulty in defining welfare (some of which we discussed in Chapter 1), for welfare is essentially a subjective measure. Amartaya Sen (1985), who has written extensively about the concept of poverty, argues strongly against both relative and subjective measures of poverty because they detract from an "irreducible absolutist core" that is implicit in the concept of poverty. According to Sen, poverty should be defined in relation to the ability to function with respect to nourishment, participation in society, and transport. Any relative or subjective evaluation can be influenced by the psychological need of the individual doing the evaluation. For example, two different individuals in similar economic circumstances may well give different judgements on their own status depending on their aspirations, social roles, and past experience.

We can conclude that there is no generally agreed on definition of an ideal poverty line. In a survey of the literature from various countries shows that the number of poor households depends very much on the definition of poverty line. Therefore the choice of a poverty line becomes ideological. An absolute poverty line based on the cost of consuming bare essentials will show fewer poor people.[9] According to *The Globe and Mail* in 1993 (February 24, 1993), Conservative backbenchers in Canada had become so frustrated at the number of children reported poor in Canada that they were trying to develop a new method of measuring poverty.

In Canada, provincial welfare authorities tend to use absolute measures of poverty; that is, they establish the incomes necessary to meet the needs of families of various sizes. The Canadian Council of Social Development, on the other hand, defines a family of three as poor if its income is less than 50 percent of the average income of Canadian families. To calculate the poverty line for families of other sizes, a scaling formula is used. For example the poverty line for a family of one is 50 percent of that for a family of three.

Statistics Canada, presumably for political reasons, has not developed a poverty line. Instead of poverty, it uses the concept of low income. The agency calculates a low-income cut-off point by estimating the average amount a family spends on food, shelter and clothing, and then adds an arbitrary 20 percent to the figure. For example, in 1978, the average family spent 38.5 percent of its income on food, clothing, and shelter; therefore the low income cut-off point was set at 58.5 percent. If you spent more than 58.5 percent of your income on food, clothing, and shelter, you belonged in the low-income category. Low-income cut-offs are calculated for families of different sizes. In 1988, the two-person family low-income cut-off was $15,264, whereas the cut-off used by the Canadian Council on Social Development was $18,832 (Economic Council of Canada, 1992, p. 20). In a comparison, the official U.S. poverty line in Canadian dollars was $9,948 for a two-person family.[10]

Statistics Canada is considering changing its low-income cut-off (commonly abbreviated to LICO) to a relative-income measure based on 50 percent of adjusted median family income (abbreviated to LIM = low income measure). The adjusted median family income is arrived at by dividing each family income by the size of the family (where the first adult is counted as one person and each additional adult as 0.4 of a person, recognizing the presence of some economies of scale in running a family)[11]. The low-income measure gives a cut-off for a family of two of $14,685 for 1988.

According to the figures published by Statistics Canada using the 1978 base for low-income cut-offs, 11.5 percent of all Canadian families and 32.1 percent of unattached individuals were classified as low-income in 1991.[12] There were substantial provincial variations. The Atlantic provinces have an average incidence of 13 percent for families;

Newfoundland had the highest in the country with 15.8 percent. Low incomes were also widespread in Quebec (13.9 percent) and in the Prairie provinces (Manitoba has 15.1 percent). The corresponding figures for Ontario and British Columbia were 9.7 percent and 9.2 percent respectively.

Poverty is a predominantly female phenomenon: 37.6 percent of families headed by women were poor, compared to only 8.1 percent of families headed by men; 35.9 percent of unattached women were poor, compared to 27.9 percent of unattached men. (In families consisting of married couples, the husband is defined as the head of the family). The incidence of low incomes also increases with the number of children and decreases with age among the working population.[13] The incidence of poverty is higher among young families and individuals than others. Of families headed by someone younger than 24 years, 33.9 percent were poor. The low-income rates of young people appear to be particularly sensitive to fluctuations in the economy. In 1987, their incidence of low income was much lower: 25.1 percent. Young people are more likely to be unemployed during recessions.

It helps to be employed. Only 8.4 percent of families with the head of the family in the labour force fell in the low-income category. (The figure for individuals was 21.2 percent.) Low-income families also have a high proportion of seasonal workers. Lack of education also increases on the likelihood of becoming poor. Of families headed by persons with less than nine years of education, 15.2 percent were poor, and of individuals with the same education level, 47.3 percent were poor. With a university degree, the incidence was 5.3 percent for families and 19.3 percent for unattached individuals.

By international standards, Canada's incidence of poverty is high. Again the Luxembourg income study offers some interesting comparisons. This study defines people as poor if their adjusted disposible incomes are below half of the median income in each country. Table 6.4 gives some comparable data.

The statistics on poverty come as no surprise, given the earlier comparative statistics on income distribution. The relative-poverty measure used in the study makes income distribution a determining

TABLE 6.4

Incidence of Poverty of Persons in Various Demographic Groups,
1979–83, Selected Countries

	All persons	Single persons	Lone parent with children	Couples with > 2 children	Elderly couples	Elderly single
Australia	11.4	17.8	55.4	10.3	7.3	30.1
Canada	12.3	19.9	46.3	11.5	12.0	32.0
Israel	11.0	9.3	22.6	9.8	13.2	23.4
Germany	4.9	9.9	7.2	1.3	8.6	12.9
Netherlands	7.5	18.6	21.0	3.0	2.3	2.0
Norway	4.8	12.9	8.1	1.9	2.9	4.9
Sweden	5.0	14.0	9.8	4.6	0.6	0.9
Switzerland	8.2	15.1	21.2	6.0	4.0	16.9
United Kingdom	11.7	12.6	29.3	7.5	23.6	51.5
United States	16.6	19.6	54.0	12.1	15.0	39.6
Average	9.4	15.4	28.6	6.7	8.9	21.4

Source. Smeeding (1991), p. 48.

Note: The statistics for elderly are for the 65–74 age group. All persons includes all persons in families.

factor. Countries with the most uneven income distribution also have the highest incidence of poverty. The United States has by far the highest incidence of poverty, followed by Canada, the United Kingdom, and Australia. The lowest poverty rates are in Sweden, Norway, and Germany. Canada has the highest poverty rate for single persons. In most of the countries studied, single parents, who are predominantly female, have the highest poverty rates, but the differences between countries are substantial. The Canadian incidence is almost five times that of Sweden and Norway. These differences are presumably due not only to differences in tax and transfer policies but also differences in the availability of day care and in the enforcement of child support payments. In all countries except Norway there is a higher incidence of poverty for couples with more than two children.[14] Single elderly people also fare badly in all countries except Sweden. This group consists predominantly of women.

Though the incidence of low income has declined in Canada since the 1960s, it varies with the state of the economy[15] (see Table 6.5). The low-income rates go up in a recession and fall during economic upturns (note the effects of the 1982–83 recession). This is not surprising since unemployment rises and earnings fall during a recession. Some families and individuals are clearly on the borderline of poverty, and a recession is likely to push them over. There is plenty of evidence from the United States that the income distribution widens when the economy shrinks and narrows when the economy expands, indicating that the poor gain when the economy expands and lose when it contracts. Blank and Blinder (1986) estimated that an increase in the prime-age male unemployment rate of 2 percent, maintained for two years, would subtract 0.3 percent from the lowest quintile and add 0.9 percent to the poverty rate for all persons. Ellwood and Summers (1986) showed that almost all the variations in the poverty rate until the early 1980s could be traced by movements in median family income. Prager (1988) established the same statistical link for Canada, albeit somewhat more weakly. It seems that in both countries the 1981–82 recession disproportionately affected the poor. The number of people living in poverty increased more than the decline in median income would have predicted.

The question often asked is whether there is an underclass, that is, a group of people who are persistently poor and whose children are also likely to be poor. Evidence from the United States shows that most of the poor do not remain poor all their lives. Only about 40 percent of the poor are persistently poor, and 50 percent of these are old or disabled (Ruggles 1991). Approximately 80 percent of the remainder are headed by an unmarried person with children. Do children of poor parents also become poor? Not necessarily. While those born into

TABLE 6.5
Incidence of Low Income Families and Unattached Individuals,
1981–1991

Year	Families (%)	Unattached Individuals (%)
1981	11.3	37.5
1982	12.6	37.1
1983	13.8	41.9
1984	13.9	37.7
1985	12.6	36.9
1986	11.8	34.6
1987	11.3	33.5
1988	10.5	33.1
1989	9.6	30.5
1990	10.7	30.1
1991	11.5	32.1

Source: Statistics Canada, Income Distribution by Size (cat. 13–207), Table 66.

poverty are more likely than others to be poor as adults and to have children who become poor, only one in five persons who was poor as a child will become a poor adult (*ibid.*).

Studies for Canada also indicate that the population of low-income people fluctuates considerably. The Economic Council of Canada (1992) reports the results from a longitudinal study that followed a sample of individuals between 1982 and 1986. Over half of the families had experienced a change in their relative position in the family-income distribution scale in the four years. Thirty-nine percent of families in the lowest quintiles had moved to a higher quintile by 1986, and 40 percent of those in the lowest quintile had moved down from a higher quintile (Economic Council of Canada, 1992, p. 14). The fluctuations in family incomes are due to two factors: variations in earnings and variations in family status (marriage, separation, divorce, children). Sixty-three percent of the families did not change their family status in the period; forty-seven percent of these moved to a different quintile. But of the 37 percent of the families whose status changed, 32 percent moved to a higher quintile and 30 percent to a lower. Marriage and divorce had the largest influence on incomes. The National Council of Welfare (1990, p. 19) estimates that the 1987 poverty rate for adults would have been 2 percentage points lower if the family structure in society had remained the same as it was in 1971. The annual rate of movement into and out of poverty is about 27 percent. A large proportion of those who escape poverty will re-enter it fairly soon. It is estimated that nearly one in three Canadians is likely to experience poverty at least once in their working careers (*ibid.*, p. 27). In short, if there is a permanent underclass, it is relatively small.

The high unemployment rate and its link to poverty and low-income status have greatly heightened the sense of economic and social insecurity among Canadians. Fifty percent of middle-income Canadians surveyed believed that they were worse off in 1992 than in 1987, and 63 percent expected their standard of lining to remain the same or worsen in the future. Only 14 percent expected their children to be better off than they were — 54 percent expected them to be worse off. Seventy-six percent believed that their current economic difficulties were caused by fundamental rather than cyclical changes in the economy (The National Forum on Family Security, 1993, p. 3–4). A survey done in 1992 for the Canadian Mental Health Association and the Canadian Psychiatric Association found that the heightened insecurity has resulted in higher stress levels and that the highest levels were reported in Ontario and the Prairie provinces (*ibid.*, p. 4). Almost 50 percent of the respondents felt "really stressed" at some time during any given week, and one-third felt "really depressed" once a month or more. The main causes of depression were work and financial worries.

There is evidence that stress, combined with a feeling of lack of control, is bad for the physical health. A study of British civil servants showed that the proportion of people who thought they had little control over their work was much higher in the lower tiers than in the higher tiers. The lower-level civil servants were four times more likely to die of a heart attack than the upper level civil servants. (Keating and Mustard, 1993, p. 94).

We can summarize. The best way of avoiding poverty and ill health is to be married, to be a man, to have fewer than two children, to be middle-aged, to have a post-secondary education, and to have a full-time job. We have already discussed the changes in the labour markets and the evidence of increased earning disparities among the working populations in the previous chapter, as well as the increases in the unemployment rate and duration of unemployment. We have also established that a post-secondary education decreases the likelihood of being unemployed and also of being poor.

On Being Female and on Having Children

Most poor people are female.[16] Why? One of the reasons is that women earn less than men. In a survey of male-female wage differentials in 1980, quoted by Gunderson (1989), the ratio of women's earnings to men's earnings ranged from 0.54 in Japan, to 0.64 in Canada, 0.83 in Italy, and 0.9 in Sweden. Even in the old Soviet Union, where wages were set by a state committed to equality of the sexes, women on the average earned only 70 percent of what men earned. In theory, the market rewards a person according to the value of what that person produces in his or her occupation; in other words, people are paid according to their productivity. Since a person with more education and experience should be able to contribute more to output they should be paid more. Large wage differentials that are not related to productivity differentials can only persist if persons in high-paying occupations can prevent other workers from entering these occupations and bidding down wages, or if the occupational requirements are so specific and demanding that few people can qualify. The question then is whether women earn less because they are less productive (owing to lack of experience, education, and training), or because they are are denied access to better-paying occupations (a practice known as occupational segregation), or because they are paid less just because they are women (a practice called wage discrimination). Occupational segregation could be caused by disciminatory barriers to entry or a preference by women for occupations that are compatible with childrearing.

Statistical analysis tries to correlate the earnings gap with variables for differences in education, age, race, training, and on-the-job experience. In the Canadian case, several studies have shown that 10 percentage points of the estimated wage gap of 35 percent is explained by productive characteristics, 20 percentage points by occupational segregation, and the remaining 5 percentage points (or according to some studies up to 10 percentage points) by pure wage discrimination (Robb 1987). Results from other countries are not very different. Most studies find a residual wage gap that is attributed to wage discrimination. These studies also include control variables whose values themselves could be affected by discrimination (Gunderson, 1989, p. 51).[17] Specific variables that are important in explaining the male-female wage differential are factors outside the labour market such as differences in household responsibilities (the gap is the largest between the earnings of married men and married women); differences in labour market experience, including the continuity of the experience and seniority; and differences in the type of education (women's education tends to put less emphasis on occupational skills) (*ibid.*).

In most studies occupational segregation is an important factor explaining the gap. Most of the low-paying occupations are dominated by women, and they are often described as female ghettoes. Most women are employed in activities related to various aspects of communication: clerical, secretarial, organizational, or transactional (cashiers, tellers); the next largest group is in retailing, catering, and general services; next a considerable number are in semi-professional, supervisory, and technical occupations (such as nursing); managerial and professional women are in the next group; and at the top are the few women who are employed in the highest levels of the judiciary, government, industry, the arts, and institutions (Peitchinis, 1989, p. 101). Women are more concentrated in low-paying jobs than men. The whole structure of female employment takes the shape of a triangle with the majority at the base of the triangle in the communication sector; the occupational structure for men, on the other hand, looks like a barrel with approximately equal numbers at the bottom and the top. The majority of men are in the middle in supervisory, technical, semi-professional, professional, and managerial occupations (*ibid.*).

The question why occupational segregation exists is an interesting one, that has received much attention in feminist research. It is certainly neither new nor unique to industrialized societies. Historical and anthropological surveys of the sexual division of labour show that the hunting of large animals, fishing, smelting ores, metalwork, mining, quarrying, and lumbering were almost always male tasks, while dairy production, cooking, carrying water, and gathering vegetables were most commonly done by women.[18] In most societies the provision of food, care of the home, child care, nursing of the sick, teaching, and manufacture of clothing are done by women, either as subsistence labour or as unpaid housework. In industrialized societies women often perform commercialized forms of these same activities, which centre on the care and serving of other people (Bradley, 1989, p. 9). The descriptions of women's work have certain common features:

"It is usually indoor work, considered to be "lighter" than men's work; it is clean, safe, physically undemanding, often repetitive and considered boring, requires dexterity rather than "skill", often has domestic associations; it tends to lack mobility, being tied to a particular work station; it may well have associations and requirements of beauty and glamour. By contrast, if we visualize typical men's work, we tend to evoke images of the outdoors, of strength and physicality; men's work may be heavy, dirty, dangerous, it is often highly mobile . . ., it requires "skill" and training. It is frequently highly technical, based on mechanical knowledge or scientific expertise; at the highest level, it requires characteristics of creativity, innovation, intelligence, responsibility, authority and power....

These typical ascriptions were already being elaborated in 1861, and jobs were allocated to men and women in terms of matching up to some or other of these criteria. During the remaining decades of the nineteenth century ... the familiar modern sexual division of labor in factories and offices, schools and hospitals evolved, and the related notions of fit work for the sexes became a commonplace of our culture. (Bradley, 1989, p. 9).

The origins of segregation and the persistence can be explained by the sexual division of labour within the household, women's childbearing role, authority relations in the family, the influence of domestic ideology elaborated by the Victorian middle classes, religion, attitudes of employers to female workers, and processes of socialization in the home, at school, and later (*ibid.*, p. 23).

Nakamura and Nakamura (1986) found that women's labour supply and choice of occupation are affected less by expected wages than their expectations for their future and their family circumstances. Using information from case studies, Nakamura and Nakamura divide married women into different categories on the basis of their taste for work. Women in one category see themselves as short-term workers who may enter the workforce occasionally when their family needs money. The husband may still be in training for a career, or they may work, for a short time, to cover a large expense. As they did not originally plan to work, they have not invested in occupational education or training, though they may have invested in a substantial amount of schooling developing personal interests and acquiring other sorts of skills. Because economic needs have brought these women into the labour market, they cannot afford any training that is at the expense of current earnings, and if their employers are aware of their short-term interest in the labour market, they are unlikely to make investments in their training. The situation of many women in this category could be radically altered by divorce.

The second group of women expect to work most of their lives out of necessity. Many of these women would not work if they were in more affluent circumstances. They may feel that they have to work because the long term earning prospects of their husbands are poor, or they expect their marriage to break up. Many of these women may have come from low-income families and have not had access to much education or training (Nakamura and Nakamura 1985).[19] Because they work out of economic necessity, they may not be able to sacrifice any of their earnings to take special training. Their employers may also be reluctant to invest in their training because of the women's low initial levels of education and because they cannot distinguish between women who have a short-term commitment and those with a long-term commitment to the labour force.

The final category of working wives are those who work more or less because they want to, rather than out of a need to support the family. These women could be expected to be well-educated and to have highly-paid spouses and relatively few children. If this categorization of women is accurate, occupational segregation will decrease if young girls form a more accurate expectation of their likely status as married women, and if there are better opportunities for training.

There is evidence that occupational segregation is decreasing and that more women are entering non-traditional occupations, but the process is painfully slow. Affirmative action programs and the legislation of equal pay for work of equal value appear to be effective in narrowing the wage gap if properly implemented (Gunderson 1989).

Affirmative action programs involve strenuous attempts to seek out women candidates for non-traditional jobs and giving women candidates preferential treatment if their qualifications are equal. Equal pay policies require employers to give equal pay for the same work within the same establishment. Equal pay legislation has been on the books in most countries for a considerable time but has not been very effective. Legislation requiring equal pay for work of equal value (pay equity) is a far more radical approach, and has been in effect in Quebec since 1976 and in the federal government since 1978. Equal pay for work of equal value requires employers to compare wages and salaries in dissimilar occupations, using job evaluation procedures, in which each component of a job, such as responsibility, danger, and skill, is given a point score. Female wages are then to be adjusted to male wages in those cases where the job evaluation scores show that the jobs are of equal value. Where pay equity has been in place, it has raised women's wages by 10–20 percent (Gunderson, 1989, p. 68).[20]

Women's childbearing role does not only affect earnings differentials, but also poverty levels. The highest poverty rates are found for single mothers, and the poverty rates for married couples increase with the number of children (Smeeding 1991). The growth in the number of single parents can explain why poverty is a predominantly female phenomenon. A fivefold increase in the divorce rate resulted in an increase in the proportion of single-parent families from 6 percent of all families in 1961 to 13 percent of all families in 1986 (Gunderson and Muszynski, 1990, p. 16). Over 80 percent of these single parents are women. Single parents are less likely to be employed than the male heads of two-parent families, often because of their child-care responsibilities. In 1990, only 55 percent of single parents were employed, compared to 85 percent of fathers in two-parent families. Among those who were employed, 29 percent of lone-parent families were below the low-income cut-off, compared to only 6 percent of two-parent families. Of the ones who received assistance, 37 percent had incomes $10,000 below the poverty lines and 52 percent had incomes between $1,000 and $9,999 below (Oderkirk 1992). The earnings of married women drop considerably when there are two or more children, thus reducing family income. The poverty rate for children, according to the new Statistics Canada low-income measure, has fluctuated between 15 and 18 percent, the higher percentage occurring during the recessions.

Estimates by the Economic Council of Canada show that divorce increases the probabilility of becoming poor for both men and women but more so for women. On average the incomes of women (after adjusting for family size) fell by 39 percent in the year following a divorce, while that for men (adjusted for family size) fell by 7 percent. However, among women the poverty rate of women increased by 37 percent and among men by only 2 percent. A study by the Department of Justice showed that only 68 percent of divorces in 1989 involving dependent children resulted in a child-support order. The average order per child was approximately $250 a month (Economic Council of Canada, 1992, p. 49). Divorce also appears to have an effect on the children's school work. Sixty-nine percent of 15-year olds from two-parent families accumulated eight or more school credits. Fifty-nine percent of children of single-female-parent families achieved the same number of credits, and 54 percent of children of single-male-parent families.

It is obvious from the large number of children in low-income families that we do not look after our children well in Canada. The human capital invested in our children is the most important asset we bequeath to future generations. Poor children may have difficulties ranging from restricted access to recreational activities and reduced acceptance by peers, to poor health, malnutrition, and inadequate shelter, all of which may have an effect on their schooling and therefore on their future prospects. There is some evidence to show that the way a newborn child is treated in its first year of life is crucial for its later social and academic development. Children brought up in poor socio-economic environments often have difficulties adjusting at school, resulting in high drop-out rates and poor academic performance (Keating and Mustard, 1963, p. 96). Our current incomes are not sustainable unless we invest sufficiently in our children. The records of other countries show that we could do better. We need more effective laws to guarantee child support for single parents, and we need better child care. We also need adequate policies for closing the gender gap in earnings.

The Economic Status of Visible Minorities and Aboriginal Peoples

No discussion about poverty in Canada would be complete without an examination of the economic status of visible minorities and aboriginal peoples in Canada. According to statistics for 1986, members of minority groups were less likely to be in the labour force than other Canadians, were more likely to be unemployed, and had lower than average earnings (Christofides and Swidinsky 1994). A recent study by Christofides and Swindinsky (*ibid.*) based on the 1989 Labour Market Activity Survey estimated that the average hourly wage was $14.73 for white males, $12.48 for minority males, $11.33 for white women, and $10.97 for minority women. The differences in wage rates could be explained partly by productivity differences. However, 46.2 percent of the difference between white male and minority male wages could not be explained. The corresponding figure for minority females was 70 percent.

Visible minority women are at a particular disadvantage in labour markets. Christofides and Swindinsky point out that minority women are likely to fall outside the scope of pay equity legislation since they tend to be segregated into small, low-wage establishments and industries. Therefore, pay equity legislation might narrow the overall wage gap between males and females, but might actually widen the gap between white women and minority women.

Most Canadians are familiar with the poor living conditions and low economic status of aboriginal peoples. Statistics indicate a suicide rate almost three times that of the general population with most of the suicides occurring in the younger age groups. There are also large differences in life expectancy and infant mortality between aboriginal groups and other Canadians. Life on many reserves is characterized by crowded houses, lack of sanitation, high alcoholism rates, and a high incidence of accidental deaths. Our prison population has disproportionate representation from aboriginal peoples.[21]

According to the 1986 census, some aboriginal ancestry was reported by 711,725 Canadians (approximately 2.8 percent of the total Canadian population). Of these, 263,245 were registered Indians (status Indians under the Indian Act), 33,460 were of Inuit origin, and 415,025 were of Métis origin or were non-status Indians (Larocque and Gauvin, 1989, p. 7). The size of the aboriginal population in relation to the total population varies from province to province. New Brunswick and Prince Edward Island, together with Quebec, have the lowest proportion of aboriginal people (1.3 percent); Manitoba has the highest (8.1 percent). In comparison, 58.7 percent of the population of the Northwest Territories claim aboriginal origin (*ibid.*, p. 9). Most status Indians live in British Columbia, and most non-status Indians and Métis live in Ontario. Most status Indians (62.4 percent) live on reserves. Table 6.6 gives some information on factors describing the economic conditions for registered Indians compared to the rest of the Canadian population.

TABLE 6.6

Economic Conditions of Registered Indians in Comparison to
Other Canadians, 1986

	Registered Indians	Others
Average income before taxes	$ 9,900	$18,800
Proportion of income from employment	50%	70%
Proportion of income from transfer payments	45.6%	19.4%
Employment rate	31.4%	59.8%
Persons with less than grade 9 education	44.7% (on reserves)	
	37.2% (off reserves)	17.1%
Persons living in crowded dwellings (>1 person/room)	28.9%	1.7%

Source: Larocque and Gauvin, 1989.

A new study by George and Kuhn (1994), based on 1986 census data, showed that the average wage gap between aboriginal peoples living off reserves and outside Yukon and the Northwest Territories and other Canadians was only 11 percent (6.5 percent for women and 11.6 percent for men). When the sample includes only individuals who report their background as exclusively aboriginal, the wage gap widens to 18.1 percent for men and 10.8 percent for women. The researchers also show that 50 percent of the differences in pay can be explained by differences in observable characteristics such as education. However, aboriginal peoples living on reserves have substantially lower wages than those outside, and education makes no difference to their earnings. This finding is consistent with the results of a study by Drost (1994), who found that post-secondary education and training had little effect on the unemployment rate of aboriginal men living on reserves. In general, unemployment among aboriginals is higher than among any other ethnic group in Canada, and is approximately 2.5 times the national average.

The reasons for the relatively low economic status of aboriginal peoples and some visible minorities are difficult to pinpoint and also controversial. Traditional economic theory would argue that their earnings are low because their productivity is low; therefore any investments in human capital in the form of education and training would their improve earnings capacity and give them the opportunity to acquire better-paying jobs. Indeed, according to George and Kuhn (1994), 30–40 percent of the already small wage gap for aboriginals living off reserves could be eliminated by more training and education.

Critics of orthodox human capital theory point to the fact that despite large investments in education and training, substantial earnings gaps still exist between aboriginal peoples living on reserves and other Canadians. Earnings differentials are not necessarily caused by differences in human capital. Two theories that attempt to explain persistent earning differentials are **segmentation** or **dual labour market theories.**[22] According to segmentation theory, there are two labour markets in operation: primary labour markets and secondary labour markets. Primary labour markets are characterized by high wages, employment stability, opportunities for advancement, efficient management, and strong labour unions. High wages induce management to raise productivity to offset the increased costs. Improvements in productivity require additional training for workers and opportunities for advancement. The large investment in training requires stable jobs so that the employers can obtain a return on their investment. Secondary labour markets, on the other hand, are characterized by unstable jobs with high turnover, low wages, few opportunities for advancement, and labour-intensive technology. The low wages give little incentive to improve production technology, and therefore productivity and wages stagnate. Because of the lack of skills, the jobs are dead-end. Examples of these types of jobs are dishwashing and cleaning jobs. Over time, workers in both markets develop characteristics appropriate to their particular market. Workers in primary markets tend to be dependable, conscientious, punctual, and anxious to learn new skills. Secondary-market workers, because of the lack of possibilities for advancement, have poor work habits and weak job attachment. There is little mobility between the two sectors, partly because of discrimination and partly because workers in the secondary market have acquired undesirable characteristics.

In the case of aboriginal peoples living on reserves, the reserve system combined with easy access to welfare may be detrimental to their realizing their potential because reserves isolatae people from better opportunities and could create unfavourable work attitudes. Drost (1994) found that the most important variable explaining the unemployment rate among aboriginals was a variable for social assistance. Being on social assistance increased the probability of being unemployed by 34 percent.

Workfare and Welfare

It is well-known that most welfare or social assistance programs act as disincentives to work, since the more you work, the less assistance you receive. Any increase in social assistance payments, with the good intention of combating poverty, will further decrease any incentives to take low-paying jobs and will therefore make the recipient less likely to acquire enough skills and experience to become independent. Studies from the United States, surveyed by Sawhill (1988) show that one dollar in social assistance is translated into a net increase in income between 29 and 77 cents as a result of the reduced work effort. If we add to this the disincentive effects of having to tax the non-poor, the net total increase in income may be as little as 11 cents.[23] Various solutions have been proposed to get around this trade-off between equity and efficiency, including guaranteed income schemes and welfare tied to training or work.

Guaranteed income (or negative income tax) was seen as a good way of reforming the welfare system in the seventies and the eighties. There are many variants of these schemes, but they have in common a guarantee of a certain minimum income to everyone. People whose earnings are below the guaranteed level will be taxed at a low rate. In current practice, if a person on social assistance earns any money, their social assistance is reduced by the amount of the earnings. In other words, earnings are in effect taxed at 100 percent. Under guaranteed income, earnings below the guaranteed income level would not lead to an equivalent reduction in payments from the government. The government would apply a "negative income tax," which would be less than 100 percent, say 50 percent. Thus, one-hundred-dollar increase in earnings would reduce payments from the government by $50 rather than $100. Earnings above the guaranteed income level would be taxed at the "normal" income tax rates. The system would be administratively efficient because it would operate under the current tax system, and it would not discourage people from earning additional income to the same degree as the current system of social assistance. It would, however, be very expensive. There is also some concern that if everybody were guaranteed a certain level of income, it would discourage some people from looking for work. Several guaranteed income schemes were run as pilot projects in the United States as part of the "war on poverty." The first was the New Jersey Graduated Work Incentive experiment, which began in 1968. It was followed by four others. Canada started its own experiment in Manitoba in 1975 (the Manitoba Basic Annual Income Experiment, or Mincome). Over a period of three years, one thousand families were randomly assigned to different negative income tax programs or to a control group that received no benefits. The participants were interviewed three times a year about their work effort. In analyzing the data from the experiment, Hum and Simpson (1991) estimate that the negative effects on work effort were very small, in fact considerably smaller than the studies done on the U.S. experiments.

Training or "workfare" (welfare with a requirement to work) are often thought to offer long-term solutions to poverty. The arguments in favour or against often run along ideological lines. People on the left of the political spectrum tend to accept the premise that work is superior to welfare, but they continue to emphasize the reduction of poverty over the reduction of dependence. They believe that the only thing that stops welfare recipients from earning a decent living is their lack of education and training and the lack of adequate day-care facilities if they have children. They advocate voluntary participation in programs that provide intensive education and training and programs that guarantee affordable child care for those who leave welfare to work. Conservatives, on the other hand, tend to emphasize the reduction of dependence over the reduction of poverty. Many argue that jobs are available and people on welfare are unwilling to work or have unrealistic expectations about their job prospects. Programs are favoured that set clear expectations for recipients, and that require participation in program activities or regular employment. Conservatives doubt that the provision of more training and education will enable people to get off welfare or that such programs are cost-effective (Gueron, 1990, p. 83–84).

The idea that welfare recipients should have to work if they are able-bodied goes back a long time. The British Poor Laws of the sixteenth and seventeenth centuries first made the distinction between the "deserving" poor and the "undeserving" poor. The "undeserving" poor were able-bodied adults and their dependents, and they had to work as a condition for receiving subsistence-level relief.[24] The word "workfare" which is short for work for welfare, is new. At first it referred to the practice of requiring unpaid work in exchange for benefits (Evans, 1993, p. 56). Workfare has been tried on a limited scale in the United States and also in Canada.

Bassi and Ashenfelter (1986), who provide a summary of the evidence from training programs, conclude that the programs have not been a total failure but that the benefits have been very modest. Their largest impact has been on women and visible minorities. On the other hand, a survey of the effectiveness of seven welfare employment programs in the United States showed that in most cases the programs led to a measurable increase in employment and earnings, which continued for the three years the studies lasted. The programs also led to welfare savings, even though they were smaller than the gains in earnings (Evans 1993). Gueron (1993) points out that even though the programs were successful in reducing welfare costs and increasing employment, they did not necessarily lead to a reduction in poverty. That was because many of the jobs were minimum-wage jobs that did not pay enough to raise the people out of poverty.

Conclusions

In our survey, we found that the distribution of income has remained relatively constant in Canada for the last 30 years. This does not mean, however, that the social safety net in which we take such pride has been a complete failure. The data show that without these social policies our income distribution would have been worse. Our distribution of income is more equal than that in the United States but less equal than the distribution in many European countries, which spend more money than we do on social programs. We can draw the same conclusions about the incidence of poverty. The total incidence has not changed much, but is very sensitive to the state of the economy. We have proportionally fewer poor people than the United States but far more than many European countries. We have a particularly high incidence of poverty among single parents, most of whom are women. This is particularly worrying because of the potential long-term adverse effects on the children. We looked at some of the reasons for the higher incidence of poverty among women, such as wage differentials between men and women, child-care responsibilities, and changes in marital status. Much of the earnings differential between males and females can be attributed to occupational segregation, which has a long history and appears to exist in most societies. We also found substantial wage differentials between visible minorities and whites in Canada; the most disadvantaged were visible minority women. There are also differences in wages and unemployment rates between people of aboriginal origins and others. We looked at the effects of affirmative action and equal pay for work of equal value. Finally, we examined the effectiveness of training and workfare on getting people out of poverty.

TOPICS FOR DISCUSSION

1. As you know from the previous chapter, some economists believe that people who are out of work are voluntarily unemployed. Using the same logic, can one argue that people are voluntarily poor?

2. There is some evidence that equal pay for work of equal value legislation increases unemployment among women in some industries. Taking that into account, do you think such legislation is a good idea?

RECOMMENDED READING

The New Face of Poverty: Income Security Needs of Canadian Families (Economic Council of Canada 1992) and *Family Security in Insecure Times* (National Council of Welfare 1993) contain good discussions of the problems of poor families in Canada. You might also want to read Christopher Sarlo's *Poverty in Canada* (1992) for an interesting contrast. The research studies done for the Abella Commission (*Research Studies for the Commission on Equality in Employment* 1985) are excellent sources of information on income and employment opportunities for different minority groups in Canada.

References

Bassi, Laurie J. and Orley Ashenfelter. "The Effect of Direct Job Creation and Training Programs on Low Skilled Workers." In *Fighting Poverty*, eds. Sheldon H. Danziger and Daniel H. Weinberg (1986): 133-52.

Blank, Rebecca M. and Blinder, Alan S. "Macroeconomics, Income Distribution, and Poverty." In *Fighting Poverty*. (*ibid.*): 180-209.

Bergmann, Barbara R. "Does the Market for Women's Labour Need Fixing ?" *The Journal of Economic Perspectives* 3 (Winter 1989): 43-61

Bradley, Harriet. *Men's Work, Women's Work: A Sociological History of the Sexual Division of Labour in Employment*. Minneapolis: University of Minnesota Press, 1989.

Canada. The National Forum on Family Security. *Family Security in Insecure Times*. Ottawa: National Forum on Family Security, 1993.

Canada. Economic Council of Canada. *A Lot to Learn. Education and Training in Canada*. Ottawa: Ministry of Supply and Services, 1992.

Canada. Economic Council of Canada. *The New Face of Poverty. Income Security Needs of Canadian Families*. Ottawa: Ministry of Supply and Services, 1992.

Canada. National Council of Welfare. *Women and Poverty Revisited: A Report by the National Council of Welfare*. Ottawa: Ministry of Supply and Services, 1990.

Christofides, L.N. and Swidinsky, R. "Wage Determination by Gender and Visible Minority Status: Evidence from the 1989 LMAS." *Canadian Public Policy-Analyse de Politiques* 20 (March 1994): 34-52.

Danziger, Sheldon H. and Daniel H. Weinberg eds. *Fighting Poverty: What Works and What Doesn't.* Cambridge: Harvard University Press, 1986.

Drost, Helmar. "Schooling, Vocational Training and Unemployment: The Case of Canadian Aboriginals." *Canadian Public Policy-Analyse de Politiques* 20 (March 1994): 52-66.

Ellwood, David T. and Lawrence H. Summers. "Poverty in America: Is Welfare the Answer or the Problem." In *Fighting Poverty*, eds. Sheldon H. Danziger and Daniel H. Weinberg (1986): 78-106.

Evans, Patricia M. "From Workfare to the Social Contract: Implications for Canada of Recent US Welfare Reforms." *Canadian Public Policy* 19 (March 1993): 54-68.

George, Peter and Peter Kuhn. "The Size and Structure of Native-White Wage Differentials in Canada." *Canadian Journal of Economics* 27 (February 1994): 20-43.

Gueron, Judith M. "Work and Welfare: Lessons on Employment Programs." *The Journal of Economic Perspectives* 4 (Winter 1990): 79-99.

Gueron, Judith M. "Welfare Reform in the United States: Strategies to Increase Work and Reduce Poverty." In *Income Security in Canada: Changing Needs, Changing Means*, ed. Elizabeth B. Reynolds. Montreal: Institute for Research on Public Policy, 1993: 171-87.

Gunderson, Morley. "Male-Female Wage Differentials and Policy Responses." *Journal of Economic Literature* 27 (March 1989): 46-72.

Gunderson, Morley and Leon Muszynski. *Women and Labour Market Poverty.* Ottawa: The Canadian Advisory Council on the Status of Women, June 1990.

Hagenaars, Aldi J. M. "The Definition and Measurement of Poverty." In *Economic Inequality and Poverty*, ed. Lars Osberg (1991): 134-57.

Hum, Derek and Wayne Simpson. *Income Maintenance, Work Effort and the Canadian Mincome Experiment.* Ottawa: Ministry of Supply and Service, 1991.

Jenkins, Stephen. "The Measurement of Income Inequality." In *Economic Inequality and Poverty*, ed. Lars Osberg (1991): 3-39.

Keating, Daniel P. and Fraser J. Mustard. "Social Economic Factors and Human Development." In *Family Security in Insecure Times*. The National Forum on Family Security (1993): 87-107.

Larocque, Gilles Y. and Pierre R. Gauvin. *1986 Census Highlights on Registered Indians: Annotated Tables.* Ottawa: Quantitative Analysis and Socio-Demographic Research, Finance and Professional Services, Indian and Northern Affairs Canada, 1989.

Lightman, Ernie S. "Work Incentives Across Canada." *Journal of Canadian Studies* 26 (Spring 1991): 120-37.

McConnell Campbell R. and Stanley L. Brue. *Contemporary Labor Economics.* 2nd edition. New York: McGraw-Hill Book Company, 1989.

Nakamura, Alice and Masao Nakamura. "A Survey of Research on the Work Behaviour of Canadian Women." In *Work and Pay: The Canadian Labour Market*, Research Coordinator Craig Riddell, Toronto: University of Toronto Press, 1985: 171-219. Prepared for the Royal Commission on the Economic Union and Development Prospects for Canada.

Oderkirk, Jillian. "Parents and Children Living with Low Incomes." *Canadian Social Trends* (Winter 1992).

Osberg, Lars ed. *Economic Inequality and Poverty: International Perspectives.* Armonk, New York: M.E. Sharpe, Inc., 1991.

Peitchinis, Stephen G. *Women at Work: Discrimination and Response.* Toronto: McClelland and Stewart Inc., 1989.

Prager, Carol A.L. "Poverty in North America." *Canadian Public Policy-Analyse de Politiques* 14 (March 1988): 52-66.

Rawls, John. "Social Unity and Primary Goods." In *Utilitarianism and Beyond,* eds. Amartaya Sen and Bernard Williams (1992): 159-87.

Robb, Roberta Edgecombe. "Equal Pay for Work of Equal Value: Issues and Policies." *Canadian Public Policy-Analyse de Politiques* 13 (December 1987): 445-61.

Ruggles, Patricia. "Short- and Long-Term Poverty in the United States: Measuring the American Underclass." In *Economic Inequality,* ed. Lars Osberg (1991): 157-93.

Sarlo, Christopher A. *Poverty in Canada.* Vancouver: The Fraser Institute, 1992.

Sawhill, Isabel V. "Poverty in the U.S.: Why Is It So Persistant." *Journal of Economic Literature* 26 (September 1988): 1073-120.

Sen, Amartaya and Bernard Williams eds. *Utilitarianism and Beyond.* Cambridge: Cambridge University Press, 1982.

Sharzer, Steven. "Native People: Some Issues." In *Research Studies of the Commission on Equality in Employment.* Ottawa: Ministry of Supply and Services, 1985: 547-49.

Slesnick, Daniel T. "Gaining Ground: Poverty in the Postwar United States." *Journal of Political Economy* 101 (February 1993): 1-39.

Smeeding, Timothy M. "Cross-National Comparisons of Inequality and Poverty Position." In *Economic Inequality and Poverty,* ed. Lars Osberg (1991): 159-87.

Vaillancourt, Francois. "Income Distribution and Economic Security in Canada." In *Income Distribution and Economic Security in Canada,* Research Coordinator Francois Vaillancourt. Toronto: University of Toronto Press, 1985: 1-77. Prepared for The Royal Commission on the Economic Union and Development Prospects for Canada.

Wien, Fred. *Rebuilding the Economic Base of Indian Communities: The Micmac in Nova Scotia.* Montreal: The Institute for Research on Public Policy, 1986.

Endnotes

1   This is from the law of diminishing marginal utility. Total utility increases with the amount of good or income a person has, but it does so at a decreasing rate.

2   Discussions in economics about the measurability of utility have gone on for years. Economic analysis is built around the notion of ordinal (as opposed to cardinal utility), where all that is required is for an individual to be able to catagorize all states of affairs in terms of better or worse or the same. For a modern discussion of the implications of utilitarianism on which most economics is based, see Sen and Williams (1982).

3   This section is much influenced by Osberg (1985).

4   See for example Jenkins (1991).

5   See *Income Distribution by Size in Canada*, (Statistics Canada Cat. 13-207) various issues.

6   This section is based on Haagenaars (1991).

7   This may be a questionable assumption. There is some evidence from studies in Australia and Britain that women who live in families where the total family income is adequate are individually deprived because they do not have any control over family resources nor have adequate personal spending money (Gunderson and Muszynski, 1990, p. 12).

8   There have also been attempts to create subjective poverty lines building on the notion that relative poverty is a state of mind. To what extent do you feel relatively deprived? These attempts are not quite as ridiculous as they would seem. (People were not considered poor because they felt deprived because they did not own a Ferrari). People are asked to give the minimum amount needed to get along for their own households. (Hagenaars, 1991, p. 139).

9   For examples, see Slesnick (1993) and Sarlo (1992).

10 The poverty threshold is set at three times the minimum income required for a non-farm family to purchase what the U.S. Department of Agriculture refers to as a minimum diet (Economic Council of Canada, 1992, p. 20).

11 Each child is counted as 0.3 of a person except in families of one adult where the first child is counted as 0.4 of a person. See Statistics Canada, *Income Distributions by Size in Canada*, 1991 cat no. 13-207 (Ottawa: Ministry of Supply and Services, 1992) p. 185-86.

12 The low income measure places 12.3 percent of families and 30.2 percent of unattached individuals below the cut-off.

13 This has to be qualified. The incidence of low incomes for families with no children under eight years old is 6.9 percent, with one child 16.9 percent, with two children 14.9 percent, and with more than two children 22.9 percent.

14 Table 6.4 does not give the poverty rates for couples with less than two children. In general, couples with no children have less incidence of poverty than any socio-economic group. (Smeeding, 1991, p. 48).

15 The incidence of low income among families, in 1961 was 27.9 for families and 49.2 for unattached individuals. In 1971 the corresponding figures were 18.3 and 43.1.(Vaillancourt, 1985, p. 18).

16 According to the new low-income measures of Statistics Canada, the proportion of female, low-income, non-elderly adults was 55.8 percent in 1991. (Calculated from Appendix, Table 2 from Statistics Canada, Income Distribution by Size, 1991) Note, however, that females did not always constitute the majority of poor. In 1971 they were 45.6 percent of those in poverty. However, even at that time they had a larger probability of being poor. 16.9 percent of women were poor compared to 13.3 percent of men. (Gunderson and Muszynski, 1990, p. 7-8).

17 For an interesting discussion of this issue, see Bergmann (1989). She argues that economists have been loath to recognize the existence of discrimination because

according to a very influential article by the Nobel Prize winner Gary Becker who argued that if a firm discriminated it would fail. If a firm excluded women or visible minorities from employment, and if these cheap substitutes were as productive as white males, another firm would realize the opportunity for profit, and would hire these people. This firm could then drive the discriminating firms out of business because it could produce at lower cost. However, as she points out, in the real world few firms exist who would violate social customs which they themselves support and enjoy for the purpose of making money. It is also assumed that competition is sufficiently intense to drive discriminating firms out of business.

18   This is based on Bradley (1989), p. 8-9.

19   One example comes from the Toronto Board of Education. In Ontario the students in high school are streamed into advanced, general, and basic programmes. The advanced programme is seen as a preparation for university, the general for community colleges, and the basic for entry into the labour force. In 1987, 72 percent of Grade 9 students were enrolled in the advanced stream, 21 percent in the general, and 7 percent in the basic. Ninety-four percent of students from high socio-economic background were in advanced program compared to 60 percent of students from families where parents were "unskilled". (Economic Council of Canada, 1992, p. 11). Better educated parents are more likely to be able to assist and encourage their children at school. They can afford to give their children extra professional help and send them to different and reputedly better schools if necessary.

20   It would be expected that pay equity policies would lead to increased unemployment for females as in a sense these policies are comparable to minimum wage policies. Even though the evidence is not clear, the effects on employment so far have not been large (Gunderson, 1989, p. 68).

21   See for example Scharzer (1985).

22   For a survey of traditional and radical theories attempting to explain native socio-economic development, see Wien (1986), p. 79-115. For a general survey, see McConnell and Brue (1989).

23   These figures come from estimated labour supply elasticities. Hum and Simpson (1991) in their evaluation of the Mincome experiment (see below) arrive at considerably lower labour supply elasticites, indicating that the negative impact of transfers on work effort is very small.

24   For a discussion, see Evans (1993) and Lightman (1991).

7

Canadian Competitiveness

After reading this chapter you should understand what most economists mean by the term "competitiveness." You will be able to explain how economists view economic growth, and the difference between the new growth theory and the more traditional theory. You should be able to make a similar distinction between the modern and more traditional theory of international trade. You will also be able to discuss whether Canada is competitive, and the likely reasons behind our low productivity.

While there is little agreement on the precise definition of competitiveness, most people believe that if we are not competitive our living standards will suffer. Competitiveness can refer to the performance of the whole economy (national competitiveness) as well as to the performance of individual sectors. National competitiveness can be defined as:

> the degree to which [a country] can, under free and fair market conditions, produce goods and services that meet the test of international markets while simultaneously maintaining and expanding the real incomes of its citizens (President's Commission on Industrial Competitiveness 1985),

or

the ability of a country to realise central economic policy goals, especially growth in income and employment, without running into balance-of-payments difficulties (Fagerberg 1988)

or

a country can be said to be competitive if it maintains a growth rate of real income equal to that of its trading partners in an environment of free and (long-run) balanced trade (Markusen 1992).

Those definitions essentially emphasize the long-run growth of real incomes and the connection between economic growth and trade. Trade promotes growth if a country specializes in producing and exporting products with high productivity growth.

The sector definition of competitiveness is usually framed around an industry. There are two versions of it. One states that an industry is competitive if its productivity is higher than that of its competitors; and the other states that it is competitive if its per unit costs are lower than, or equal to, those of its competitors (Markusen, 1992, p. 8). Per unit costs depend on productivity, cost of labour and other inputs, and the exchange rate.

What would happen if many of our exports were no longer competitive on world markets? There would be a balance of payments deficit and the Canadian dollar would fall in value because the supply of Canadian dollars on the foreign exchange markets would be greater than the demand for Canadian dollars. A fall in the value of the dollar would stimulate exports and make imports more expensive and therefore serve to correct the deficit. Because of the high prices for imports our real incomes would fall. The decline in the value of the dollar could also lend to inflation if the economy is in a recovery phase, causing speculators to sell Canadian dollars, thereby driving the dollar down further. Instead of allowing the dollar to drop in value, the federal government might try to finance the deficit by borrowing money from abroad, which would become increasingly expensive given our large foreign debt and its effect on bond ratings. Interest rates would have to rise, which would have an adverse effect on employment and output. The alternative would be to reduce our consumption of imports and other products by raising taxes or cutting government expenditures, which would also decrease real incomes and therefore our well-being.[1]

As the concept of "competitiveness" is related to economic growth and international trade, it is essential that we understand both. We will first survey growth theory and see what factors have been shown to be identified with growth. Next we will survey trade theory with a particular emphasis on the theory of comparative advantage, which is really a theory of competitiveness. We will also examine our current trading pattern and the competitiveness of some Canadian industries.

Determinants of Long-Run Growth

Economic thinking about determinants of growth has been strongly influenced by the work of Robert Solow, a Nobel Prize winner in economics. Solow (1956) took as his starting point a standard production function: $Y = f(K, L, A)$, where output (Y) is a function of labour (L), capital (K), and a measure of technical change (A).

Assuming constant returns to scale and perfect competition, he was able to demonstrate that the savings rate (S/Y) was a crucial determinant of output growth. The higher the savings rate, which in a closed economy will be equal to the ratio of investments to GDP (I/Y), the larger the capital stock (K) and therefore the higher the level of output.[2] The optimum level of capital stock would be the capital stock that maximized the current level of consumption. This level of capital stock would be the level at which the marginal product of capital, net of depreciation, was equal to the rate of population growth. It was therefore possible to determine if a country should increase or decrease its capital stock through investments or disinvestments. When a country has reached this optimum capital stock, it will be in a steady state; that is, it will not grow, but income will be maintained at a high level. Other results from the model are that the higher the population growth, the higher the growth rate but the lower the per capita income; and that the economies of countries with low per capita income are likely to grow faster than countries with high per capita income. Low-income countries are likely to have little capital, and therefore the marginal product of capital will be high. Any new investment will therefore lead to large increases in output. (This is called the **catch-up or convergence hypothesis.**)

Solow also developed a methodology for testing the model, the **growth accounting method.** Simple manipulation of the production function shows that the growth in income (output) can be decomposed into growth in labour, growth in capital, and growth in technical change (growth in **total factor productivity**).[3] It can also be shown that the total factor productivity is equal to the growth in the average product of labour minus the growth in the capital/labour ratio multiplied by the share of capital in total income. Applying his model to U.S data for 1909-49, he found that although output per worker had doubled in the 40-year period, only 12 percent was explained by an increase in the amount of capital per worker; the remaining 88 percent was explained by technical change, or growth in total factor productivity, which in the estimation process appears as residual. Further refinements of the model, which involved disaggregating labour into various groups, such as skilled and unskilled labour, led to quite similar results. The most recent attempt is by Maddison (1987), who estimated that changes in total factor productivity accounted for 50-80 percent of total growth for six industrialized countries for the period 1950-73. He also decomposed total factor productivity by taking into account such factors as structural change, regulation, higher energy prices, and economies of scale. In doing so he was able to explain over 70 percent of total growth. All the countries studied experienced a decline in total factor productivity after 1973; the largest decline was in Japan.

Fresh evidence on the determinants of growth has been introduced by a new data set (the Penn World Table).[4] This data set contains comparable real GDP-per-capita estimates for 138 countries for the years 1960-88. The data show that Taiwan, South Korea, Hong Kong, Japan, and China have achieved remarkable growth rates. In fact, most countries, with the exception of some African countries, experienced growth during the period. The data also confirmed a slowdown in economic growth after 1973.

Working with the same data, Barro (1991) showed that the growth rate of real per capita GDP was positively correlated to the initial human capital as measured by the level of education of the labour force, and negatively correlated with the level of real per capita GDP. This finding gave support to the catch-up hypothesis. He also showed that countries with higher human capital had lower fertility rates and higher rates of physical investment. Growth was negatively correlated with the share of government consumption in GDP.

DeLong and Summers (1991), who also used the same data, found a strong relationship between the rate of investment in machinery and equipment and growth in per capita income. Each extra percentage point of GDP invested in equipment is associated with increase in GDP growth of one-third of a percentage point per year. They argued that the social return to investment in equipment is far above the private return, and is about 30 percent a year. They also found support for Solow's theoretical connection between population growth and per capita income (the higher the population growth, the lower per capita income). Unlike Barro, they found only weak support for the convergence of per capita incomes.

Brander (1992), in his survey of the findings based on the Penn World Tables, points out that most of the variations in per capita GDP were not explained by the models. Indeed, the growth rates of some countries in Asia are far too high, and the growth rates of some of the African countries too low to be explained by the traditional growth variables.

To explain growth by saying that most is caused by a residual (or growth in total factor productivity, or technological change) is not very helpful. The new, so-called **endogenous growth models**, developed by Romer (1986) and others, try to make technological progress and its determinants explicit variables in explaining economic growth.[5] The common belief among economists used to be that technological progress flowed from scientific discoveries that were subsequently applied to technology. But that belief was dispelled by Schmookler (1966). In his study of almost a thousand inventions he found that the stimulus to innovation was the recognition of a costly problem to be solved, or a profitable opportunity to be seized. Most inventions resulted from conditions in the market rather than from discoveries by the scientific community. Henry Ergas, as reported in *The Economist* (January 11, 1992), found three sets of factors important in explaining why innovations occur and why some countries are more likely to innovate than others. One set of factors including the quality of a country's scientific base, the presence of research institutions, and the quality of the education system, influenced the inputs into innovation. Another set influenced demand (such as sophisticated customers who called for constant innovation). A third set referred to the industrial structure of a country where conditions for intense competition were combined with a mechanism for firms to share the financing and diffusion of scientific research.[6]

The new growth models also emphasize the importance of externalities. Capital investments create externalities in the sense that they improve not only the productivity of the investing firm or worker, but also the productivity of other firms and workers. Knowledge gained by one firm tends to spill over into the knowledge of other firms. Knowledge is seen as an additional factor of production, and countries have to invest in knowledge in the same way as they invest in machinery. New investment may require investment in more knowledge, and more knowledge in turn may spur investments in more capital. (Note the findings above of De Long and Summers 1991.) Trade could also increase the advantage that an innovating firm has in capitalizing on its knowledge. If a firm is restricted by the home market for sales of a new product, the profits (or rents) that firm would earn from its innovation before imitators are attracted would not be as large as if the firm could sell the product globally. Therefore trade could act as an additional spur to innovation and explain the high growth rates achieved by some "trade-oriented" countries. In a study of more than a hundred countries, Syrquin and Chenery (1989) found that between 1952 and 1983 those with an outward orientation achieved an economic growth rate of 5.22 percent and a growth in total factor productivity of 2.2 percent; the corresponding figures for inward-looking countries were 4.28 percent and 1.6 percent. A link between exports and economic growth was also documented by Romer (1986) and Baldwin (1992).

Nevertheless, there may be some cases where an export orientation does not necessarily maximize long-run growth. Grossman and Helpman (1994) argue that countries like Canada and Australia, that are endowed with an abundance of natural resources may become so dependent on resource exports and resource-related activities that little investment takes place in the generation of new knowledge through R&D, to the detriment of long-run growth. We will return to this point below.

The emphasis on knowledge has also led to more emphasis on human capital to explain economic growth. Most of the studies have shown a positive correlation between the level of education and per capita income growth.[7] Nevertheless, there is some evidence that not all education is necessarily productive. For example, some people may use their education to engage in rent-seeking activities rather than wealth-creating activities. Rent-seeking occurs when an individual or group tries to enlarge its share of the economy at the expense of somebody else. Mancur Olson (1982) has argued that income growth may depend on how large the rent-seeking sector is in a country compared with the wealth-creating sector. Lobby groups are obviously rent-seeking, for their purpose is to get a better deal for their groups. Labour unions often engage in rent-seeking, and so do lawyers. Indeed, there is some evidence that enrolments in law schools have a negative effect on growth. Murphy et al. (1992) found that the economies of countries with relatively high enrolments in law schools grow more slowly than other countries. Similarly, countries with relatively high enrolments in engineering schools grow more quickly than others. They argue that a high enrolment in engineering ensures the training of entrepreneurs of high quality and therefore results in a high rate of technological progress and growth. With proportionately more talent going into law, by implication there is less talent in entrepreneurship and more in rent-seeking and therefore the result is lower growth. A positive effect on growth of a large number of scientists and engineers employed in research was also found by Romer (1986).

The New Trade Theory

In its emphasis on technology and externalities, the new trade theory has followed a similar development to the new growth theory. Traditional trade theory believed that the basis of trade was embedded in differences between nations. Trade was a way for countries to benefit from those differences. The **Ricardian theory** emphasized the importance of differences in per unit labour requirements, that is, labour productivity, in determining comparative advantage and therefore trade. The **Heckscher-Ohlin theory** of trade, which used to dominate textbooks in international economics, emphasized differences in factor endowments. Assume, for example, that there are two countries, Canada and China, and that there are only two factors of production, labour and capital, and that China has relatively more labour than capital compared with Canada. With these assumptions it is easy to understand that in the absence of market imperfections, labour is relatively cheap in China compared to capital, and in Canada capital is relatively cheap. Therefore, China can produce labour-intensive products, such as textiles, relatively cheaply compared to Canada, and Canada can produce capital-intensive products, such as cars, more cheaply. However, it is obvious that in reality, labour-intensive countries like South Korea, Japan, and China can compete very successfully in producing capital-intensive products like cars.

The Heckscher-Ohlin theory can explain trade at a simple level if we bring in more specific factors of production such as natural resources. Compared to most countries, Canada is well-endowed with forests. Therefore Canada can produce and export products that use forests, for example, pulp and paper. Similarly, countries with very skilled work forces tend to export knowledge-intensive products. However, since the Second World War, a large and growing part of world trade has consisted of products whose characteristics cannot easily be attributed to specific inherent advantages of a particular country. A growing proportion of trade is intra-industry trade, where countries both import and export a certain product. For example, Canada both exports and imports cars, a possibility that traditional trade theory would deny.

It is now clear that traditional trade theory, in its emphasis on perfect competition, neglected product differentiation and the advantages of specialization in cases of increasing returns to scale. For example, the economies of scale in the manufacture of aircraft are so large that the world market is large enough for only two firms. Much of the trade today results from advantages gained from economies of scale and technological leadership. The new trade theory has abandoned the emphasis on perfect competition and instead has brought in oligopoly, game theory, and strategic behaviour in general.[8] In the presence of economies of scale, for example, there is nothing to say *a priori* why a market would be captured by one country rather than another. It could be luck, or it could be because one country entered the market first, an advantage that would increase with time as the country gained more experience in production. Innovating countries could become quite rich, because at first they could earn high rents from an innovation. Over time these rents would be whittled away by imitators, but by then the innovating country might have introduced another product onto the world market. Innovation, as is recognized by the new endogenous growth theory, has substantial externalities. Know-how spills over to other industries through diffusion.

Given that comparative advantage in some products is not determined by a country's physical or other characteristics, comparative advantage, or competitiveness, is continually evolving. Indeed, in theory, comparative advantage can be engineered through **strategic trade policies**. A government could subsidize industries, such as high-tech industries, that generate high rents and that have substantial spillover effects on other industries. Whether this is a practical policy is of course open to debate.[9] Most economists have doubts about the ability of governments to predict which industries will be successful. And such policies could encourage industries to spend substantial sums of money to persuade politicians to give them subsidies.

Porter's Diamond

The publication of Michael Porter's *The Competitive Advantage of Nations* in 1990 had considerable influence in business and government circles on discussions of what determines competitiveness. The book, which capitalizes on the new trade and growth theories, develops a specific theory of what makes some nations more successful than others.

The theory is based on case studies of industry successes in ten industrialized countries (not including Canada). Porter believes that productivity is the only meaningful concept of competitiveness at the national level.[10] Trade and foreign investment increase productivity and living standards by allowing a country to specialize in the products and services in which its firms are more productive than its foreign competitors, and to import products in which it is less productive. Investment abroad can have a similar effect on productivity by allowing firms to shift their less productive activities abroad, and giving them a base for increasing their exports and for channelling profits back to the home country, where they will raise incomes. For the purpose of his study he argues that an industry in a particular nation has achieved international competitive advantage if it has substantial and sustained exports to a wide array of other countries or significant outbound foreign investment based on skills and assets created in the home country (Porter, 1990, p. 25).

Porter claims that the competitive advantage of a particular industry is determined by the interaction of four factors (see Figure 7.1): factor conditions, demand conditions, related and supporting industries, and firm strategy, structure, and rivalry.

Factor conditions refer to the quantity and quality of human resources; physical resources (land, water, and forests); knowledge resources (scientific, technical, and market knowledge); capital (the availability of financing); and infrastructure (transportation, communications, and health care). A country's firms may gain a competitive advantage if they have inexpensive or high-quality factors necessary for production in a certain industry. Competitive advantage also depends on how efficiently the available factors are employed. Porter argues, however, that it is important to realize that since some factors of production are highly mobile, unskilled workers are vulnerable to competition from low-wage countries. Porter also makes a distinction between basic factors, such as natural resources, unskilled and semi-skilled labour, and debt capital; and advanced factors, such as a modern digital data communications infrastructure, engineers, computer scientists, and university research institutes. The latter are far more

Figure 7.1
Porter's Diamond

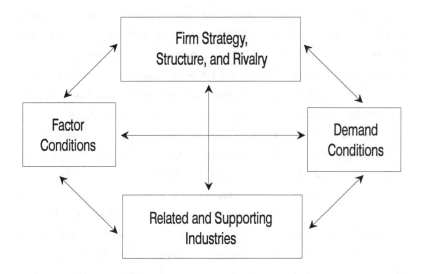

Source: Porter (1990), p. 127.

important in a competitive economy. They are more scarce in the sense that they require large investments in both human and physical capital. It becomes a circle because the institutions, like universities, that are required to create advanced factors require the very factors that are being created. Porter particulary emphasizes the role of education in creating competitive advantage (*ibid.*, p. 628–30). The educational and training system must be competitive and must set high standards for the students. He argues that most students should be given some form of occupational training in their education, that there should be close links between educational institutions and employers, and that firms should invest heavily in training.

Porter's research showed that the second factor, home demand, was important in nearly every successful industry studied. A large home market can of course ensure that a firm reaps the benefits of economies of scale, but the quality of home demand is more important than the size of the market. Home demand determines how firms interpret and respond to the buyers' needs. If home demand gives local firms a clearer and earlier picture of market needs than other firms, a competitive advantage will develop. He points out that it is not unusual for a national interest or favourite pastime to serve as the foundation for competitive industries. The British who are passionate gardeners are good at making garden tools. The Italians are reputed to love fast cars, beautiful clothes, and good food, all of which they export.[11] Canadians, who like hockey, have developed a competitive industry making skates.

The third determinant of national advantage is the presence of internationally competitive supplier industries. Indeed, Porter found that it is unusual for an industry to be competitive alone. Instead there are frequently clusters of industries that are related to each other and all of which have achieved competitiveness. For example, the Swedish strength in fabricated steel products, such as ball bearings and cutting tools, was helped by their strength in specialty steels. The Japanese machine tool industry developed out of the country's leadership in numerical control units and motors.

The final determinant is the nature of domestic rivalry as well as the strategy and structure of the firm. Of these, Porter particularly emphasizes rivalry. Intense rivalry among firms provides a stimulus to improvement and an essential motivation for firms to make the investments necessary for competitive advantage. The strategy and structure of firms vary widely from country to country, and nations will tend to succeed in industries where the management practices and modes of organization common in the national environment are well-suited to a particular industry's success. For example, in Germany, many executives have science and engineering backgrounds, which give them an advantage in industries, like machinery and chemicals, where the improvement of product and process is important. A global outlook, as manifested in linguistic ability and an interest in travel, are also important.

Porter also recognizes the importance of both chance and government in promoting invention and entrepreneurship. An industry may be well-positioned to take advantage of an unexpected breakthrough in technology or a surge in world demand. Government policy can influence each of the four determinants. And as a buyer, government can also influence industry standards.

We will now try to apply what we have learnt from the new growth theory and the new trade theories, and from Michael Porter to an analysis of Canadian competitiveness.

Canadian Productivity

Even though our labour productivity as measured by real GDP per capita is the fourth-highest in the world (see Chapter 1), other countries are rapidly catching up. Our total factor productivity in manufacturing has been persistently low compared to that of the other G-7 countries. The Economic Council of Canada (Rao and Lemprière, 1992, p. 8) estimates that the total annual growth in factor productivity in the business sector was 2.6 percent for 1962-73, 0.4 for 1974-79, and 0.9 for 1980-88. Growth in labour productivity, which is one of the determinants of growth in total factor productivity, showed a similar pattern. Table 7.1 shows that we have consistently ranked fifth or sixth among the G-7 countries. A study by Griliches (1988) shows that, compared to 12 other countries, Canada ranked second-last in terms of growth in labour productivity in manufacturing for the period 1979-86. And Canada's performance in the service sector as measured by value added per worker was below the OECD average.[12] It is perhaps not surprising then that the average Canadian family experienced essentially no gain in real after-tax income between 1980 and 1989.

A recent disaggregated study by Denny et al. (1992) provides some interesting information on Canadian total factor productivity growth for 1953-86, compared to growth in the United States and Japan. The following is a summary of their conclusions:

1. Both Canada and Japan have improved their productivity in relation to that of the United States during the period. All three countries did have a slowdown in productivity growth from 1973 to 1980. The largest slowdown was in Japan, and the smallest in Canada. Productivity growth did not return to its earlier levels in the 1980s.

217

2. The best performer in all countries was the electrical equipment industry, followed by wood, textiles, precision equipment, and transportation equipment. Low increases in productivity growth were found in food, tobacco, paper, petroleum, and primary metals. The authors argue that productivity growth in an industry is determined largely by the state of knowledge in that industry.

3. In 14 of the 18 Canadian industries, productivity growth declined after the 1973-80 period. The four industries with an improvement in productivity were leather, wood, printing, and electrical machinery. In Japan and the United States, fewer industries had higher productivity growth rates in those years compared to Canada. On the other hand, in 11 of the 18 Canadian industries, productivity growth declined by more than 75 percent, and in five of these, productivity growth was negative—furniture, paper, primary metals, transportation equipment, and non-metallic minerals. This record was marginally better than the U.S. record and marginally worse than that in Japan. In the eighties, the paper and non-metallic minerals industry continued with negative productivity growth and were joined by tobacco, machinery, and miscellaneous manufacturing. Rao and Lemprière (1992) attribute the slowdown in productivity growth after 1973 to low capacity utilization caused by weak demand, the sharp increase in real energy prices, a lower rate of substitution of capital and intermediate inputs for labour, and a shift of resources from industries with high productivity to those with low productivity. Similar results were reported by Helliwell *et al.* (1986).[13]

Canada's Comparative Advantage

Over time a nation tends to specialize in the products in which it is competitive, that is, in products that either have a lower price than the products of competitors or have other features, such as quality or delivery conditions, which make the products desirable.[14] Clearly productivity is only one determinant of price. There are other factors that

TABLE 7.1

Average Annual Growth in Real GDP per Employed Person,

G-7 Countries, 1962-90

Country	1962–73	1974–79	1980–90
Canada	2.4	1.3	1.1
France	4.7	2.5	2.1
Italy	5.6	2.8	1.9
Japan	7.9	2.9	2.9
United Kingdom	3.0	1.3	1.5
United States	1.9	0.0	0.9
West Germany	4.1	2.7	1.4

Source: Rao and Lempière (1992, p. 15).

enter into the costs of production, such as labour costs, taxes, capital costs, and exchange rates. A low exchange rate can give exporters a temporary advantage, whereas a high exchange rate can make it difficult to compete. Canadian labour costs have been growing faster than the growth in productivity. The result is that our per unit labour costs rose almost twice as fast as U.S. per unit costs in the 1980s (Porter, 1991, p. 81).

One method of showing which industries have established themselves as being competitive in world markets is to calculate **revealed comparative advantage**. Revealed comparative advantage is the ratio of a country's share of world exports of a particular product to that same country' share of total world merchandise exports. If this ratio is greater than one, the country is deemed to have a comparative advantage in that product. We have to be careful in interpreting data for revealed comparative advantage. If an industry exports because it is heavily subsidized, its revealed comparative advantage does not signify any inherent advantage or competitiveness.

Canada's revealed comparative advantage in some industries is shown in Table 7.2. The table shows that Canada has a revealed comparative advantage in the exports of products based on our rich endowments of natural resources, and that this situation has changed little over the last 20 years. In that respect we are similar to Sweden. However, there is an important difference. Canada's exports are far more concentrated than the great majority of other industrialized countries. Canada's top 50 industries in terms of world export shares accounted for 21.6 percent of Canadian exports in 1989; the comparable figure for Sweden was 11.7 percent (Porter, 1991, p. 28). Porter (1991) identifies five major competitive industrial clusters in Canada: forest products, materials and metals, petroleum and chemicals, transportation, and food and beverages. He argues that few of these clusters show signs of any capacity to grow by moving into new segments or related industries. In other words, linkages are not well-developed.

While our current living standards show that we have benefited from our resource orientation, there are problems for the future. I have already alluded to the fact that the world economy is becoming less dependent on resources because of changes in technology (see Introduction). In Chapter 4 we saw that our resources do not appear to be well managed. The resource industries also suffer from low productivity growth, which will result in slower growth in wages and profits in these industries (Denny *et al.* 1992).

Reasons for Poor Canadian Productivity Growth

As productivity growth is the basis for economic growth, it is clearly important to understand the reasons for our poor productivity performance. Earlier much effort and research went into explaining the reasons for the differences in the level of productivity between Canada and the United States. Most of these differences were thought to be caused by scale effects. Canadian plants were usually smaller than U.S. plants and therefore did not achieve economies of scale. The reason for the smaller plants was thought to be the high level of protection in Canada compared to that in the United States. Firms operating in

TABLE 7.2
Revealed Comparative Advantage in Selected Commodity Groups,
Canada, 1971-73 and 1987-89

Commodity	1971-73	1987-89
Pulp and waste paper	6.8	7.9
Cork and wood	3.8	5.2
Electric current	3.7	4.3
Paper, paper board, and articles made of paper pulp, paper or board	4.0	3.6
Gas, natural and manufactured	5.5	3.2
Crude fertilizers and crude minerals	2.8	3.0
Metalliferous ores and metal scrap	4.0	2.8
Manufactured fertilizers	2.5	2.7
Road vehicles	2.7	2.7
Coal, coke, and briquettes	0.8	2.5
Cereals and cereal preparations	2.3	2.5
Non-ferrous metals	2.5	2.0
Fish, crustaceans, and molluscs	2.2	1.8
Oil seeds and oleaginous fruits	1.7	1.7
Live animals	1.0	1.5
Cork and wood manufactures	1.5	1.5
Inorganic chemicals	1.1	1.4
Animal oils and fats	0.9	1.4
Power-generating machinery and equipment	1.8	1.3
Hides, skins, and fur	0.8	1.1
Beverages	1.4	0.7

Source: Economic Council of Canada (1992), p. 14.

Note: Revealed comparative advantage is the ratio of a country's share of world exports in a particular product to that country's share of total world exports of merchandise.

Canada set their prices at a level equivalent to the U.S. price plus the Canadian tariff and therefore could continue to compete without being particularly efficient.[15] This theory, which became known as the **Eastman-Stykolt hypothesis**, served as a basis for many of the studies attempting to estimate the effects of free trade with the United States (see Chapter 10). This analysis, however, was essentially static and was not designed to explain differences in productivity growth. Instead, we will follow the new growth and trade theories in examining the importance of technology, research and development (R&D), education, and training. We will also look at some of the other factors emphasized by Porter, such as the competitive environment in Canada.

Research and Development and The Diffusion of Technology

Many studies have attempted to quantify the effect of research and development on productivity. They show that the private rate of return from research and development is higher than the rate of return on investment in physical capital, and that it lies between 10 and 40 percent.[16] The spillover effects are substantial, with social rates of return 50-100 percent higher than private rates of return. Other findings are that rates of return are higher on basic research than on applied research or development; company-financed R&D gives higher returns than publicly financed R&D; and the return is higher for process R&D as opposed to R&D on new products. R&D and investments in plant and equipment are complementary, for investment in one encourages investment in the other. The Canadian studies do not show as strong a link between R&D and productivity improvements as the American studies.[17]

It is well known that Canada has a poor record in R&D. Figure 7.2 shows that in 1989 Canada ranked eighth in expenditures on R&D. Industry financed only 41.7 percent of our R&D, a proportion lower than in most industrialized countries with the exception of Italy (Department of State 1991).

The new growth theory emphasizes the reinforcing links among investments in machinery and equipment, research and development,

Figure 7.2
Gross Expenditure on R&D as a
Percentage of GDP, Selected Countries, 1989

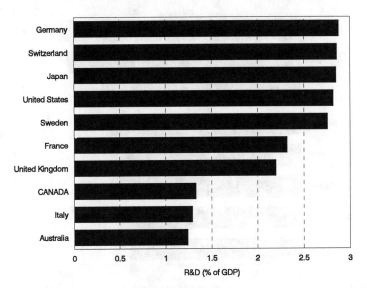

Source: Human Resources Development Canada. Profile of Post-Secondary Education in Canada, 1993 edition, p. 39. Ministry of Supply and Services, 1994.

and growth. Empirical support for the importance of machinery and equipment was given by De Long and Summers (1991) (see above). Canada's overall investment has increased since the 1970s and is about 25 percent of GDP; investment in machinery and equipment is 7 percent of GDP. In real terms it has grown faster than that of other G-7 countries (Porter, 1991, p. 9). However, even though investments in machinery and equipment have increased, they are still lower than in other advanced countries (see Figure 7.3).

Other indicators of the quantity of R&D are the number of patents granted and the proportion of the labour force in science and engineering. Canada does not rank high on either of these indicators. In a ranking of the number of patents secured per 100,000 inhabitants, Canada is outperformed by eight out of ten industrialized countries, led by Switzerland.[18] A ranking of the number of scientists and engineers engaged in

Figure 7.3
Machinery and Equipment,
Investment in Selected Countries, 1980-89

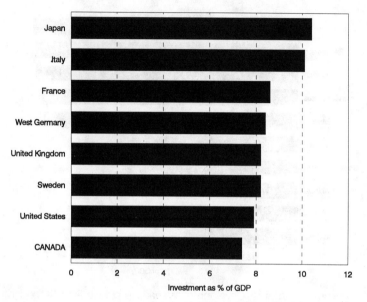

Source: OECD, Economic Outlook, December 1990, Table 2.

R&D per thousand inhabitants places Canada fifth in a group of eight countries (Department of the Secretary of State, 1992, p. 33).

We do not fare much better in individual industries. In 1987, Canadian R&D activities were higher than the G-7 average in only two industries: electronics and computers.[19] The Economic Council of Canada (1992, p. 36) also found that while there was a 40 percent increase from 1980 to 1987 in the Canadian propensity to do R&D in manufacturing, there was a 500 percent increase in the propensity of Canadian branch plants in the United States to do R&D; in other words Canadian companies appear to be shifting their R&D to the United States.

Nobody knows why industry in Canada invests so little in R&D. Many have argued that the presence of so many multinational corporations in Canada could be the cause, since they may do most of their

R&D at their head offices in other countries. However, Safarian (1969) and others showed that foreign-owned subsidiaries did at least as much R&D as Canadian-owned firms. Grossman and Helpman's finding from their theoretical model which showed that staple-exporting countries such as Canada may under-invest in R&D could be worth exploring (Grossman and Helpman, 1994).

Not only do we have a poor record in R&D, but we also have a poor record in the adoption of existing manufacturing technologies in design and engineering (computer-aided design and manufacturing, or CAD/CAM); in fabrication and assembly (numerical control and computerized numerical control, NC/CNC; and flexible manufacturing systems, or FMS); automated material handling (automated storage and retrieval systems, or AS/RS) and communications and controls (local area networks).

In a survey of the literature, McFetridge (1992) shows that an early adoption of advanced manufacturing technologies is influenced by the size of the firm, the growth rate, management education, and interaction with suppliers. In Canada, foreign-owned firms were more likely than Canadian firms to adopt new technology. Adoption rates were the highest in western Canada, and the lowest in the Atlantic provinces.

Flexible manufacturing, in particular, offers the advantage of being able to tailor a product to the needs of a particular customer with little downtime. According to a survey by the International Institute for Applied Systems Analysis (as reported by Boyer, 1991), there were eight hundred flexible manufacturing systems in operation in 1989. Twenty-one per cent were in operation in Japan, 17 percent in the United States and only 0.4 percent in Canada. The same survey found that flexible manufacturing had reduced the time between order and delivery by a factor of 5.6, increased labour productivity by a factor of 5.9, and decreased unit cost by a factor of 1.6.

Advanced manufacturing technologies are prevalent in certain industries. However, they are less likely to be adopted in Canada than in the United States (see Figure 7.4). Moreover, use in the United States is lower than that in other countries, such as Japan and West Germany. According to earlier studies, one determinant of adoption is firm size. But, even allowing for the smaller average firm size in Canada, our adoption rate is lower (McFetridge, 1992, p. 38). It is also interesting to note that the gap in use is greater for NC/CNC machines, an old technology that has been available for over 30 years, than for CAD technology, which began to be used only 20 years ago (*ibid.*, p. 44). This seems to suggest that the ultimate penetration of mature technologies is lower in Canada than in other countries. Why is that so? Are the costs of adoption higher in Canada than in other countries? Do Canadian companies pay more for equipment than their U.S. counterparts, or do they have greater difficulties in finding skilled personnel? Are there differences in tax treatments or in management structures, or are there differences in the competitive environment? We don't know.

Education and Training

As mentioned above there is now a strong emphasis in growth theories on education as a vehicle for promoting growth and improvements in productivity. This belief in education has also been embraced by the media, which frequently inform us that in the new global economy we can earn a living only by living by our wits. In order to do so our education system must turn out people who are literate, numerate, and adaptable. The education system must also provide a basis for "lifelong learning."

There have been several reports about the mediocre performance of Canadian students on international tests in mathematics and science. The results of a basic literacy survey have also cast doubts on the quality of our schools. One survey in 1990 found that only 42 percent of business leaders and 60 percent of labour leaders believed that Canada's schools were educating and training Canadians adequately. Thirty-six percent of business leaders and 51 percent of the labour leaders judged illiteracy to be "very significant" or "somewhat significant" among Canadian workers (Economic Council, 1992, p. 7).

And yet, compared to most other countries, we have spent a large portion of GDP on education. Figure 7.5 shows that we have spent more on the average than other rich countries, with the exception of

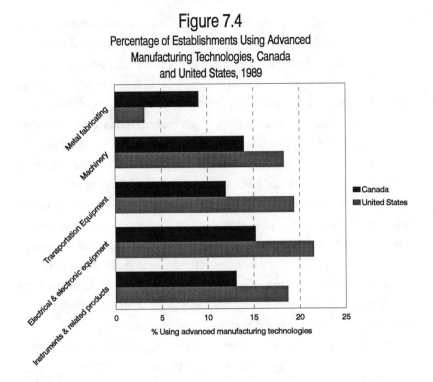

Figure 7.4
Percentage of Establishments Using Advanced Manufacturing Technologies, Canada and United States, 1989

Source: McFetridge (1992), p.33.

Sweden.[20] It is possible, however, that our money could have been better spent. Our high school drop-out rate in Canada is relatively high. Fifteen to 20 percent of Canadians between 25 and 34 did not complete high school, and even though Canadians are more likely than people in other countries to go to college or university, the proportion who graduates is relatively low (Economic Council of Canada, 1992, p. 111). The question is whether we get value for the substantial amount of money we have put into education. Have we underinvested or overinvested?

The contribution of education to the economy can be examined in several different ways. One is to estimate the productivity of the education sector as a whole; another is to evaluate the contribution of education to the economy through the growth-accounting method devised by Solow; or a third is to use rate-of-return calculations. We will look at each in turn.

There are only a few studies of the efficiency of the education sector. West (1988) made an attempt to calculate the total factor productivity of post-secondary education in Canada 1975-84 by dividing an index of output (the value of the educated students) by an index of inputs (cost of educating the students, including the students' time). If no allowance was made for any changes in the quality of the output, total factor productivity declined by 4 percent. If such an allowance was made, factor productivity increased by 2 percent — not a very large figure over ten years. These findings, which are not inconsistent with findings in other countries, are not surprising in view of the fact that in almost every industry the introduction of technology has led to substantial improvements in productivity. No such changes have occurred in teaching. However, West argues that the dominant cost of a university education is that of foregone student earnings. Therefore large productivity improvements in education would probably be associated with economies in the use of the students' time. He notes that it is possible to decrease the time spent at university. An example is the new private university in Buckingham in England, where degrees can be earned in two four-term years.

There is no study of the productivity of primary and secondary education, but in view of the large cost increases that have occurred in this sector, it is unlikely that it is more productive than the post-secondary sector. For example, average class sizes decreased in all provinces from 1960 to 1986 (Easton, 1988, p. 47). In 1960 the average student-to-teacher ratio was 26:1; in 1986, 18:3. Smaller classes can be justified if the effect on quality is larger than the effect on costs. Unfortunately, the question of quality is difficult to settle. Easton (1988, p. 69) quotes surveys of the literature that found that out of 112 studies of the effect of teacher/student ratio on performance, 9 show a statistically significant positive effect, 14 show a significant negative effect, and the remaining 89 show no effect at all. It seems that smaller classes are unlikely to have a significant effect on quality.

It is difficult to compare the quality of output in Canada with that in other countries since most provinces have abandoned province-wide testing and we have no national equivalent to the U.S. SAT scores. Porter (1991, p. 209) claims that Canada is virtually alone among the

Figure 7.5
Total Public Expenditures for Education as a Proportion of GNP, Selected Countries, 1965-88

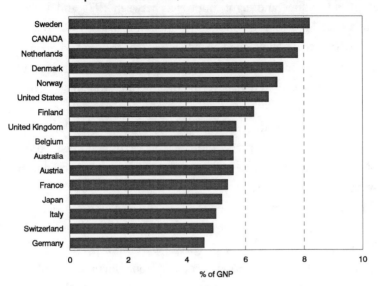

Source: Department of the Secretary of State (1992), p.37.

major OECD countries in having no national educational standards. In a survey of the evidence, including several studies of students' knowledge in science and mathematics by the International Association for the Evaluation of Educational Achievement, the Economic Council of Canada (1992) concluded that Canadian mathematics and science education is relatively strong up to the age of nine or ten. By 13 or 14, however, Canadian students are falling below the mean for industrial countries. There are also substantial variations among the provinces; in general the western provinces score better than the eastern provinces.

The Statistics Canada study of adult literacy showed that 16 percent of Canadian adults could not read well enough to handle most everyday essential reading.[21] Reading ability depended on the province where the person was educated. Education in one of the western provinces resulted in significantly better reading ability. There were also differences between occupations: only 50 percent of workers in agriculture and other primary industries could handle everyday reading requirements. There was some indication that literacy and numeracy levels, as measured in grades four and eight, improved between 1973 and 1980 but declined after 1980 (The Economic Council of Canada, 1992, p. 23).

To what extent has Canadian education contributed to economic growth? Studies for Canada have found that, since 1962, education has contributed approximately half a percentage point annually (Economic Council of Canada, 1992, p. 3). During the fast-growing sixties, the share of the total growth attributed to education was less than 10 percent. It rose to about 25 percent during the 1970s and declined to 16 percent during the eighties.[22] Calculations of the returns to education show a similar pattern.

Private rates of return to education are calculated by identifying the rate of interest, or discount rate, that equates the present value of costs and the present value of benefits. Apart from personal satisfaction, the benefit from education is the additional income, net of taxes, that individuals will earn from increased schooling, while the costs are the sum of the direct costs of education, such as tuition fees and books, and the indirect costs in foregone earnings. Social rates of return to education are calculated by including taxes in the benefits and adding to the private costs the costs to society of educating the student. The costs to society are substantial, for elementary and secondary education in Canada is financed publicly, and post-secondary education is heavily subsidized. Table 7.3 gives estimates for the social and private returns to a high school education in Canada.

The large differences between the regions are due to the differences in industrial structure and the composition of the labour force. It appears that in most parts of the country the cost of dropping out of high school is particularly high for women.

The rates of return to men for a university education are not as high as those for high school education (see Table 7.4). On the basis of these data, an investment in a university education gives a good return for a man, particularly in the Maritimes or Quebec. Table 7.5 gives statistics on the rate of return in Ontario for different programs. Medicine

TABLE 7.3

Private and Social Returns to Completing High School,
Canada and Provinces, 1985

	Men		Women	
	Private	Social	Private	Social
		(percent)		
Canada	29.0	11.2	33.2	8.4
Atlantic provinces	28.5	12.9	19.6	2.7
Quebec	11.3	4.4	21.8	7.4
Ontario	31.7	12.9	32.6	8.8
Manitoba and Saskatchewan	39.4	16.1	47.3	12.3
Alberta	28.7	10.7	40.1	10.0
British Columbia	4.0	13.9	45.5	10.6

Source: Economic Council of Canada (1992), p. 2 based on Vaillancourt.

and dentistry offered the highest returns in Ontario, and it is unlikely that the situation is different in other provinces. What is the social rate of return? Again the difference between the social and the private return is that the social return includes the full cost to society of educating the student. Table 7.3, 7.4 and 7.5 indicate that the social return is always less than the private return. West (1988) argues that if it is assumed that students at university forego income equal to 75 percent of the income of a school leaver (taking into account summer employment), then the social rate of return is 9.27 percent for Canada as a whole. If it is assumed that some of the earnings differential can be attributed to ability rather than the university education as such, the rate of return is of course smaller. If it is assumed that 35 percent of the income differential between individuals with and without a post-secondary education is related to ability, the social rate of return is 6.95 percent, which is still higher than the estimates for rate of return on physical capital.

TABLE 7.4

Private and Social Rates of Return to University Education for
Canadian Men, 1981.

Region	Private Returns	Social Returns
	(percent)	
Atlantic provinces		
3 years	14	9
4 years	12	8
Quebec		
3 years	14	10
4 years	13	9
Ontario		
3 years	11	8
4 years	9	7
Prairies provinces		
3 years	9	7
4 years	7	6
British Columbia		
3 years	10	7
4 years	8	6

Source: Vaillancourt and Henriques (1988), p. 63.
Note: The authors were unable to provide reliable estimates for women
because of statistical difficulties.

As mentioned above, the social rate of return calculations do not
include any estimates for externalities. The external benefits of education include income gains of persons other than those who have received
the additional education; income gains of subsequent generations from a
better-educated present generation; the means of ensuring occupational
flexibility of the labour force; and the creation of an institutional environment that stimulates research in science and technology. One could

TABLE 7.5
Rates of Return for Selected Bachelor and First Professional
Degree Programs, Ontario, 1985

Program	Private		Social	
	Men	Women	Men	Women
		(percent)		
Arts and Science				
Teaching	4.0	10.2	3.8	8.6
Other occupations	4.4	6.9	3.6	3.8
Commerce				
Accountants	13.1	20.6	11.4	17.1
Managers	14.0	15.2	12.1	11.8
Social work (BSW)	—	9.0	—	5.6
Law	13.6	—	11.6	—
Engineering	14.0	—	10.7	—
Architecture	6.0	—	4.5	—
Nursing	—	17.8	—	11.8
Pharmacy	17.4	20.7	14.0	13.1
Medicine	21.6	19.6	15.2	12.2
Dentistry	22.4	—	15.5	—
All occupations	14.0	15.2	12.1	11.8

Source: Stager (1989), p. 71.

also argue that education can foster political stability by developing an informed electorate, competent political leadership, and social cohesion by the transmission of a common cultural heritage. Haveman and Wolfe (1984) claim that the standard estimates of rate of return capture only three-fifths of the full value of education in the United States.[23] Much of the new literature on growth theory and trade theory emphasizes the importance of external benefits to education. It is likely that the external benefits of an engineering education in particular are likely to be quite high because of the links between the number of engineering graduates and economic growth. There is no study in Canada that includes the external benefits in estimating the rate of return.

Others argue that rate-of-return calculations do not capture the fact that education can be used as a form of job-market signalling. In this case, education can be socially wasteful. The argument is as follows: Assume that employers use the quantity of education as an indicator of an employee's productivity. Educated workers therefore are paid more. Assume also that less able people find it more costly than able individuals to acquire a given level of education. Consequently, the best workers will then have an incentive to obtain a diploma or a degree because they can be expected to receive a higher wage than the less educated workers. This type of education therefore signals productivity but does not improve it. Thus the only function of education is to redistribute income, in the process leading to lower net output, because of the diversion of resources into education (West, 1988, p. 70). There is, however, little evidence in support of this hypothesis.

Others argue that the rates of return to education are overstated because many professionals, such as doctors, dentists, and accountants, are able to increase their wages through restrictions on entry. Others also claim that rate-of-return calculations do not include the costs of raising the required funds for publicly subsidized education. Usher (1986) has argued that the total cost of raising one dollar in taxes is $1.80. If this is included in rate-of-return calculations for post-secondary education, the social rate of return would be only 5.59 percent (West 1988), less than the rate of return on investment in physical capital.

Much attention has been paid to training and the lack of training in Canada. According to a Statistics Canada survey, employers in Canada spent $1.4 billion on training, which is the equivalent of $100 per worker and 0.3 percent of GDP (Premier's Council Report, 1990, p. 91). Studies for the United States report training expenditures at least twice that of Canada, and other studies show that the U.S. provides less training than other countries. The federal government spends about $1 billion on training, and provincial governments an additional $2.2 billion. Twenty-eight percent of the total Canadian labour force aged 17 and over took part in some kind of training (Economic Council of Canada, 1992, p. 46) in 1989-90; 6 percent took full-time courses, and the remaining 22 percent, part-time or short-term courses. About one-third of firms in Canada provide formal training. Large firms are more likely to do training than small firms. Porter (1991, p. 210) points out that, compared to other OECD countries, our labour market policies concentrate on income support through unemployment insurance rather than labour market training. Only a small percentage of the unemployed receive training while they are out of work. Our apprenticeship programs, which appear to be outdated, suffer from restricted access and high drop-out rates (Premier's Council, 1990, p. 120-27).

There are no Canadian studies of the returns to training to society, the individual, or the firm.[24] U.S. studies have shown that training improves productivity in the sense that workers' wages increase; there is assumed to be a direct link between wages and productivity. Training also decreases the probability of becoming unemployed. There are few conclusive studies on the effect of training on firm productivity.

Other Factors

Porter (1991) claims that, with few exceptions, Canadian competitiveness as described by the four factors in the "Porter diamond" is not well developed:

> Historically, there has been little pressure for Canadian firms to upgrade or expand their sources of advantage beyond basic factor advantages, or preferred access to the home market. Canadian firms have often adopted inward-looking, cost-based strategies. The size or sophistication of Canadian domestic demand has proven to be a spur to innovation, and an advantage, in only a few of the industries studied. Weak related and supporting industries have reinforced a narrow cost orientation. Limited domestic rivalry, coupled with historic protection, has reduced the incentives for many Canadian firms to innovate and improve their performance relative to other international competitors. Canadian government policy, though well-intentioned and helpful in

some industries, has historically tended to foster reliance on basic factors and dependency on government and has insulated the economy from external pressures (Porter, 1991, p. 141).

Porter identifies particularly the lack of local rivalry as a problem. While an openness to international trade encourages competition, the evidence from a large number of country and industry studies shows that there is a strong association between domestic rivalry and success in international markets. Domestic rivalry puts pressure on firms to innovate and to export, nullifies the effects of factor advantages, and promotes upgrading. Porter argues that the lack of domestic rivalry in Canada can be attributed to the traditionally high tariff protection in Canada, high levels of concentration in many industries, a historically ineffective competition policy, and interprovincial trade barriers. Compared to other countries, Canadian concentration ratios appear to be high (Khemani 1986). Canadian competition laws have been weak. It was not until recently that the Competition Bureau was given enough power to assess the anti-competitive effect of mergers.[25]

Interprovincial trade barriers are a serious impediment to competition. One study (Porter, 1991, p. 306) estimates that there are over five hundred interprovincial trade barriers in operation. Most involve discriminatory government procurement practices, agricultural support programs like marketing boards, policies like provincial licensing requirements that restrict labour mobility, and distribution regulations (for example, beer cannot cross provincial boundaries). These barriers inhibit trade and the flow of capital and labour between provinces, effectively encouraging inefficient firms. The lack of rivalry also appears to have made Canadian firms more profitable. Pre-tax profits as a proportion of GDP have been consistently higher in Canada than in the United States and other countries (*ibid.*, p. 313).

Porter also claims that Canadian consumers are less demanding than consumers in the United States and in other countries. They are less likely to complain and are also less likely to try new products. Many Canadian firms compete on price rather than quality and have therefore developed conservative buying habits with respect to new technology and innovation. Similarly, governments have not used their influence as buyers to encourage product developments in their procurement policies.

Porter argues that Canadians have not benefited as much from from foreign investment as we could have if we had been able to provide a more favourable "diamond." Porter's ten-nation study finds three reasons for foreign direct investments: to get access to basic factors of production; to gain access to a market, and to establish or acquire a home base. Much of foreign investment in Canada, particularly in the resource sector, has been of the first type; that is multinational firms seeking access to natural resources. The high tariffs under John A. Macdonald's National Policy also led to market-access investment in manufacturing. Little foreign investment in Canada is of the third type, which offers the widest benefits to a nation's economy. The home base is the place where the multinational firm contributes the most to the local economy. It is the locus of innovation and productivity growth, and the place where the most beneficial externalities to other industries occur. Factor sourcing and market-access investments normally involve lower productivity than home-base activities and provide fewer beneficial externalities. These type of investments also tend to be less permanent. According to Porter, there appears to be a tendency for some successful Canadian firms to shift their home bases to the United States, which points to underlying weaknesses in the Canadian economy. This contention is consistent with the Economic Council's observation that Canadian affiliates in the United States increased their R&D faster than firms located in Canada.

Conclusions

In our survey we have noted serious weaknesses in our competitive position. Our production costs have increased faster than those of other countries. If our productivity increases had outstripped cost increases, our situation would not be so serious. However, study after study has noted our low growth in total factor productivity as well as in one of its components, labour productivity. This is particularly the case for our resource industries, where our comparative advantage appears to lie. Our resource sector also suffers from problems related to sustainability (see Chapter 4).

Recent developments in trade and growth theory emphasize the importance of interactions among research and development, education and training, and investments in machinery and equipment in promoting growth and developing comparative advantage. We spend less on research and development than most other industrialized countries, and our record of research and development as measured by the number of patents and the number of scientists and engineers employed in research is worse. We are also less likely than other countries to adopt new technologies in production. On the other hand, we have spent more on education than most countries, but there is some evidence from the quality of output, particularly in schools, that the money is not well-spent. We may also have underinvested in engineering education. Our training record is also worse than that of other countries.

Porter also argues that there are other features of our economy that do not promote competitiveness; two of these are the lack of intense competition within Canada because of the legacy of a weak competition policy and interprovincial barriers to trade. Our consumers, be they governments, industries, or private individuals, also appear to be less demanding than consumers in other countries. Unless we correct some of these underlying weaknesses, it is possible that our current living standards will be jeopardized.

TOPICS FOR DISCUSSION

1. Why do you think so few students study science and engineering? Do you think governments should try to steer more students into these subjects, and if so, how?

2. Would a strategic trade policy be a good idea for Canada? Is there any evidence it has been successful anywhere else?

3. President Clinton has stated that each nation can be compared to a big corporation competing in the global marketplace. Do you

think a nations's problems of competition are virtually the same as those of the corporation?

RECOMMENDED READING

For a good discussion of the whole notion of competitiveness, read Krugman's 1993 article in *Foreign Affairs* and the editorial comment on the article in the April 30, 1994, issue of *The Economist*. Harris and Watson (1993) give an interesting comparison of the ideas of Porter, Reich, and Thurow as they pertian to competitiveness. You will find excellent discussions of Canada's competitiveness in Courchene and Purvis (1993) and in Porter (1991).

If you are interested in history, Landes (1969) gives an interesting account of the importance of technological change in the industrial revolution.

References

Baldwin, R.E. "Measurable Dynamic Gains from Trade." *Journal of Political Economy* 100 (1992): 162-74.

Barro, Robert J. "Economic Growth in a Cross Section of Countries." *The Quarterly Journal of Economics* 301 (May 1991): 407-45.

Betcherman, Gordon. "Research Gaps Facing Training Policy-Makers." *Canadian Public Policy* 19 (March 1993): 18-29.

Boyer, Marcel. "Presidential Address: Leadership, Flexibility and Growth." *Canadian Journal of Economics* 24 (November 1991): 751-74.

Boothby, Daniel. "Schooling, Literacy and the Labour Market: Towards a 'Literacy Shortage'?" *Canadian Public Policy* 19 (March 1993): 29-36.

Brander, James A. "Innis Lecture: Comparative Economic Growth: Evidence and Interpretation." *Canadian Journal of Economics* 25 (November 1992): 792-819.

Canada. Economic Council of Canada. *Pulling Together. Productivity, Innovation and Trade*. Ottawa: Ministry of Supply and Services, 1992.

Courchene, Thomas J. and Douglas D. Purvis eds. *Productivity, Growth and Canada's International Competitiveness*. Queen's University, Kingston, On.: John Deutsch Institute for the Study of Economic Policy, 1993.

Daly, Donald J. "Porter's Diamond and Exchange Rates". Research Paper, March 1993, Faculty of Administrative Studies Research Program.

De Long, Bradford J. and Lawrence H. Summers. "Equipment Investment and Economic Growth." *The Quarterly Journal of Economics* 106 (May 1991): 445-503.

Denny, M.J., M. Bernstein, Nakamura S. Fuss, and L. Waverman. "Productivity in Manufacturing Industries: Canada, Japan and the United States, 1953-86: Was the 'productivity slowdown' Reversed?" *Canadian Journal of Economics* 25 (August 1992): 584-604.

Denny, Michael and Thomas A. Wilson "Productivity and Growth: Canada's Competitive Roots." In *Productivity, Growth and Canada's International Competitiveness*, eds. Thomas J. Courchene and Douglas D. Purvis (1993): 7-59.

Easton, Stephen T. *Education in Canada: An Analysis of Elementary, Secondary and Vocational Schooling*. Vancouver: The Fraser Institute, 1988.

The Economist "Innovation, the Machinery of Growth," January 11, 1992. "The Economics of Meaning," April 30, 1994.

Fagerberg, Jan. "International Competitiveness." *The Economic Journal* 8 (June 1988): 355-74.

Griliches, Zvi. "Productivity Puzzles and R&D: Another Nonexplanation." *The Journal of Economic Perspectives* 2 (Fall 1988): 9-23.

Grossman, Gene M. and Elhanan Helpman. "Endogenous Innovation in the Theory of Growth." *The Journal of Economic Perspectives* 8 (Winter 1994): 23-45.

Harris, Richard G. and William G. Watson. "Three Visions of Competitiveness: Porter, Reich and Thurow on Economic Growth and Policy." In *Productivity Growth and Canada's International Competitiveness*, eds. Thomas J. Courchene and Douglas D. Purvis (1993): 233-81.

Helliwell, John F., Mary E. MacGregor, and Tim Padmore. "Economic Growth and Productivity in Canada, 1955-90." In *Economic Growth: Prospects and Determinants*, Research Coordinator John Sargent. Toronto: University of Toronto Press, 1986: 26-65. Prepared for The Royal Commission on the Economic Union and Development Prospects for Canada.

Khemani, R.S. "The Extent and Evolution of Competition in the Canadian Economy." In *Canadian Industry in Transition*, Research Coordinator Donald G. McFetridge. Toronto : University of Toronto Press, 135-76. Prepared for The Royal Commission on the Economic Union and Development Prospects for Canada.

Krugman, Paul R. ed. *Strategic Trade Policy and the New International Economics*. Cambridge Mass: The MIT Press, 1986.

Krugman, Paul R. and Maurice Obstfeld. *International Economics: Theory and Policy*. 2nd Edition. New York: HarperCollins Publishers Inc., 1991.

Krugman, Paul R. "Competitiveness: A Dangerous Obsession." *Foreign Affairs* 73 (March-April 1994): 28-44.

Maddison, Angus. "Growth and Slowdown in Advanced Capitalist Economies." *Journal of Economic Literature* 25 (June 1987): 649-99.

Landes, David. *The Unbound Prometheus*. Cambridge: Cambridge University Press, 1969.

Markusen, James R. *Productivity, Competitiveness, Trade Performance and Real Income: The Nexus Among Four Concepts*. Ottawa: The Ministry of Supply and Services, 1992.

McFetridge, D.G. *Advanced Technologies in Canada: An Analysis of Recent Evidence on Their Use*. Ottawa: Ministry of Supply and Services, 1992.

Mohnen, Pierre. *The Relationship Between R&D and Productivity Growth in Canada and Other Major Industrialized Countries*. Ottawa: Ministry of Supply and Services, 1992.

Murphy, Kevin M., Andrei Schleifer and Robert W. Vishny. "The Allocation of Talent: Implications for Growth." *The Quarterly Journal of Economics* 106 (May 1991): 503-31.

Olson, Mancur. *The Rise and Decline of Nations*. New Haven: Yale University Press, 1982.

Ontario Premier's Council. *People and Skills In The New Global Economy*. Toronto: Queen's Printer for Ontario, 1990.

Porter, Michael E. *The Competitive Advantage of Nations*. New York: The Free Press, 1990.

Porter, Michael and the Monitor Company. *Canada at the Crossroads: The Reality of a New Competitive Environment*. Ottawa: Business Council on National Issues and the Ministry of Supply and Services, 1991.

President's Commission on Industrial Competitiveness. *Global Competition: The New Reality*. Washington D. C., 1985.

Rao, P. Someshwar and Tony Lempière. *Canada's Productivity Performance*. Ottawa: Ministry of Supply and Services, 1992.

Romer, Paul M. "Increasing Returns and Long-Run Growth." *Journal of Political Economy* 94 (October 1986): 1002-37.

Romer, Paul M. "The Origins of Endogenous Growth." *The Journal of Economic Perspectives*. 8 (Winter 1994): 3-23.

Safarian, A. E. *The Performance of Foreign-Owned Firms in Canada*. Montreal: The Private Planning Association, 1969.

Schmookler, Jacob. *Invention and Economic Growth*. Cambridge: Harvard University Press, 1966.

Solow, Robert M. "A Contribution to the Theory of Economic Growth." *Quarterly Journal of Economics* 70 (February 1956): 65-94.

Stager, David A.A. *Focus on Fees: Alternative Policies for University Tuition Fees*. Toronto: Council of Ontario Universities, 1989.

Trebilcock, Michael. "The Evolution of Competition Policy: A Comparative Perspective." In *The Law and Economics of Competition Policy*, eds. Frank Mathewson *et al.* Vancouver, B.C.: The Fraser Institute, 1988: 1-27.

Vaillancourt, Francois and Irene Henriques. "The Returns to University Schooling in Canada." *Canadian Public Policy — Analyse de Politiques*. 12 (September 1986): 449-458.

West, Edwin G. *Higher Education in Canada: An Analysis*. Vancouver: The Fraser Institute, 1988.

Endnotes

1   In this situation economists talk about reducing net absorption which is the same thing.

2   For a full derivation of the results, see for example Mankiw (1992), Chapter 4.

3   Assume the production function is of the Cobb-Douglas type $Y=AKbL^{(1-b)}$, where Y is output, A technology, K capital, and L labour. b and $(1-b)$ is the share of the return to capital and labour in the economy. It can then be shown through differentiation that $dY/Y=dA/A + bdK/K +(1-b)dL/L$, that is the growth in output can be decomposed into the growth in total factor productivity and the growth of capital and the growth of labour, the last two weighted by their income shares. The growth in total factor productivity dA/A can be shown to be equal to the growth in the average product of labour minus the change in the capital/labour ratio multiplied by b.

4   For a survey and discussions of the findings of the new data set, see Brander (1992).

5   For a survey, see Romer (1994) and Grossman and Helpman (1994).

6   For a development of these ideas, see Porter's diamond below.

7   Correlation, of course, does not imply causation. The demand for education expands with income, so like the chicken and the egg, we do not know which came first. However, the consensus appears to be that education has a positive effect on economic growth.

8   For a good introductory discussion, see Krugman and Obstfeld (1991).

9   For a good discussion, see Krugman (1986).

10   Daly (1993) argues that most studies have shown that wage rates and exchange rates are more important than productivity in explaining competitiveness.

11   The importance of home demand was also stressed in the product cycle theory of trade.

12   See Denny and Wilson (1993). They emphasize, however, that because of the difficulties of measuring productivity in services, the data are not necessarily correct.

13   See also the symposium on the slowdown in productivity growth in the Fall 1988 issue of *The Journal of Economic Perspectives*.

14   Fagerberg (1988) emphasizes the importance of technological competitiveness and other features of a product such as the speed of delivery.

15   For a survey of these studies, see Baldwin and Gorecki (1986).

16   The information in this section is based on a summary of the studies on the effect of R&D on productivity growth, Mohnen (1992).

17   See Mohnen (1992), p. 6 and Rao and Lempriere (1992): p. 39.

18   The number of patents may of course be influenced by the requirements in each country for patents. Patents may be easier to obtain in some countries than in others.

19   Economic Council of Canada (1992) p. 37. However, Porter (1991) using 1989 data adds the aerospace industry to the other two.

20 However, in 1989 Canadian expenditure on education dropped to 6.2 percent of GDP and to fifth place.

21 The same survey, however, indicates that there is likely to have been substantial improvements in literacy since the Second World War, reflecting rising levels of schooling. For a discussion of the survey results and their interpretation, see Boothby (1993).

22 The decline in the early eighties is seen as an aberration caused by the severe recession (Economic Council 1992).

23 Some would argue that there may be significant negative externalities. Certain types of education could lead to social unrest, encourage useless academic research, and impede the ability of the labour force to adjust to changing technology (see West, 1988, p. 69).

24 The following is based on Betcherman (1993).

25 For a discussion, see Trebilcock (1988).

Part Two

Towards More Efficient,
Equitable, and Sustainable
Economic Policies

Wbox E WILL FINALLY TURN OUR ATTENTION TO POLICIES.
The previous chapters occasionally referred to the
need for better policies, but the focus was on the
problems and challenges we face, not on the solutions. We start
Chapter 8 with a recapitulation of what the major problems are and
then continue with a discussion of the difficulties in implementing
good economic policies in general, and in Canada in particular.
Good economics is not necessarily good politics. Chapter 9 will
focus on the record of monetary and fiscal policies in Canada, the
problems caused by our high debt levels, and the debate about the
merits of having an economy with no inflation. In Chapter 10 we
will discuss the merits of the Canada–U.S. Free Trade Agreement
and the North American Free Trade Agreement, as well as the larger trade issues arising from Canada's participation in the General
Agreement on Tariffs and Trade (GATT). The many and varied proposals for reform of our unemployment insurance system and our

social policies will be discussed in Chapter 11. We will also discuss proposals for reform of the education system. Following Chapter 11, there is a brief concluding chapter, summarizing what we have learnt and the recommendations arising from our findings.

8

The Policy Environment

After completing this chapter you will be able to discuss the limitations of economics as a policy-oriented discipline and economists' traditional approach to economic policy making. You will also be familiar with the particular difficulties for Canadian policy makers.

A Recapitulation

Radical changes in communications technology have transformed the world economy by making it far more interdependent, a process we refer to as globalization. According to Sylvia Ostry (1990), there were three phases of globalization: (1) the lowering of tariff barriers and the expansion of trade immediately after the Second World War, (2) the freeing of capital flows, and (3) the emergence of the trans-national corporation that buys materials and services throughout the world, and locates production wherever it is advantageous to do so, because of the availability of low-cost factors of production or of scarce factors such as highly trained labour and technical expertise. The second and third phases of globalization were made possible by the changes in computer technology that affected both communications and production.

Drucker (1986) (see Introduction) also pointed out that globalization and changes in technology led to some fundamental changes in how economies function, namely, in the traditional links between the industrial economy and primary products, between production and employment, and between capital movements and trade. Drucker claims that those links have been severely weakened. Computer technology and new materials technology have reduced the need for primary products, a development of considerable concern for countries like Canada, whose high living standards have partly resulted from the export of resources. An illustration of the weakened link between production and employment is that in the recent recovery from the 1991-92 recession where output is growing without a significant fall in unemployment.[1] Firms that survived the recession became "lean and mean" and shed their excess labour.

One result of the high mobility of capital is that governments are severely constrained in their ability to pursue economic policies. Any attempt of a country to tax capital at a higher rate than in other countries could lead to a flight of capital from the country. Environmental taxes in one country, province, or state could cause corporations to move to places without such taxes. In fact, threats of moving were used extensively in Ontario by the business community in an attempt to prevent the newly elected NDP government from passing new labour legislation pertaining to strikes. A decrease in U.S. tax rates by the Reagan administration precipitated a similar tax cut in Canada. Similarly, monetary policy is dictated by international markets. The lowering of interest rates for domestic policy purposes may lead to a flight of capital and thus to a drop in the value of the Canadian dollar on foreign exchange markets. In 1994, for example, the Bank of Canada was forced to follow the U.S. Federal Reserve Board in raising interest rates, even though the Canadian economy showed no signs of inflation and unemployment was above 11 percent.

Another result of globalization discussed in the Introduction is that unskilled production work will move to places where labour is the cheapest, for example Mexico. Rich countries will try to maintain their living standards by competing for high-productivity, high-paid jobs that require a high level of education, training, and sophistication, and large expenditures on research and development. In Reich's terminology, the labour markets are splitting into "good" jobs performed by symbolic analysts, and "bad" jobs performed by routine production workers and in-person service workers. As a result inequalities in society will increase. We already saw evidence of this in Chapter 6.

Globalization also poses difficulties for the nation state, not only by making it difficult for the state to perform its traditional functions, but also by threatening its long-term survival. The threat to the nation state is more subtle. Courchene (1992) describes four different influences, two tending towards supra-national bodies or treaties and two towards disintegration. One influence towards supra-national bodies is the growth in the importance of trans-national corporations, which tends to take sovereignty away from the nation state. The other influence is the need to strengthen supra-national treaties or bodies and establish new ones to deal with global problems. One example is the proliferation of environmental treaties and bodies. Another is the new and expanded role of the United Nations in peacekeeping. Add to this the development of trading blocks in which varying amounts of authority are ceded to an international body, as in Europe and in North America under NAFTA.

According to Courchene, one of the disintegrating influences of globalization that pulls authority downwards from the nation state, is the advances in telecommunications that give more power to the individual citizen, because the government no longer has a monopoly in controlling the flow of information. In the Introduction, I also referred to the decline in deference to the state. The other disintegrating influence is the rise of the power of large cities. Indeed, Courchene argues that the cities are the vehicles by which globalization occurs. The cities (such as Montreal, Toronto, and Vancouver) are the centres of global communications and trading networks. But the influence of cities is nowhere recognized in the institutional and regulatory framework for policy making.

I also pointed out in the Introduction that the disintegrating influences appear to have led to the rise of various interest groups. People appear to identify more with their own group interests, be they racial, ethnic, or local than with any national interest, perhaps because central authority has become more diffused. Courchene quotes the sociologist Daniel Bell (1987) who says, "The nation state is becoming too small for the big problems of life, and too big for the small problems of life."

Add then our unique Canadian problems to the global environment, and the picture becomes extremely complex. Free trade with the United States, in combination with the already continuous changes brought on by globalization, caused massive structural changes to the Canadian economy. Like other countries we are suffering from very high unemployment (see Chapter 5), made worse by the recent recession, which was brought on by inappropriate monetary and fiscal policies. An analysis of our income distribution in Chapter 6 showed that had it not been for our social policies, our income distribution would have deteriorated substantially. Now the continuation of many of our social policies is in doubt because of the large debt carried by both the federal and provincial governments. As it is, too many of our children are poor, which means that the social capital we are leaving to future generations is deteriorating: our social policies are not sustainable. Our survey of the environment in Chapters 3 and 4 also indicated that our use of our environment and natural resources is not sustainable, nor is are our living standards because of our external debt load. Because of our low productivity growth, which was discussed in Chapter 7, we will have increased difficulty remaining competitive, which is another threat to our living standards. Our fundamental responsibility as a nation is to create good jobs for the majority of our citizens in a sustainable economic environment, and to maintain a social safety net to help people who cannot work to live in dignity.

Is Economics Up to the Challenge?

What is the future of economics as a discipline? Can economics contribute to a solution to the problems facing Canada and the rest of the world? Economics as a discipline has undergone a substantial transformation in the last 30 years. It has become more abstract, more theoretical, and more mathematical. In the process it has gained through the refinement of its analytical tools. It has also lost because analytical rigour has often been at the expense of reality and usefulness for policy makers. Traditionally, economic theory was tied to the need for government policies. Adam Smith, David Ricardo, and John Maynard Keynes formulated their theories with concrete policy issues in mind; this link between theory and policy has now been compromised.

On the other hand, economic principles have made inroads into other social sciences, notably sociology, through the analysis of marriage, divorce, suicide, and reproductive behaviour by the Nobel Prize winner Gary Becker; and into political science in public choice theory, which is basically an application of maximizing behaviour to agents in the public sector.[2] But, other disciplines have made few inroads into mainstream economics. There is some interest in behavioural economics, which is evolving out of a collaboration between economists and psychologists who are trying to analyze how economic agents actually behave, which is not necessarily in the rational manner economists assume.

The shortcomings of economics are not unrecognized by mainstream economists. In celebration of the centenary of the journal of the Royal Economic Society, *The Economic Journal*, a number of prominent economists were asked to speculate on the future of economics.[3] Many welcomed the increased use of mathematics with its analytical rigour, but they had reservations about its ultimate usefulness:

There can hardly be any argument with the proposition that the use of mathematical methods has not solved all problems in economic analysis, and that some problems lend themselves more readily to statistical, experimental, historical or other lines of attack. While formal mathematical theory has made invaluable contributions in fields where its success might have caused considerable surprise in an earlier day — fields such as public finance and industrial organisation — each of these areas surely still leaves considerable scope for other research procedures. And there are still other areas, for example, labour economics, in which this is probably even truer. The trouble is that if individuals are not respected for the pursuit of alternative approaches, if only those whose writings are pockmarked by algebraic symbols receive kudos, one can expect a misallocation of resources like that which always results from a distortion of relative prices.

The second consequence follows from the first; not only can we expect more than the optimal amount of study and publication to be based on mathematical methods, but we can expect people to be induced to adopt this approach even though they are relatively poorly endowed with the requisite talents. Graduate programmes, for example, will be burdened with a spate of dissertations that qualify primarily as mathematical (or econometric) exercises whose sole raison d'être seems to be the opportunity they afford to their authors to display whatever facility they can muster in manipulation of the tools of abstraction. Even the most mathematically-oriented of our colleagues will undoubtedly agree that this is what has already happened (Baumol, 1991, p. 2-3).[4]

Critics also point out on the short-run orientation of current economics. As was mentioned in Chapter 7, we do not know very much about the determinants of long-run growth. Nowhere is this failure so obvious as in development economics, where despite enormous infusions of aid and much research, many parts of the world have failed to grow and develop, leaving their populations in a continual state of misery. The short-run orientation also is evident in environmental economics, where the process of discounting future costs and benefits does not give adequate weight to the future of the environment, or indeed to the future of the human race. Note here, however, that most mainstream economists would probably not agree that discounting is a problem (see the discussion in Chapter 2).

Other economists argue for the need to study institutions and how they influence economic behaviour (Baumol, 1991; Buchanan, 1991; Galbraith, 1991).[5] There are also a number of economists who have left traditional, neoclassical economics and, with the help of sociologists, political scientists, and environmentalists, have developed alternative approaches to analyzing economic problems. Examples are the new fields of institutional, evolutionary, and ecological economics, as well as socioeconomics. What these approaches have in common is that they consider the economy to be only one dimension of human life.[6] Other dimensions are the ethical, social, and ecological, which are inseparably linked to the economic dimension. It is rare that any of these dimensions can be analyzed in isolation from the others, nor are they measurable. Love, altruism, duty, respect, beauty, and dignity are powerful influences on economic behaviour, and are intrinsically linked to human welfare, but they cannot be analyzed exclusively in terms of price and self-interest. Furthermore, the economy's physical through-put of matter and energy is subject to the absolute limits of the biosphere and solar flows and to the laws of thermodynamics. These limits and laws place unavoidable constraints on the long-term growth of GDP and therefore on the possibility of continually increasing our welfare through increased consumption.

These ideas are developed most thoroughly by Herman Daly and John B. Cobb (1989), whose book *For the Common Good: Redirecting the Economy Toward Community, Environment and a Sustainable Future*, launches a full-scale attack on neoclassical economics for its failure to deal with the serious problems of today, particularly as they pertain to the environment. Daly, who is an economist with the World Bank, and Cobb, who is a theologian, argue that economics has been caught in a **fallacy of misplaced concreteness**, in which thinkers forget how much abstraction is involved in their thought and draw unwarranted conclusions about the real world. One example of the fallacy is the theory of the circular flow of income, which is built on the assumption that one person's welfare is independent of that of others. Since this assumption is not realistic, economists try to deal with the effects of one person's production and consumption on others through the notion of externalities. Daly and Cobb argue, though, that when vital issues have to be classified as external to the process, it is time to restructure the basic concepts of the discipline.

Another example of the fallacy of misplaced concreteness is the treatment of land and natural resources, which are considered to be a nearly perfect substitute for capital, a belief that clearly contradicts the laws of nature (for a discussion of the laws of thermodynamics, see Chapter 1).

Another example is the theory of comparative advantage, which is based on the assumption that capital is immobile between nations and mobile within a single country. If capital is internationally mobile, the theory of comparative advantage does not hold: rather trading is determined by absolute advantage. What matters is not relative prices and costs but absolute ones. In the countries where investments are not being made, opportunities for workers decline and their wages will go down.[7] The reason why trade between high-wage and low-wage societies has not threatened high wages until recently is that the high wages were based on the lack of heavy capitalization and advanced technology in the low-wage countries. But now low-wage countries attract both capital and technology. Daly and Cobb propose that unlimited free trade should be abandoned and that governments should promote a policy of balanced trade and self-sufficiency both at the national and community level.

But Daly and Cobb do not propose that the market be abandoned as the arbiter of claims on resources. In relying on the market, however, they argue we have to be wary of the tendency for competition to disappear over time; of the corrosiveness of self-interest on the moral fibre of the community that was evident in the excesses of the late eighties (aptly described by Tom Wolfe in *The Bonfire of the Vanities*); and of the existence of public goods and externalities. We should also remember that an allocation based on the market does not give us a just income distribution. They also introduce the idea that there is an optimum scale to economic activities, optimum, that is, in relation to the environment. Economic activity should not exceed the **carrying capacity** of the ecological systems.

Economists as Policy Makers

What do economists know about policy making and policy analysis? In general, it appears not much. They are prepared to deal with the normative theory of policy, such as whether or not the authorities should intervene or the market should be left alone. And if intervention is deemed necessary, economists will debate such questions as how we can best attain the goals; how we can achieve full employment; how we can "grow" the economy as Clinton is reported to have said; or how we can achieve a pollution-free environment. But the positive analysis of public policy, which looks at how and why the government chooses to intervene on some occasions and not on others, perhaps contrary to the advice of economists, is an area that appears to be dominated almost entirely by political scientists.[8]

Alan Blinder, in a lighter vein, coined "Murphy's Law of Economic Policy":

> Economists have the least influence on policy where they know the most and are most agreed; they have the most influence on policy where they know the least and disagree most vehemently (Blinder, 1987, p. 1).

Blinder argues that the reason for this law is that politicians choose solutions they think are politically sound. Good economics often does not make for good politics because of the public's ignorance of basic economic principles, unthinking attachments to myths and slogans, and interest-group politics. As an illustration, he points to the Laffer curve and the Reagan tax cuts:

> One day in 1974, a then obscure but now famous economist named Arthur Laffer took a napkin in a Washington restaurant and drew on it a curve that looked like a little hill sitting on its side. As it rose to a peak, the curve indicated that increasing a tax rate that is low or moderate normally leads to higher tax revenues. But as it descended, the curve suggested that very high tax rates may so discourage the activity being taxed that tax receipts actually fall as the tax rate rises.
>
> Laffer's reasoning was incontrovertible. To prove the basic proposition requires nothing more than some elementary mathematics. But then, in a remarkable and unsupported leap of faith, Laffer convinced first himself and then several influential journalists and politicians that the downhill side of what came to be called the "Laffer curve" . . . might actually describe the U.S. income tax . . . Laffer and Company convinced themselves that the government might actually collect more revenue by cutting personal income-tax rates. . . . Laffer's inspiration must have been other-worldly, for in this world there never was any evidence to suggest that the U.S. income-tax system was in the range of confiscatory taxation where lower rates produce higher revenues. Indeed, there was ample evidence to the contrary . . . Laffer's flight of fancy captured the imagination of candidate Ronald Reagan in 1980, and after the election Peter Pan economics became the official policy of the United States government. Within months, Congress was joyfully participating in the mass self-delusion of the day by enacting a gigantic tax cut that was premised in part on optimistic forecasts that the budget deficit would shrink, not rise. No amount of congressional testimony, op-ed pieces, or speeches by spoilsport economists could deflect the political joyride . . . the rest [is] history — with which we are still living as the nation grapples with the mammoth deficits that were born of the actions of 1981 (Blinder, 1987, p. 3-4).

The theory of economic policy was first developed by the Nobel Prize winner Jan Tinbergen in the 1950s. It is a normative theory of how economic policy makers should behave.[9] Tinbergen argued that the first step in policy making is for the policy maker to specify the goals for economic policy. These goals are included in the social welfare function that is to be maximized. One obvious goal for maximization is economic well-being, but as we know already, no single measure can capture economic well-being. Therefore we have to concentrate on certain features of well-being, such as employment. The second step is for the policy maker to identify the target to be reached, such as an unemployment rate of 7 percent or 5 percent or 3 percent. Third, the instruments that are available to reach the targets must be identified (monetary policy, fiscal policy, or structural policies). It is possible that the instruments are constrained by some overriding policies or commitments. For example, if exchange rates are fixed and capital is fully mobile, monetary policy is restricted to a choice of the level of the exchange rate. Once the exchange rate is chosen, monetary policy must be used to maintain the exchange rate. It cannot be used to stabilize the economy at the same time. Tinbergen proved that the number of targets must be equal to the number of instruments. If there are two targets, two instruments must be used to reach these targets, and the instruments must be independent of each other.

Finally, in order to choose the optimal value of policy instruments, the policy makers must have a model of the economy that can link the instruments to the targets. Most countries have large-scale econometric models of their national economies that are reasonably accurate, at least in predicting changes in the short term. Where the models fail is in their inability to predict the the shocks to which all economies are subjected, such as wars or crop failures.

The experience in some former socialist countries and developing countries has made this traditional view of economic policy making increasingly untenable and raises some fundamental questions about the policy environment (Rodrik 1993). Why are reforms that will eventually benefit most people resisted in some countries and not in others? Why are some reforms reversed, and why do some countries go through cycles of progressive policies followed by retrenchment?

To answer those and similar questions, several economists have tried to build new models integrating economics and politics. Most of these models treat policy reform not as a result of consensus, but rather as the outcome of a power struggle between classes or interest groups that will all be affected in different ways by the reforms. For example, one model (Alesina and Drazen 1991) shows how distributional struggles over the benefits of reform could lead to delays in its implementation. It is assumed that there are two groups in society, capital and labour, and each group incurs rising costs if reform is delayed. The group that is the first to consent to the reforms is assumed to bear the major cost of the reforms. The cost of waiting is unknown to each group. This creates an incentive for each group to wait for the other group to consent to the reform. Reform takes place when one of the groups decides that it will gain more from assuming the cost of reform than from waiting longer for its rival to do so. This model can be used to show that the situation can deteriorate considerably before decisive action is taken to stop inflation or to bring a budget deficit under control. While these type of models can provide some interesting insights, it is too early to say whether they can be useful in policy making.

Problems in Policy Formulation in Canada

A country's ability to adjust to changing conditions depends on the nature of its fundamental institutions, its governmental and judicial structures, its process of decision making, and its ability to create a consensus on change among the majority of the electorate. In this section we shall look both at institutions and at the difficulties of creating consensus.

Canadian society is faced with formidable difficulties in responding to change, as a result of our history and our evolution.[10] Canada is one nation politically, but it consists of two or more distinct societies split by language and culture. The French-speaking part of Canada considers that it has not only a different language, but also a different history, a different culture, and different aspirations from the rest of Canada. The English-speaking part of Canada, on the other hand, has never had a homogeneous identity despite its common ethnic origin (British) and some shared values. Canada's large land mass inevitably fostered different interests and identities, and the situation was further complicated by large-scale immigration of people from different cultures. Multiculturalism has transformed what used to be called English Canada into something very different, at least in the larger cities. There is also greater acceptance of the native people's right to govern themselves. We are a country uncertain of our identity trying to define what it is to be Canadian. The result has been a never-ending search for a constitutional formula capable of reconciling political nationhood first with the existence of two distinct societies (Quebec and the rest of Canada) and now with a greater awareness of a third, consisting of the native communities. This search culminated and failed again in the October 1992 referendum on constitutional proposals embedded in the Charlottetown Accord. The regional nature of the Canadian economy, the tensions between the two levels of government, the tensions between Quebec and the rest of Canada, and the uneven results of the structural changes in the economy have so far prevented a resolution of our constitutional impasse and the development of new, innovative, and effective economic policies.

The ability of the federal government to effect change is very limited in Canada, more so than in most other countries. Formerly, under the British North America Act of 1867, and now under the Constitution, education is a provincial jurisdiction; therefore any attempt to adopt uniform standards or a common approach to educational policies would require the agreement of all the provinces. The same applies to the labour relations legislation. Any regulations concerning specific industries could involve either the provincial or federal government, depending on the industry (for example banking and the aeronautics industry fall within the purview of the federal government, while securities and insurance are provincial). Since the Constitution gives the federal government very little power over nation-wide trade, there is a proliferation of provincial barriers to trade. In an emergency, however, the Government of Canada, under the peace, order, and good government clause, can legislate on any subject.

In the areas of social policy, the environment, and immigration, the powers are mixed. Social services change fall under provincial jurisdiction, while employment services, including unemployment insurance, are federal. Guaranteed-income schemes could be introduced by the provinces, or by the federal government under its spending and taxing powers. In the environmental area, the division of powers is particularly confusing. Earlier constitutional decisions held that the regulation of pollution was a provincial matter, but in a 1988 decision, the Supreme Court of Canada upheld federal powers where the particular problem at hand requires national treatment (Johnson, 1990, p. 268-69). We have frequently ended up with overlapping powers and duplication of services.

The mechanism for forging inter-governmental cooperation is through constitutional amendments that grant the federal government additional powers to meet new national responsibilities, and through the use of federal spending powers. Under Established Program Financing, for example, provincial legislatures enact national standards and goals as part of their provincial programs in return for partial federal funding. But Established Program Financing has been weakened substantially by the need for the federal government to control the deficit (Courchene, 1992, p. 128-30). The federal government has frozen cash transfers under established programs for health and education, and under the present scheme an increasing share of the financing of these functions will fall on the provinces. The large debt will make it impossible for either level of governments to fund any new spending.

Then there is the question of consensus. We appear to be a fractious people. Canada has spent a huge amount of time and effort in attempting to remove the causes of regional discontent. The policy of national bilingualism is enshrined in the Constitution; equalization of provincial revenues to guarantee an equivalent level of public service across the country is also enshrined in the Constitution; large amounts of federal expenditures are allocated to regional economic development; the provinces are empowered to opt out of some national programs (Quebec administers its own pension plan and income tax scheme); and elaborate consultations are held with the provinces on national policies (Johnson, 1990, p. 276). But, there is no sign that those measures have decreased regional discontent.

In order to get agreement among the general public on the need for action in the policy area, it is essential for economists to communicate effectively with politicians and the public. It is also essential for economists to agree on the nature of the problem and the nature of the solution. Despite impressions to the contrary, mainstream economists do in general agree on major issues, at least as they pertain to microeconomics. Where there is disagreement is in macroeconomics, as was evident in our analysis in Chapter 5. As we already discussed, when Keynesianism ruled, economists agreed on principles of macroeconomics. We also have seen how the Keynesian consensus was eroded in the 1970s and 1980s by a combination of economic forces and intellectual and ideological currents. The new orthodoxy (the new classical economics) that replaced Keynesianism espoused market efficiency and denounced government intervention; it probably reached its peak at the same time as communism fell in eastern Europe. The emphasis is on the individual, and the welfare state is considered an obstacle to efficiency and motivation. Privatization and deregulation were the rallying cries of the period. It is interesting to note that the new classical economics did not attract many adherents in Europe. Blinder (1990) points out that the new classical theory could succeed only in a country and at a time when right-wing ideology was on the ascendency, as it was in the United States in the 1970s and 1980s. These developments also influenced Canadian economists.

Blinder (1990) argues that there is a rising tide of new Keynesianism with its emphasis on monopolistic competition, economic shocks, menu costs, efficiency wage theories, and hysteresis which appear to explain the current economic situation. In contrast the new classical theory had little success in explaining the real world.

Whether a new consensus will emerge is difficult to say. The more activist Clinton administration in the United States may swing the tide in the profession. Canadian society has of course never embraced individualism to the same extent as American society. The Canadian outlook is more in keeping with peace, order, and good government than with the American life, liberty, and the pursuit of happiness.[11]

There is also the additional need for economists to devise policies that are realistic politically or they will never be adopted. This may be the greatest difficulty of all.

Conclusions

This chapter has provided a recapitulation and general overview of the difficulties of globalization for Canada as well as other specific problems that Canada has to deal with. We surveyed the state of the discipline of economics with an emphasis on its contribution to economic policy. Economists tend to see economic policy in isolation from all the other forces that operate on the electorate and politicians.

The current situation presents Canada with enormous difficulties. Can economics and economists help? Obviously economics must be part of the solution. The discipline has much to contribute despite the turmoil in the field of macroeconomics. However, for economists to become effective in the policy field, it is essential that they make an effort to educate the general public about basic economic principles, and also that they themselves become more familiar with the positive theory of policy making. Why does good politics often lead to bad economics? How can Murphy's Law of Economic Policy be broken?

Despite this rather pessimistic survey of the fractiousness of Canadian society, there is one observation we did not make. Canadians have proved themselves adept at making compromises and practising the rather difficult art of "muddling through." The defeat of the Charlottetown Accord did not lead to disaster. Most people drew a sigh of relief. If there is a will to overcome our problems, there is always a way.

TOPICS FOR DISCUSSION

1. Do you think Canada is ungovernable? What could be done to build consensus on economic policies? Do you think economics is too difficult for the electorate to understand?

2. Do you think Daly and Cobb's proposal of limiting international trade and promoting self-sufficiency is realistic? Which interest group would be served by such a policy? Who would lose?

3. Can you think of some examples of Murphy's Law of Economic Policy in Canada?

RECOMMENDED READING

For interesting alternative approaches to economics, read Daly and Cobb's *For the Common Good* (Daly and Cobb 1989) and Ekins and Max-Neef's *Real-Life Economics* (Ekins and Max-Neff 1992). Lipset (1990) gives a fascinating account of the differences between Canadian and American societies in his *Continental Divide*. Johnson's article in *Perspectives 2000* (Johnson 1990) gives an excellent summary of the difficulties of making economic policies in Canada.

References

Alesina, Alberto and Drazen, Allan. "Why Are Stabilizations Delayed?" *The American Economic Review 81* (December 1991): 1170-88.

Baumol, William J. "Toward a Newer Economics: The Future Lies Ahead. "*The Economic Journal 101* (January 1991): 1-8.

Bell, Daniel. "The World and the United States in 2013." *Daedalus 116* (Summer 1987): 1-33.

Blinder, Alan S. *Hard Heads Soft Hearts: Tough Minded Economics for a Just Society.* Reading, Mass: Addison-Wesley Publishing Company, 1987.

Blinder, Alan S. "Economic Policy and Economic Science: The Case of Macroeconomics." In *Perspective 2000*, Newton *et al.*(1990): 283-95.

Buchanan, James M. "Economics in the Post-Socialist Century." *The Economic Journal 101* (January 1991): 15-21.

Courchene, Thomas J. *The Courchene Papers*. Oakville: Mosaic Press, 1992.

Daly, Herman E. and John B. Cobb. *For the Common Good: Redirecting the Economy Toward Community, the Environment, and a Sustainable Future.* Boston: Beacon Press, 1989.

Drucker, Peter. "The Changed World Economy." *Foreign Affairs 64* (Spring 1986): 768-92.

Ekins, Paul and Manfred Max-Neef. *Real-Life Economics: Understanding Wealth Creation.* London: Routledge, 1992.

Frank, Robert H., Thomas Gilovich, and Dennis T. Regan. "Does Studying Economics Inhibit Cooperation." *The Journal of Economic Perspectives 7* (Spring 1993): 159-73.

Galbraith, John Kenneth. "Economics In the Century Ahead." *The Economic Journal 101* (January 1991):

Johnson, A.W. "Global Force and National Policy Making." In *Perspective 2000*, S T. Newton *et al.* (1990): 261-78.

Lipset, Seymour Martin. Continental Divide. The Values and Institutions of the United States and Canada. New York: Routledge, 1990.

Lipsey, Richard. "A Crystal Ball Applied to Canadian Economics." *Canadian Journal of Economics* 26 (February 1993): 70-77.

Newton, K., T. Schweitzer and J.P. Voyer. *Perspective 2000: Proceedings of a Conference Sponsored by the Economic Council of Canada*. Ottawa: Ministry of Supply and Services, 1990.

Ostry, Sylvia. "Economic Factors and Impacts." In *Penser Globalement, Think Globally*, eds. Diane Wilhelmy and Pierre Coulombe. Toronto: IPAC, 1990. Proceedings of the 42nd Annual Meetings of the Institute of Public Administration of Canada.

Rodrik, Dani. "The Positive Economics of Policy Reform." *The American Economic Review* 83 (May 1993): 356-61.

Sachs, Jeffrey D. and Felipe B. Larrain. *Macroeconomics in the Global Economy*. Englewood Cliffs, New Jersey: Prentice Hall, 1993.

Endnotes

1   Deficit-induced trimming of the civil service by both provincial and federal governments obviously did not help any recovery in employment.

2   This may not be a good thing. Recent empirical research has shown that training in economics appears to make people less cooperative and more likely to act in their own self-interest (Frank *et al.*, 1993).

3   See also the twenty-fifth anniversary symposium of the Canadian Economics Association in the *Canadian Journal of Economics*, February 1993.

4   For a similar argument about Canadian economics, See Lipsey (1993).

5   Galbraith has in most of his writings emphasized the importance of power in economic relations and the exclusion of power from economic analysis.

6   An interesting collection of writing in this genre is Ekins and Max-Neef (1992, p. 423-26) from which this summary is taken.

7   However, traditional trade theory also predicts that in a perfectly competitive world with factors immobile between countries, and where comparative advantage is based on different factor endowments, factor price equalization will occur and real wages will decline in high-wage countries.

8   Public choice theory is an exception. Public choice theory treats the political mechanism, for example voting, as the means by which preferences are transmitted to policy makers.

9   This section is based on Sachs and Larrain (1993, Chapter 19).

10   This section has benefited from Johnson (1990).

11   For an interesting book on the differences between Canadian and American society, see Lipset's *Continental Divide* (1990). The phrase "peace, order, and good government" appears in the Canadian constitution in describing the powers of parliament. The phrase "life, liberty, and the pursuit of happiness" can be found in the American constitution.

9

Monetary and Fiscal Policies

After completing this chapter you will be able to discuss the appropriateness of Canadian monetary and fiscal policies in the eighties and nineties and the merits of a zero-inflation policy. You will also be able to assess the advantages and disadvantages of stringent rules against budget deficits and whether fiscal policies would be more effective if the provinces had a larger role.

The Debate over Monetary and Fiscal Policies: Rules versus Discretion

There are two questions about monetary and fiscal policies that need to be settled. The first is whether the government should intervene in the economy at all; the second is whether the government should be made to follow rules imposed by the legislature.

The first question about government intervention is not easy to answer. The macroeconomic theory surveyed in Chapter 5 tells us that monetary and fiscal policies can be effective in stabilizing the economy. The question is whether they are effective in practice. Unfortunately, the answer is not clear. It was not until after the Keynesian revolution that governments assumed a responsibility for economic stabilization.

Most Keynesians, comparing data from before the Second World War with data from after the war, have argued that real GDP and unemployment have become far more stable because of Keynesian policies. Romer (1986), however, argues that this is not the case, and that the measured increase in stability after the Second World War is the result of the availability of more accurate data after the war: in other words, increased stability is a statistical fluke. She tries to prove her case by constructing more accurate data for the earlier period, as well as constructing less accurate data for the postwar period in order to achieve comparability. Her findings are still controversial. As yet, history cannot settle the debates, mainly for lack of data. If it is true that stabilization policies have not been effective, how can it be explained?

One reason is the long delays between the time a problem is recognized by the policy makers, and the time they take action (**the inside lag**). For example, any change in fiscal policy requires approval by Parliament, which can take a long time. There is also a lag between the time a policy is implemented and the time it takes effect (**the outside lag**). This lag is particularly long for monetary policy, which works through interest rates, which in turn affect investment and consumption. Investment plans in particular are often made far in advance, and therefore a change in monetary policy is not thought to influence real GDP until at least two years later.

Therefore, if stabilization policy is to work, forecasting has to be accurate; otherwise by the time a stimulus takes affect, the economy may already be into an upturn. A mistimed stimulus could rapidly make the upturn inflationary. Though short-term forecasting is reasonably accurate, long-term forecasting is not, since the forecasting models cannot foresee wars, natural disasters, and the results of election.[1] (see Chapter 8).

Another criticism of active stabilization policies is that neither policy makers nor forecasters have an adequate understanding of how the economy is affected by their expectations. Expectations are very important because they affect the behaviour of consumers, investors, and other economic agents. Unless it is known how people change their expectations in response to a new policy, we do not know how effective the policy will be. (For a discussion of the Lucas critique and the theory of rational expectations, see Chapter 5.)

Some would also argue that the fundamental problem is that stabilization policies are left to politicians, who often act out of a desire to be re-elected, rather than in the interest of the long-term well-being of the electorate. In fact, there is evidence in the United States that politicians tend to inflate the economy before an election.

A further problem for stabilization arises from the **time inconsistency** of policy.[2] Time inconsistency arises when a policy that makes sense today no longer makes sense to policy makers when the time comes to act on it. Without binding rules, a government always has the option of switching to what it later believes to be a better policy. And often politicians make promises that they cannot or do not intend to keep. Three examples are Mulroney's promise of no free trade with the United States, George Bush's promise not to raise taxes ("read my lips"), and Trudeau's promise not to impose wage and price controls. The result is that the electorate treats politicians with utmost cynicism and will usually take any promises with a grain of salt. Moreover, when people realize that the government is likely to change its mind, they will anticipate a policy change and behave in ways that makes it impossible for policy makers to achieve their original goals. Thus, announced policy of zero inflation may not have the desired effect on expectations because the public knows that if the policy of zero inflation creates too much unemployment, the government will inflate the economy again. The problem for a government is how to achieve credibility.

The widespread distrust of politicians has led to the suggestion that economic policy should be put outside their influence by making politicians follow certain prescribed rules. For example, monetarists sometimes argue that the Bank of Canada should keep the money supply growing at a fixed rate. Monetarists believe that short-term fluctuations in the economy are caused almost entirely by fluctuations in the money supply. Therefore if the money supply is controlled, economic fluctuations would not occur. The link between the money supply and economic activity can be described by the equation $MV = PQ$, where M is the supply of money, V is the velocity of circulation of money, P is the price level, and Q is the quantity of goods and services produced. PQ is therefore the money value of aggregate economic activity. If there is to be a direct link between aggregate economic activity and the money supply, the velocity of circulation must be constant. During the 1980s the velocity of circulation varied considerably. For this reason most economists believe that a policy controlling the growth in the money supply would be unwise. Another suggestion is that the central bank be required to follow rules specifying how monetary policy will be conducted under various economic circumstances. For example, the central bank could set a target for the inflation rate (note the discussion below of the zero inflation rate target).[3]

Rules are also often proposed for fiscal policy. Under a balanced budget rule, for example, politicians could not spend more than the tax revenue. This suggestion is often heard in Canada as an effective way of controlling expenditures by profligate federal and provincial governments. In the United States, the constitutions of 49 states limit deficit spending, and those of ten states limit expenditures and taxes. However, because of the effects of automatic stabilizers, it would be extremely difficult to enforce balanced budget rules, at least if the budget was to be balanced over a budget year. Government budgets would then be pro-cyclical since governments would have to raise taxes during a recession and lower them during inflationary periods, or cut expenditures during recessions and increase them during inflationary periods. Most economists would agree, though, that the budget should be balanced over a business cycle.[4]

Canadian Monetary and Fiscal Policies: Recent History

Although one chapter has already been devoted to our unemployment record, it is useful to summarize the main features of our macroeconomic performance, and how the federal government and the Bank of Canada responded.[5] Table 9.1 summarizes the salient features.

The 1980s were a decade of lower inflation than the 1970s. In all the OECD countries inflation rose on average by only half as much as in the 1970s, a trend that has continued into the 1990s. In early 1993, the annual rate of inflation in the OECD countries was 2-4 percent; Canada's was 1.5 percent. Through the eighties, all countries had very

TABLE 9.1.

Economic Indicators, Canada, 1980-1993

Year	Growth of GDP (1986 prices) (%)	Unem-ployment (%)	Increase in CPI (%)	Bank Rate (%)	Exchange Rate (Canada/ U.S.) ($)	Federal Deficit (current dollars)	Current account balance (current dollars) ($ million)
1980	1.5	7.5	10.2	12.89	1.169	-10,663	-1,793
1981	3.7	7.6	12.5	17.93	1.199	-7,315	-6,884
1982	-3.2	11.0	10.8	13.96	1.234	-20,281	2,004
1983	3.2	11.9	5.8	9.55	1.232	-24,994	2,102
1984	6.3	11.3	4.4	11.31	1.295	-30,024	1,686
1985	4.8	10.5	4.0	9.65	1.366	-31,424	-3,095
1986	3.1	9.6	4.1	9.21	1.389	-23,617	-11,394
1987	4.2	8.8	4.4	8.40	1.326	-20,704	-11,601
1988	5.0	7.8	4.0	9.69	1.231	-19,166	-13,883
1989	2.3	7.5	5.0	12.29	1.184	-21,195	-22,886
1990	-0.5	8.1	4.8	13.05	1.167	-25,492	-25,709
1991	-1.2	10.3	5.6	9.03	1.146	-30,737	-29,035
1992	0.9	11.3	1.5	6.78	1.209	-26,403	-27,683
1993	2.7	11.2	1.8	5.09	1.290	-30,216	-25,219

Source: The Canadian Economic Observer (cat. 11-010), various issues.

high nominal interest rates, which because inflation was falling, translated into record high real interest rates. (The real interest rate is the nominal rate minus the inflation rate.) Canada had the highest real interest rate of any G-7 country. Nominal interest rates started to decline in 1991, but because inflation was low, real interest rates remained high.

The 1980s were also a decade of high unemployment and slow economic growth. Canada had an average unemployment rate in the 1980s of 9.3 percent, compared to 6.7 percent in the seventies. In

France, the United Kingdom, and Germany, unemployment was twice as high in the eighties as in the seventies. That was despite the fact that most countries provided a considerable fiscal stimulus by running large deficits. In the OECD countries, the average deficit rose from 2.4 percent of GDP from 1974–79 to 3.4 percent in 1980-89. Canada's average deficit in the eighties for all levels of government was 4.6 percent of GDP. Large deficits resulted in large increases in the debt-to-GDP ratios in most countries (see Chapter 1). Only Italy had a worse ratio of debt to GDP than Canada.

The very high Canadian interest rates in the late eighties led to large capital inflows which increased the value of the Canadian dollar, making it very difficult for Canadian industry to remain competitive. The current account balance deteriorated substantially, creating "twin deficits," a situation that also occurred in the United States.

Those developments were partly a result of monetary and fiscal policies and partly a cause of them.[6] The 1970s were a decade of very high inflation caused by high prices for commodities, in particular oil. The three-year program of wage and price controls instituted in 1975, combined with the Bank of Canada's policy of monetary austerity (the policy of "gradualism"), brought inflation down in the late seventies. However, another round of increases in prices of commodities, particularly food and oil, led to more inflation. Between 1978 and 1981 world market prices for crude oil increased by 159 per cent, for wheat and barley by 79 percent, and for paper and allied products by 59 percent (Barber, 1992, p. 103).

Late in 1979, interest rates were being pushed up in the United States because of a restrictive monetary policy. The Bank of Canada followed suit, and Canadian interest rates climbed to record high levels. The bank believed that Canadian rates had to follow U.S. rates to prevent a depreciation of the dollar that would have caused further inflation. In 1980, the monetarist policies of the Federal Reserve Board in the United States led to extremely volatile interest rates. The prime lending rate in the United States rose from 15.25 percent at the beginning of the year to 20 percent in April, 11 percent in August, and 21.5 percent in December. This volatility caused difficulties for the Bank of Canada. In trying to moderate these trends, the bank had to allow the exchange rate to drop to 0.8249 in December, and interest rates followed downwards. In order to make interest rate adjustments easier, the Bank of Canada, in March 1980, introduced a floating bank rate: every week the rate was set at one-quarter of one percent above the average established in the weekly auction of 91-day treasury bills issued by the Government of Canada.

In 1980, the economy experienced a moderate downturn. Inflation was rising rapidly, and so were wage settlements. In 1981, inflation soared to 12.4 percent, and average wage settlements 13.3 percent. Part of the higher inflation was caused by the higher energy prices, which, under the National Energy Program, were phased in more slowly in Canada than in other countries. Late in the year, the economy slipped into a deep recession, hardly before it had recovered from the 1980 downturn. By the end of 1982, Canada had had six consecutive quarter declines in real GDP and a total decline of 3.2 percent in that year. Unemployment rose to a post-war high of 11.8 percent; inflation moderated somewhat. The federal deficit increased in one year from $7 billion to $20 billion, owing to increased transfer payments in the form of unemployment insurance and interest on the public debt.

The severe slump experienced in Canada in 1982 can be attributed to the severity of the world recession, which adversely affected the export sector, and the anti-inflationary monetarist policies pursued in the United States and Canada. The resulting record-high interest rates dampened spending. In 1982, the Bank of Canada abandoned its policy of gradualism, a policy involving monetary targeting that it instituted in 1975. The bank no longer found monetary aggregates to be reliable indicators of economic activity, largely because of the extensive financial innovations that took place in the early eighties among banks and near-banks in the type of deposits and services offered.

Inflation was very much on the government's mind in the 1982 budget which imposed mandatory wage guidelines on the federal public service. Known as the "six and five" policy, they were designed to limit wage increases to 6 percent and 5 percent respectively over the next two years. The government urged the provinces and the private sector to stay within the guidelines too.

Economic recovery started in the first quarter of 1983 and continued throughout the year. The first four quarters of the recovery recaptured the output lost during the recession. Inflation moderated and unemployment fell marginally. Business investment, however, remained weak.

In preparing the April 1983 budget, the policy makers were faced with difficult choices, given the size of the federal deficit, and given that recovery had barely started. A slow recovery would discourage business investment and further intensify the long-term problems in the Canadian economy. The budget aimed to give the economy an immediate boost through a stimulation of investment and employment coupled with a longer-term policy to reduce the deficit. The immediate stimulus consisted of an increase in expenditures on job creation as well as reductions in taxes. In the following year, the stimulus was to be withdrawn by an increase in personal income taxes and the gradual phasing out of the new programs. The intention was to reduce the deficit over four years.

When the February 1984 budget was being prepared, the economy was still growing strongly, but the growth had little effect on unemployment. The six-and-five guidelines were reduced to 4 percent. The budget also contained some measures to raise productivity through tax credits for profit sharing, as well as increases in the Guaranteed Income Supplement.

The first budget of the newly elected Conservative government was brought down in May 1985. The economy was still relatively strong except that unemployment remained high. As a result of the high unemployment and persistently high interest rates, the federal deficit was still high and there were no immediate prospects for a substantial reduction. The deficit became a priority in the formulation of the budget, though the government realized that with unemployment remaining high, severe fiscal restraint would not be feasible.

The budget partially deindexed personal income taxes, family allowances, and old-age security payments. Income taxes had been fully indexed since 1974. Under the new rules, exemptions and brackets in the personal income tax system would be adjusted only for inflation of more than 3 percent). There was a temporary surtax of 10 percent on individuals and corporations. The budget also included cutbacks in expenditures of government departments amounting to $500 million in the 1985-86 fiscal year and rising to almost $2 billion in 1990-91. The measures were expected to reduce the projected deficit by $4.4 billion.

Monetary policy in the mid-eighties was eased considerably in the face of a collapse in the price of oil and other commodities, resulting in renewed inflationary pressure from 1987 to 1989.[7] In January 1988, John Crow, who had been appointed Governor of the Bank of Canada the previous year, signalled the beginning of a new policy for the Bank of Canada. In a lecture at the University of Alberta, Governor Crow stated that the aim of monetary policy should be to achieve stability in the value of money, which means achieving and maintaining stable prices, that is zero inflation (Crow, 1988, p. 4). He explained that a policy of maintaining a stable inflation rate of, say, 4 percent was not a credible policy, for reasons that are explained below. There were no targets or timetables announced.

The April 1989 budget included an 8 percent surtax on individuals whose basic federal tax was more than $15,000. The budget also began a process of "clawing back" old age security and family allowance payments from taxpayers with net incomes of more than of $50,000; that threshold would be adjusted for inflation should the inflation rate exceed 3 percent.

The Conservative government also started a process of changing transfers to the provinces. The Established Program Financing is the agreement between the provinces and the federal government for sharing the costs of health care and post-secondary education. Dating back to 1977, it involves a transfer from the federal government of cash and tax points, which were to increase yearly by a factor based on the rate of population growth and the growth of GDP. In 1986, the federal government changed this formula unilaterally by limiting cash contributions to the growth of GDP minus 2 percent. In 1989 this was changed to growth of GDP minus 3 percent, and in 1990 the per capita entitlements were frozen. As the value of the tax point transfers grows with the economy, the cash component of transfers will fall to zero for Quebec as early as the mid-nineties and for the other provinces early in the next decade (Courchene, 1992, p. 206).

The zero inflation policy announced by the Bank of Canada in 1988 led to a tightening of monetary policy with very high interest rates.[8] In the 1989 budget, the Minister of Finance was faced with a substantially higher deficit because of the higher rates on government bonds. The budget contained an increase in excise taxes, and several provincial governments also followed with higher taxes. The result was higher inflation. The increase in the deficit caused by higher interest rates led to the budget of 1990 with a reduction in transfer payments to the provinces. The federal government also announced its intention to replace the Manufacturers' Sales Tax with a value-added sales tax of 7 percent beginning in January 1991.

Because the Goods and Services Tax (GST) was replacing a very inefficient tax, it was expected to lead to considerable efficiency gains.[9] However, these potential gains came at a considerable short-term cost to the economy. The Department of Finance estimates that the tax led to a decrease in GDP of 1.2 percent in 1991 and an increase in the consumer price index of 1.6 percent (Ruggeri and van Wart 1992). Clearly, the timing of the tax was unfortunate.

The 1991 budget contained a 3 percent limit on spending increases after 1991-92, and a 3 percent cap on wage raises in the civil service. The government was obviously worried about the increase in inflation, caused largely by the introduction of the GST. The budget was also accompanied by a joint announcement by Finance Minister Wilson and Governor Crow setting out a timetable for achieving price stability. For 1992 the desired inflation rate, as measured by the consumer price index, excluding food and energy, was set at 3 percent, for 1993 to 1994 at 2.5 percent, and for 1995 at 2 percent.

In 1992 inflation dropped suddenly to a rate of 1.5 percent. Interest rates also started to come down. Note, however, that real rates still remained very high (see Table 9.1).

In 1992, in an attempt to put additional control over the deficit the federal government passed the Spending Control Act, which specified that expenditure increases could not exceed an average of 3 percent a year over the 1991-96 period. Spending control did not include interest on the public debt or on some self-financing programs, such as unemployment insurance. The 1992 budget included a cut in the federal surtax. In an attempt to stimulate the housing industry, the government changed the rules for RRSP, allowing home buyers to borrow up

TABLE 9.2
Provincial Government Deficits, Canada, 1980-93

Year	Deficit ($ millions) (current dollars)
1980	–552
1981	–1,076
1982	–5,671
1983	–6,264
1984	–1,768
1985	–4,009
1986	–7,951
1987	–3,330
1988`	+ 643
1989	–1,493
1990	4,870
1991	–14,611
1992	–20,677
1993	–18,336

Source: The Canadian Economic Observer (cat. 11-010), various issues.

to $20,000 of their RRSP as a down payment without incurring taxes, provided the loan was repaid within 15 years. Later in the year, worried about the persistence of the recession, the government brought in a mini-budget with a 10 percent investment tax credit and an extension of the home buyer plan until March 1994.

Public concern about increasing debts led to a series of restrictive provincial budgets during 1993 that contained considerable cuts in expenditures and tax increases. Table 9.2 shows the increasing deficits of provincial governments. In Newfoundland and Saskatchewan, provincial bonds were downgraded from an AA to an A rating, which would make future borrowing more costly.

The provincial governments argue that part of their difficulties stem from three factors: (1) the federal government off-loading some of the costs of health and post-secondary education to the provinces through the unilateral change in the funding formula for Established Program Financing; (2) reductions in fiscal equalization; and (3) a 5 percent ceiling on the growth of transfers to the wealthier provinces under the Canada Assistance Plan. Carter (1994) shows that this is correct, estimating the revenue loss to the provinces for the 1993-94 fiscal year to be approximately $8 billion, and the cumulative loss since 1986 to be $33.6 billion in current dollars; the cuts to health and education account for $24.4 billion of the total.[10] In addition to these direct effects, cuts in federal government spending lower the tax base of the provinces and therefore further widen provincial government deficits.

The April 1993 budget of the federal government was guided by the debt and the deficit. The budget contained more spending cuts, amounting to close to $30 billion, and no tax increases. Had it not been for interest payments, the government would actually have been in a surplus position. In the 1992-93 fiscal year, the interest payments on the debt amounted to $39.5 billion and the projected deficit to $35.5 billion.

Deficits and the Debt

There are three ways of measuring the public deficit: **the national income accounts measure, the public accounts measure, and the financial requirements measure.**[11] The first of these measures the effect of the deficit on the economy, and can be used to measure the deficits of both the federal and the provincial governments. Tables 9.1 and 9.2 contain the national income measures of the deficit and Figure 9.1 shows the development of the federal debt and deficit in relation to GDP. The public accounts measure is intended to provide Parliament with the information necessary to control the government's spending estimates. It does not include non-budgetary items such as receipts and payments for unemployment insurance and the Canada Pension Plan. When these receipts and payments are added to the public accounts measure, we get the financial requirements measure, which is equal to

Figure 9.1
Canadian Net Debt and Federal Deficit as a Percentage of GDP, 1978 - 1992

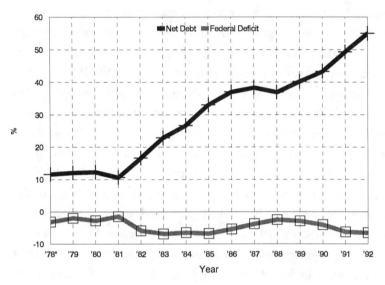

Source: OECD, Economic Outlook, December 1993, Tables A25 and A30.

the borrowing requirement of the Government of Canada. This measure is also approximately equal to the national accounts measure.[12]

There is also a difference between the actual deficit and the structural deficit. The deficit changes over the business cycle as a result of automatic stabilizers, for example, taxes and unemployment insurance payments. If the effect of the automatic stabilizers is removed from the deficit, one gets the structural deficit. The structural deficit is a useful indicator of the discretionary fiscal stance of a government.

The national debt, which is the result of the accumulation of deficits over time, is measured by the stock of net fixed-value government liabilities.

The benefits of smoothing economic cycles by borrowing (called deficit financing) are well-known. If a government borrows money during a recession by issuing bonds instead of raising taxes, income will be raised in the private sector and therefore the effects of the slump will be lessened. During expansions, the government should do the opposite: raise taxes, run a surplus, and use the surplus to pay off some of the debt.

Are large and persistent government deficits harmful? Many people think they must be, drawing the analogy with the private sector. A person who persistently spends more than he or she earns will go bankrupt. A government, however, is different. A government does not need to balance revenue and expenditures over a lifetime. A government is in a better position to raise revenue than an individual, both through its power to tax and its power to print money. Lower levels of government are less able than a central government to run deficits, since they have less power to tax and cannot print money. Bruce and Purvis (1986, p. 58) argue that the relevant criterion for evaluating the financial situation of a central government is the long-term development of the national debt in relation to GDP (the debt-to-GDP ratio).

In 1975, the total debt of the federal and provincial governments was $50 billion, or 29 percent of GDP. By early 1993 the total debt was estimated at $665 billion, or 96 percent of GDP (Carmichael 1993). It is expected that the debt-to-GDP ratio will continue to rise by 3 to 4 percent a year. The estimated federal and provincial deficits for 1993 were $58 billion, or 8.4 percent of GDP. And no relief is in sight. There is a simple formula which says that as long as the real growth rate in the economy is less than real interest rates, and as long as governments run primary deficits, there will be increases in the debt-to-GDP ratio. The projected growth rates for GDP are between 2 and 4 percent, real interest rates are 6.5 percent, and the primary deficits of provincial governments and the federal government are about 2 percent of GDP. It is obvious that the debt and the deficits are not sustainable.

"Rating agencies confirmed the quality of several provinces' debt yesterday, including Ontario's, but a Canadian Taxpayers Federation report warned dangerous debt levels persisted throughout the country.

The report, which uses World Bank methodology, found that all 10 provinces and the country as a whole can be classified as "severely indebted" and that the problem is getting worse.

The report from the Victoria-based independent research group compared the level of federal, provincial and municipal debt attributable to each province and 162 jurisdictions around the world.

Severely indebted jurisdictions are defined as having two out of three of the following: a ratio of debt to gross domestic product exceeding 50 percent, a debt to exports ratio of more than 275 percent, or an interest to exports ratio above 20 percent.

"It is surprising that the total government indebtedness of the majority of Canadian citizens is more severe than what citizens face in nations like Argentina, Burundi, Poland, Mexico and Brazil," the report said.

The report, which uses the most recent information available for each jurisdiction, found Guyana to be the most indebted. Between 1989 and 1991 that country had an average debt/GDP ratio of 800 percent. Canada's was 85 percent during the same period, the 40th-worst record. Other than Italy, Canada is the only member of the 24-nation Organization for Economic Co-operation and Development to be included on the severely indebted list.

The debt/GDP ratios for Canadian provinces ranged from 160.1 percent for Newfoundland to 50.3 percent for Alberta."

(The Financial Post, May 27, 1993).

A high debt-to-GDP ratio will affect the economy adversely in a number of ways. First, with a large number of government bonds for the private sector to channel their savings into, fewer savings are available to finance investments in machinery and equipment, assuming the government uses the revenue from the bonds to finance current consumption. Future generations will suffer because they will inherit a lower amount of capital stock, and therefore economic growth will be lower.[13]

Second, a budget deficit creates a deficit on the current account, because aggregate domestic demand will be greater than aggregate domestic supply (see Chapter 1).[14] This increased demand will spill over into greater demand for imports and will create a deficit on the current account. Thus, we get the problem of the **twin deficits**. To finance the deficit on the current account, we have to resort to borrowing abroad, which worsens the problems on the current account by leading to a large outflow of interest payments and imposing a burden on current and future generations. Some of our incomes have to be paid to foreigners. In 1992, Canada's net foreign liabilities reached a postwar record of 43.8 percent of GDP. (The previous record was 42 percent in 1961.) Today, 40 percent of the liabilities are held as long-term bonds. The federal government is responsible for one-third of the bonds, the provincial governments for 45 percent, and private corporations for the remainder (Canada, Department of Finance, 1993, p. 25). In 1990, 38 percent of all Government of Canada bonds were held abroad, compared to 15 percent in 1978. Most are held by Americans, but an increasing proportion (25 percent) are held by the Japanese (Laliberte 1991). Canada's foreign indebtedness is higher than that of any other industrialized country.

Third, when a high proportion of our debt is foreign debt, it is difficult for the Bank of Canada to operate, because interest rates have to be high enough to make the refinancing of the debt possible. It appears that provincial governments in particular will have to offer higher interest rates on their bonds because of the effects of large debts on their credit ratings by the bond agencies.

Four, the taxes needed to service the debt impose their own costs on society. As well as the administrative costs, the taxes reduce efficiency by altering incentives and encouraging the growth of the underground economy (see Chapter 1). High cigarette taxes, for example, resulted in so much tobacco smuggling that the taxes had to be reduced. The introduction of the GST did not lead to as much revenue as was expected because of tax evasion. According to Statistics Canada (*The Globe and Mail*, May 21, 1993), the federal government should have collected $39.1 billion from the GST in 1991-92; in fact it collected only $34.3 billion.

Five, a large debt-to-GDP ratio also makes the deficit very sensitive to variations in interest rates, thereby restricting the government's ability to increase expenditures. Public concern about the debt also makes it politically unacceptable for governments to pursue counter-cyclical policies during a recession. In 1993, for example, most provincial governments actually raised taxes at the beginning of a very fragile recovery.

Finally, there is the question of inter-generational equity. Government debt is a way for the current generation to pass on the burden of current programs to future generations. Assuming that the debt has been used to finance current consumption, the debt enables this generation to consume some of the production of future generations. For this reason there is a need for the political process to restrain the government from undertaking programs that offer current benefits at the expense of higher taxes or lower government services in the future, unless there are overriding economic arguments for passing on the cost. There has to be a way of enforcing fiscal prudence (Bruce and Purvis, 1986, p. 62-63).

Because of the difficulties of balancing the budget, even over the economic cycle, some economists are in favour of stabilizing the debt-to-GDP ratio. However, like a fixed-balanced-budget rule, it would require the government to pursue pro-cyclical policies over the cycle since GDP would decline and the debt would increase during recessions. Instead Bruce and Purvis favour a policy that would allow the debt-to-GDP ratio to vary over the cycle but where there would be no upward trend. They argue that the government should strive for a specified average debt-to-GDP ratio.

The Zero-Inflation Debate

In 1988, during his first year as governor of the Bank of Canada, John Crow announced that he was going to pursue a policy of price stability, which was interpreted to be a policy of zero inflation.[15] This announcement created considerable debate among economists as to whether a zero inflation rate is the "optimal" inflation rate. If it is the optimal rate, can we achieve it and what are the costs of doing so?

Persistent inflation appears to be a modern phenomenon:

Since 1933 consumer prices have risen by 950% in America and by 4000% in Britain. To put this another way, the dollar is today worth only 10 cents in 1933 money, and the pound is really worth a paltry

2½ p. Even the supposedly cast-iron D-mark has lost two-thirds of its value since it replaced the worthless Reichsmark in 1948.

Since prices have risen almost continuously since 1933, most people today expect that prices will continue to rise every year. In fact history shows that inflation is far from "normal".

In the years before 1933, prices fell in Britain and America in more years than they rose. The longest unbroken period of rising prices in both America and Britain lasted only six years. Germany's hyperinflation in 1922-23 (when the inflation rate was over 1 billion %) is well known. More interesting is the fact that unlike America and Britain, where prices drifted downwards during the 19th century, in Germany prices doubled.

After falling by 40% between 1820 and 1900, American prices more than doubled during the first world war. But by the early 1930s the average price level had fallen back to its level in 1820.

The British figures, covering the longest period, are the most revealing. During the three centuries to 1933, there were only six occasions when prices increased for more than three years in a row, mostly during wars, when government borrowing soared. Prices peaked in 1813, during the Napoleonic wars, but by the end of the 19th century had more than halved again. As in America, prices surged during 1914-20 but then fell back. By 1933 prices in Britain were hardly changed from their 1660s levels

(The Economist, February 22, 1992).

How accurately can we measure inflation? Price stability is not necessarily the same as zero inflation as measured by the consumer price index (the CPI). The consumer price index measures the prices of a fixed basket of goods in which each item is weighted by its importance in the consumer budget. The cost of the basket of goods in the base year is set arbitrarily at $100, and the cost in any other year expressed as a percentage of the base year. The contents of the basket of goods is updated every four years on the basis of consumer surveys.

There are three reasons why the consumer price index is not necessarily an accurate measure of the rate of inflation.[16] (1) There is the constant introduction of new goods to the market and (2) a change in the quality of existing goods. Both of these factors change the nature of the basket of goods more rapidly than every four years. (3) There is also the question of the substitution bias. In theory the substitution effect may be serious, but in reality it is not. Some products increase in price over the four-year cycle and consumers adjust their purchases accordingly, or products go in and out of fashion. If the price of coffee triples because of crop failure, people will drink less coffee. Therefore the weight given to coffee in the consumer price index will not be accurate after four years, and the effect on the CPI of the increase in the price of coffee will be overstated. However, it appears that consumers change their buying habits relatively slowly so the change will only have a gradual effect. A study by Genereux (1983) for Canada found that the effect of the substitution bias is to overstate the CPI by only a minor amount (approximately 0.15 to 0.20 percent).

The new-goods bias, however, may be more serious. Most new consumer goods, for example VCRs, microwave ovens, CD players, satellite dishes, and home computers, are at first very expensive. However, in a relatively short time their prices come down substantially as volumes increase. Since new goods are introduced in the CPI only every four years, it is possible that the index would miss the period of falling prices. In that case the index would again be biased upwards. Diewert (1985) thinks that the addition of the new-goods bias to the substitution bias could lead to an overestimation of the annual inflation rate by 0.5 to 1 percentage points.

Statistics Canada adjusts CPI calculations for quality changes for major commodity groups such as motor vehicles, appliances, clothing, and shelter. Fortin (1990), in a survey of the literature, argues that there is no reason why the current methods would create a bias in either direction in the calculation of the CPI. He therefore concludes that zero inflation is probably reached when the inflation rate is between 0.5 and 1 percent because of the substitution bias and the new-goods bias. To aim for zero inflation as measured by the CPI would actually be to aim for falling prices. But, falling prices are not desirable either because they too have damaging effects on the economy. For one thing, they would discourage spending since holding money would give a better return than holding goods. Furthermore, in periods of inflation nominal interest rates rise with prices, encouraging consumers to save money rather than to spend. The process does not work in reverse in periods of deflation: nominal interest rates cannot be negative. This serves as an additional incentive for people to hold on to their money and encourages further deflation.

The next question is whether a zero inflation rate, that is, a rate of 0.5 to 1.0 percent, as measured by the CPI, is desirable. What is wrong with an inflation rate of, say, 4 percent if everybody has learnt to live with 4 percent, meaning that pensions and other incomes are indexed to the rate of inflation?

One effect of inflation is on the cost of holding money. This is sometimes called "the shoe-leather effect" of inflation. Since high inflation leads to high interest rates the opportunity cost of holding money is relatively high, resulting in more money being kept in interest-bearing assets rather than cash. Therefore under inflation, people must make more trips to the bank to withdraw money. Inflation will therefore increase transaction costs (which include the shoe leather worn out by making the frequent trips). How important these transactions costs are is a matter of debate.[17]

Another effect of inflation is the need to change prices more frequently and thus to print new catalogues. This effect is known as the menu cost effect (see Chapter 5). Because of the expense of changing prices, changes may be made in big infrequent leaps, which could introduce distortions into the economy.

The government also uses inflation as a tax and is able to pay more of its bills through the printing press without having to raise taxes or borrow from the general public. The revenues generated by this tax are called **seigniorage**. The goverment will benefit even more if the tax and transfer system is not fully indexed, as is the case in Canada at present. Economists argue that the effect of inflation on the taxation of capital in particular is not efficient. Like any other tax, the inflation tax imposes a dead weight burden on society.

If inflation is unexpected, it has especially severe effects because it arbitrarily redistributes wealth among individuals. Debtors win and creditors lose. People on fixed incomes also lose. Renters lose and homeowners win, for high inflation tends to increase the relative price of housing, which is thought to be a good hedge against inflation.

It is also possible that inflation creates uncertainty and speculation about the future inflation rate. For that reason, inflation tends to divert talent into finance rather than the production of goods and services. The 1970s and 1980s saw inventions of new financial contracts, new banking techniques, and new corporate financial strategies as hedges against inflation (Howitt, 1990, p. 93). In that way, inflation reduces productivity growth. One study for Canada (Jarrett and Selody 1982) estimates that the effect of a permanent inflation rate of 1 percent a year is to reduce productivity growth by more than three-tenths of a percentage point. That does not sound like very much, but because of compounding, the present value of the gain from reducing inflation by one percentage point equals more than 16 times the current GDP, using a discount rate of 4 percent. Some economists, however, do not agree that the efficiency losses from inflation could be so large. Fortin (1990b, p. 146) points out that if these figures are correct, the reduction of inflation from 12 percent in 1980-81 to 4 percent in 1983 and after, should have raised the productivity growth rate by 2.4 percent annually. That did not happen. Lucas (1990), in surveying the literature, argues, "Despite much ingenuity on the part of theorists in identifying possible sources of inefficiency associated with inflation, there is no conclusive empirical evidence to support the view that average inflation has a negative effect on the growth rate of real GNP" (*ibid.*, p. 74).

There is some evidence that high inflation lowers productivity by leading to labour unrest. Countries with high inflation rates also have high strike records (*The Economist*, November 7, 1992). The higher the inflation rate, the more frequent wage negotiations need to be, and therefore the higher the risk of strikes. If prices were stable, wage increases would be justified only by a rise in productivity or individual performance. This situation could weaken the power of unions.

Lawrence Summers is quoted in *The Economist* (*ibid.*) as favouring an inflation rate of 2 to 3 percent rather than zero. One reason is that it would be possible to have negative real interest rates, which could pull an economy out of a recession. With zero inflation the real interest rate cannot be negative since the nominal interest rate cannot be negative. He also argues that a little inflation acts like a lubricant, helping relative prices and wages to adjust more efficiently. For example trade unions in declining industries are likely to resist a cut in nominal pay and yet be prepared to allow inflation to erode their real wages. Under zero inflation this escape would not be possible, a circumstance which could lead to greater labour unrest.

We now turn to the cost of getting to zero inflation. Using data from the early eighties, Howitt (1990, p. 105) estimates that the sacrifice ratio for Canada of reducing inflation is 4.7 percent of GNP for each percentage reduction in inflation.[18] Laidler and Robson (1993) put the sacrifice ratio at 3.6 percent. Scarth (1990), on the other hand, argues that the sacrifice ratio in getting the inflation rate down from 4 percent is higher than the sacrifice ratio was at 10 percent inflation, because the Phillips curve is flatter at lower inflation rates. Another factor that might lead to a higher sacrifice ratio is the presence of hysteresis. Workers might lose skills while they were unemployed and might therefore become permanently unemployed. And firms, because of the curtailment of their activities during the recession, might lose important markets to competitors because of lack of investments in R&D and training. The "sacrifice" would therefore affect long-term growth.[19]

Higher interest rates in combination with disinflation also lead to higher incomes for individuals holding corporate and government bonds. For this reason Peters (1990) argues that higher interest rates not only do not discourage consumer spending, but on the contrary, encourage consumption if there is a large government debt. Therefore, to achieve a certain level of nominal income contraction, interest rates would have to be raised to very high levels (Courchene, 1990, p. 182).

The cost of disinflation falls disproportionately on the poor and will therefore make our income distribution worse. From our survey in Chapter 6, we know that the poverty rate is very sensitive to the state of the economy. You are more likely to be poor when you are out of work.[20] When unemployment rises, it rises more quickly among the least advantaged groups. The high interest rate cost of disinflation also falls on those who are highly leveraged, such as debt-ridden farmers and mortgage holders. Interest rates that are higher than those in the United States also drive up the exchange rate, making it very difficult for the export sector to compete.

We can conclude that it is not clear that price stability will lead to an improvement in productivity and economic growth, particularly in view of the high cost of getting there. Because of the disproportionate burden of unemployment carried by the less fortunate in society, it is also not clear that even if productivity growth does improve, our well-being will improve.

Do We Need Provincial Stabilization Policies?

What have we learnt? It appears that some costly mistakes were made during the 1980s, the most serious being the inability of the federal government to reduce the deficit significantly in the mid-eighties. The high interest rates caused by the tight monetary policy led to a worsening of the deficit, resulting in increased fiscal stimulus, and therefore the need for an even tighter monetary policy, which in turn contributed to the severity of the recession of 1991-92. Federal tax increases implemented over the 1989-91 period can also explain the recession (Wilson, Dungan, and Murphy 1994). The high interest rates led to a very high exchange rate that made it difficult for exporters and importers to take advantage of the free trade agreement with the United States. The policies also appear to have worsened regional differences. Inflationary conditions in Ontario in particular forced the Bank of Canada to take action at the expense of other regions. Ontario's stimulative budget at the peak of a boom in 1988 was entirely inappropriate and went against the policies of the federal government. The 1991 Ontario budget repeated the pattern. Courchene wrote in 1991:

> The 1991 Ontario budget is truly a watershed document. Over a four-year period, it will effectively double Ontario's net debt—from 35 to 70 billion. No part of Canada is unaffected by its implications. It challenges the federal macro authorities approach to inflation targeting. It

creates a wedge in the nature of the social envelope across provinces and at the same time creates the perception if not the reality for the have-not provinces that Ontario may no longer be able to play its same role as paymaster for the transfer system (Courchene 1992, p. 216).

The downloading of the federal deficit, combined with irresponsible spending of some provincial governments, led in 1993 to a crisis in which, because of ballooning debts, most of the provinces, including Ontario, had to cut their spending substantially, thereby jeopardizing an already weak recovery.

There seems to be an urgent need for coordination of policy among all levels of government. In its constitutional package presented in September 1991, the federal government proposed the creation of a "Council of the Federation" to serve as an inter-governmental decision-making body, to supplement first ministers' conferences and finance ministers' meetings. The government suggested that a yearly budget timetable should be developed to allow for a better budget-making process involving both the federal and provincial governments. Economic policies would be harmonized, and guidelines would be drawn up for fiscal policies. The government also proposed the establishment of an independent agency to monitor and evaluate the macroeconomic policies of the two levels of government.

It is especially difficult to reach agreement about the need for coordination because of the long-standing conflict over shared-cost programs and the use of the federal spending power, and because of the wasteful overlap and duplication in many programs. In May 1991, the premiers of the western provinces suggested that the federal government should transfer its taxing power to the provinces so that they could stimulate their own economies as they saw fit. The debate about the desirability of provincial stabilization policies goes back to an analysis by Oates (1968)[21] which gave a rationale for leaving stabilization policies to the federal government. He made three points. If all provinces experience the same economic cycles simultaneously, there will be no point for the provincial governments to pursue their own policies. That is better done by the federal government. Second, the marginal propensity to import is likely to be higher for provincial governments than the federal government because of the strong economic linkages between the provinces. Therefore the spillover effects of provincial policies will be larger than for federal policies (the multiplier will be smaller). Third, given almost perfect mobility of capital, deficit financing of provincial governments will lead to large debts held outside each province, and will therefore be a drain on provincial wealth. Two opposing effects will occur if a provincial government increases demand through deficit financing. Demand will indeed go up immediately, but the subsequent interest payments to non-residents will drain purchasing power from the province. For these three reasons, he argued that provincial stabilization policies are not desirable.

But Oates has had many critics. Gramlich (1991) points out that the economic cycles are not necessarily co-ordinated. At the time of writing, for example, the British Columbia economy is performing much better than the economies of eastern and central Canada. During much of the seventies, the Alberta economy was booming because of the huge increases in oil prices. Furthermore, the growth of the service sector in all parts of Canada makes provincial multipliers larger (since services are usually bought locally), and therefore makes fiscal policies more effective than Oates assumed. We also know that federal deficit financing increases foreign indebtedness by creating a deficit on the current account because capital appears to be almost as mobile between countries as inside countries. Another factor is that fiscal policies work better under the fixed exchange rates that exist between the provinces. Under the flexible exchange rates faced by the federal government vis-a-vis the rest of the world, the higher interest rates caused by federal government borrowing will push up the value of the Canadian dollar. A higher value of the dollar will discourage exports and encourage imports, reducing aggregate demand and employment.[22] Gramlich argues that because the provinces do not have this problem, provincial fiscal multipliers are likely to be higher than the federal fiscal multiplier, and therefore provincial stabilization is a good idea.

However, leaving more of the task of stabilization to the provincial governments might make it more difficult to stabilize the national debt.

According to Kneebone (1989), the stability conditions necessary in a federation to keep the debt-to-GDP ratio constant are more stringent than those required in a unitary state because of the feedbacks in a federal state between the two levels of government. Macroeconomic stability is possible but is less likely if more than one level of government is running bond-financed deficits. Furthermore, provincial stabilization policies would not be an improvement over the present situation because they would not solve the problem of co-ordination:

> At this juncture of Canada's history, the issue of **intergovernmental** collaboration is extremely important for future economic performance. The proposed Council of the Federation — perhaps with a related institution, a "Federal-Provincial Commission on the Economic Union", which would be an advisory body of experts — could contribute enormously to improvement of policy performance in this area. I would propose, therefore, that these institutions be enshrined in the Constitution, with a mandate to improve the harmonization of economic policies. I also endorse the notion that an independent agency be given the mandate to monitor and assess policy in this area on a regular basis.
>
> I believe that, more importantly, these institutions could also contribute to a reversal of recent federal-provincial adversarial relationships and to the evolution of a constructive and positive dynamic built on the spirit of partnership. More than any constitutional limitations on government, that would serve to ensure the living standards and even the democratic rights and freedoms of future Canadians. That is the kind of Canada I want to live in, and that I want my children to inherit (Purvis, 1992, p. 82-83).

Conclusions

In this chapter we first surveyed the literature about rules in economic policy making. Many people would argue that, given the mess we are in, economic policy is too important to be left to politicians who appear to act in their own self-interest much of the time. Legislation might indeed be necessary to enforce some measure of fiscal prudence on governments. However, for rules to have the desired effect, they have to be simple and clear. But simple rules could have draconian results. For example, a requirement for balanced budgets would force the government to act in a pro-cyclical fashion and would intensify the economic cycles. Because of the operation of automatic stabilizers, a balanced-budget rule would require the government to increase taxes or cut expenditures during a recession. More complicated rules (such as a balanced budget over a cycle) would be impossible to administer. But simple rules might be appropriate for lower levels of government.

Our short survey of stabilization policies in the eighties and early nineties showed the roots of what has gone wrong, that is, a ballooning public debt that makes it impossible for the government to conduct appropriate stabilization policies in the face of very high unemployment. During the boom period of the 1980s, the federal government provided too much stimulus to the economy by running deficits, leaving it to the Bank of Canada to pursue restraint. Monetary restraint under the zero-inflation policy led to high interest rates that further increased the deficit and also pushed up the value of the Canadian dollar and created more unemployment. Attempts to control the federal deficit imperilled the situation for the provincial governments, whose deficits grew faster than that of the federal government. We also saw that persistent budget deficits necessarily create deficits on the current account, leading to foreign borrowing. The result is that a large proportion of our national debt is held by foreigners, and that the burden on our children has grown. Clearly there is a need for the federal and provincial governments to act together to deal with the situation.

TOPICS FOR DISCUSSION

1. Do you think that people in general have changed their inflationary expectations to expect zero inflation? If so what effect will that have on economic policy?

2. Sometimes the financial press raises the spectre of a full-fledged debt crisis. What do they mean?

3. Why did Jacques Parizeau, the leader of the Parti québécois, say that if Quebec becomes an independent country it would like to use the Canadian dollar as its currency?

RECOMMENDED READING

Good surveys of the zero-inflation debate can be found in *Taking Aim: The Debate on Zero Inflation* (York *et al.* 1990) and also *The Great Canadian Disinflation* (Laidler and Robson 1993). For critical assessments of the preoccupation with inflation, read *False Promises, The Failure of Conservative Economics* (Allen and Rosenbluth 1992) and *Hard Heads and Soft Hearts* (Blinder 1987).

References

Allen, Richard C. and Gideon Rosenbluth. *False Promises. The Failure of Conservative Economics*. Vancouver: New Star Books, 1992.

Barber, Clarence L. "Monetary and Fiscal Policy in the 1980s." In *False Promises*, Richard C. Allen and Gideon Rosenbluth (*ibid.*): 101-23.

Blinder, Alan S. *Hard Heads, Soft Hearts: Tough-Minded Economics for a Just Society*. Reading, Mass: Addison-Wesley Publishing Co., 1987.

Boothe, Paul. "Federal Budgeting in the 1990s: The End of Fiscal Federalism." In *The February 1992 Federal Budget*, eds. Thomas J. Courchene and Martin Prochowny Kingston, On: John Deutsch Institute for the Study of Economic Policy, 1992.

Bruce, Neil and Douglas D. Purvis. "Consequences of Government Budget Deficits." In *Fiscal and Monetary Policy*, research coordinator John Sargent (1986): 43-85.

Canada. Department of Finance. *The Budget 1993* Ottawa: Department of Finance, April 1993.

Carmichael, Ted. "Federal and Provincial Deficits and Debts." In *Avoiding a Crisis: Proceedings of a Workshop on Canada's Fiscal Outlook January 27 , 1993. Commentary*, eds. Irene Ip and William B.P. Robson. Toronto: C.D. Howe Institute, February 1993.

Carter, George E. "Federal Restraints to the Growth of Transfer Payments to the Provinces since 1986-87: An Assessment." *The Canadian Tax Journal* (forthcoming), 1994 Toronto: Ryerson Polytechnical University.

Crow, John W. "The Work of Canadian Monetary Policy." [speech] Eric Hanson Memorial Lecture at the University of Alberta, Edmonton. January 18 1988. Edmonton. Reprinted in the *Bank of Canada Review*, February 1988.

Courchene, Thomas J. "Rethinking the Macro Mix: The Case for Provincial Stabilization Policy." In *Taking Aim*, ed. Robert C. York (1990): 173-229.

Courchene, Thomas J. *Rearrangements: The Courchene Papers*. Oakville: Mosaic Press, 1992.

Diewert, W. Erwin. "A Note on the Neglect of New Goods Bias." [unpublished manuscript] September 1985 Vancouver: University of British Columbia.

The Economist. "Rules v. discretion," March 2, 1991," Balancing the government's books," January 25, 1992; "A short history of inflation," February 22, 1992; "The future is not what it used to be," June 13, 1992; "Zero inflation. How low is low enough ?" November 7, 1992.

The Financial Post. "Debt Imperils All Provinces, Report Warns," May 27, 1993.

Fortin, Pierre. "Do We Measure Inflation Correctly." In *Zero Inflation*, ed. Richard G. Lipsey (1990): 109-31.

Fortin, Pierre. "Can the Costs of an Anti-Inflation Policy Be Reduced ?" In *Taking Aim*, ed. Robert C. York (1990): 135-73.

Genereux, Pierre A. "Impact of the Choice of Formulae on the Canadian Consumer Price Index." In *Price Level Measurement: Proceedings from a Conference Sponsored by Statistics Canada*, eds. W.E. Diewert and C. Montmarquette (1985): 489-511.

Gramlich, Edward M. "Canadian Fiscal Federalism: An Outsider's View." In *Provincial Public Finances, Vol 2, Plaudits, Problems and Prospects*, ed. Melville McMillan Toronto: Canadian Tax Foundation, 1991.

Grubel, Herbert G., Douglas D. Purvis and William M. Scarth. *Limits to Government: Controlling Deficits and Debt in Canada, The Canada Round: A Series on the Economics of Constitutional Renewal*. Toronto: C.D. Howe Institute, 1992.

Howitt, Peter. "Zero Inflation as a Long-Term Target for Monetary Policy." In *Zero Inflation*, ed. Richard G. Lipsey (1990): 67-109.

Jarrett, Peter and Jack Selody. "The Productivity-Inflation Nexus in Canada, 1963-79." *Review of Economics and Statistics* 64 (August 1982): 361-67.

Kneebone, Ronald D. "On Macro-economic Instability under a Monetarist Policy Rule in a Federal Economy." *Canadian Journal of Economics* 22 (1989): 673-85.

Kuo, Chin-Yan and Bob Hamilton. "Reforming the Canadian Sales Tax System: A General Equilibrium Analysis." *Canadian Tax Journal* 39 (1991): 113-30.

Kydland, Finn and Edward Prescott. "Rules Rather Than Discretion. The Inconsistency of Optimal Plans." *Journal of Political Economy* 85 (1977):

Laidler, David E. W. and William B.P. Robson. *The Great Canadian Disinflation: The Economics and Politics of Monetary Policy in Canada, 1988-93*. Toronto: C.D. Howe Institute, 1993.

Laliberte, Lucie. "Foreign Investment in the Canadian Bond Market, 1978 to 1990." *Canadian Economic Observer* (June 1991): 3.19-3.34.

Lipsey, Richard G. ed. *Zero Inflation: The Goal of Price Stability*. Toronto: The C.D. Howe Institute, 1990.

Lucas, Robert F. "The Case for Stable, But Not Zero Inflation." In *Taking Aim*, ed. Robert C. York (1990): 65-81.

Oates, Wallace E. "The Theory of Public Finance in a Federal System." *Canadian Journal of Economics* 1 (1968): 37-54.

Peters, Douglas. "Fallacies and Detriments of a Zero-Inflation Policy." In *Taking Aim*, ed. Robet C. York (1990): 111-21.

Purvis, Douglas D. and Constance Smith. "Fiscal Policy in Canada: 1963-84." In *Fiscal and Monetary Policy*, Research Coordinator Sargent: 1-43.

Purvis, Douglas D. "Growth and Stabilization, Burdens of Government Policy Failures: A Comment on Grubel and Scarth." In *Limits to Government*, eds. Hubert G. Grubel *et al.* (1992): 68-85.

Romer, Christina D. "Is the Stabilization of the Postwar Economy a Figment of the Data?" *American Economic Review* 76 (June 1986): 314-34.

Ruggeri, G.C. and D. van Wart. "Overoptimism and the GST: A Critical Comment on the Hamilton & Duo General Equilibrium Analysis." *Canadian Tax Journal* 40 (1992): 148-61.

Sargent, John research coordinator. *Fiscal and Monetary Policy*. Toronto: The University of Toronto Press, 1986. Prepared for The Royal Commission on the Economic Union and Development Prospects for Canada.

Scarth, William M. "Are the Costs of Getting to Zero Too High ?" In *Taking Aim*, ed. Robert C. York (1990): 81-104.

Scarth, William M. "Provincial Stabilization Policy: Coordination Issues." In *Limits to Government*, eds. Hubert C. Grubel *et al.* (1992): 44-67.

Sparks, Gordon R. "The Theory and Practice of Monetary Policy in Canada: 1945-83." In *Fiscal and Monetary Policy*, research coordinator John Sargent (1986): 119-51.

Wilson, Thomas, Peter Dungan, and Steve Murphy. "The Sources of the Recession in Canada: 1989-1992." *Canadian Business Economics* 2 (Winter 1994): 3-16.

York, Robert C. ed. *Taking Aim: The Debate on Zero Inflation*. Toronto: The C.D. Howe Institute, 1990.

Endnotes

1   See *The Economist*, June 13, 1992. Short-term economic forecasts have become more accurate. Unfortunately, the biggest mistakes are to forecast turning-points (when the economy dips into a recession). This is when accurate forecasts are most needed.

2   The original analysis of time inconsistency is from Kydland and Prescott (1977). For a clear discussion, see *The Economist*, March 2, 1991.

3   There appears to be a link between the independence of the central bank and the rate of inflation in a country (*The Economist*, March 2, 1991). The more freedom from government interference a bank has in pursuing a goal of price stability, the lower is the resulting inflation rate. Independence can be measured by characteristics such as the presence of government officials on the board of the

bank and the existence of rules forcing the central bank automatically to finance budget deficits.

4   This is easier in theory than in practice. The problem is that the business cycle is not well-defined. It is difficult to determine whether the economy is in a prolonged recession or whether it has entered a slow-growth period or whether the expansion is strong enough to generate a surplus budget. This is one of the reasons why the debt-to-GDP ratio has increased from cycle to cycle. Bruce and Purvis (1986, p. 68) argue that a cyclically balanced budget cannot be enforced.

5   The summary is based on Barber (1992).

6   For a survey, see Bruce and Purvis (1986) and Sparks (1986).

7   This section is based on Laidler and Robson (1993), p. 87-92.

8   For a criticism of monetary and fiscal policies after 1988, see Peters (1990).

9   Hamilton and Kuo (1991) estimated these gains to be in the region of 1.4 percent of GDP.

10 See also Boothe (1992).

11 This section is based on Bruce and Purvis (1986).

12 It is sometimes argued that standard accounting practices are not followed in calculating the deficit, and therefore the deficit does not give a good indication of the fiscal health of the state. The budget deficit does not separate current spending from capital investments. In business, investments are depreciated over several years; in government, investments are charged to a single year. It is therefore suggested that governments should compile public-sector balance sheets as companies do, complete with a calculation of net worth. Because of the necessity to include the capitalised value of future state pensions and social security benefits which will increase as populations get older, net worth calculations for countries would probably look pretty dismal (*The Economist*, January 25, 1992).

13 This deficit effect can be avoided. A deficit during a recession will have a beneficial effect, because the stimulus given will prevent some of the lost output effects of the recession. It will also promote investments by ensuring the economy works closer to capacity. If the government runs a balanced budget after the recession is over, private investment will decrease for reasons outlined above. If on the other hand, the government then runs a surplus which it uses to buy back the bonds, there are no long-term effects of the deficit.

14 The national income identity gives G-T=(M-X) + (S-I); i.e. a budget deficit will have no effect on the current account if there is a savings surplus in the economy. If there is not, it will lead to an equivalent deficit on the current account. The savings rate in Canada has been halved since the early eighties which explains why the current account deficit did not appear until the late eighties.

15 See Crow (1988). In this Canada was not alone. By November 1992, the Reserve Bank of New Zealand, the Bank of Japan, and the Bundesbank had all stated their intention of aiming for an inflation rate of less than 2 percent (*The Economist*, November 7, 1992).

16 The following is based on Fortin (1990).

17 For a survey of the literature, see Howitt (1990).

18 For a discussion of the sacrifice ratio, see Chapter 5.

19 However, the evidence that hysteresis in Canada is a problem is not compelling. See Laidler and Robson (1993).

20 For an impassioned analysis of the cost to the poor of anti-inflationary policies, See Blinder (1987, Chapter 2).

21 This section is based on Scarth (1992).

22 Courchene (1992) argues that this is a reason for the Bank of Canada to fix the exchange rate against the U.S. dollar. He feels that this is necessary because under free trade, goods, services, and financial flows move north-south, rather than east-west.

10

Canadian Trade Policies

After completing this chapter you will understand the case for free trade and the case for limited free trade as embodied in a free trade area. This will enable you to form your own conclusion of the likely net benefits to Canada of the North American Free Trade Agreement.

So far we have avoided a discussion of one of the most controversial policies of the Canadian government: free trade with the United States. In this chapter, I will discuss free trade in general, the evolution of GATT and Canadian trade policies, the benefits and costs of the Free Trade Agreement with the United States (FTA), and the benefits and costs of the expanded North American Free Trade Agreement (NAFTA).

The Case for Free Trade

The case for free trade is based on the theory of comparative advantage, a theory that every first-year economics student is exposed to. The theory, which goes back to Ricardo, shows that in the presence of perfect competition and different relative efficiencies in production, countries will gain from trade. If country A's opportunity cost of producing commodity x in terms of commodity y is less than that of country B, country A has a comparative advantage in the production of x (see also the discussion in Chapter 7). It can be easily demonstrated that country B will have a corresponding comparative advantage in the production of commodity y. If both countries specialize and export the commodity in which they have a comparative advantage, both countries will be better off in that they will be able to consume more of both commodities. The distribution of gains between the two countries will be determined by the terms of trade.

New research in trade theory demonstrates that if the assumption of perfect competition is relaxed, the gains from trade may be even larger than the static model predicts because of economies of scale, and the dynamic changes caused by the increased competition introduced by free trade. The newer theories of trade also take account of "learning by doing." Early entry in an export market with a new product may create an advantage that other producers will not be able to emulate. By being first, a country's producers can always make sure that it can capitalize on the high profits possible before imitators enter the market.

The prediction that free trade will make a country better off in terms of its ability to consume more goods has to be qualified. In the first place, it is well-known in international trade theory that a country whose exports or imports are large enough to affect world prices can use a tariff or export tax to turn the terms of trade in its favour. The country will be better off with a tariff than without, provided the country has sufficient information to set the tariff at the "optimum" level, and **provided other countries do not retaliate.**[1] If retaliation does occur, as it is likely to in the real world, everybody will become worse off. Second, as pointed out in Chapters 1 and 6, the notion of economic efficiency pays no attention to income distribution. A dollar is a dollar; it does not matter if an additional dollar is pocketed by a rich person or a poor person. Therefore the gains from free trade do not necessarily improve a country's well-being, since trade may have an adverse effect on the distribution of income. In fact, the gains from trade are unlikely to be evenly distributed, but given that the gainers can compensate the losers (otherwise a net gain would not have been possible), it is usually assumed that trade makes a country better off, even if compensation is never paid. It can be shown that free trade will tend to equalize factor prices around the world and to hurt a country's scarce factor of production. If, for example, Mexico has relatively more unskilled labour than Canada, free trade between Canada and Mexico will raise the wages of unskilled labour in Mexico and lower them in Canada.

Traditional trade theory also shows that regional free trade, for example in a free trade area, customs union, or common market, is not necessarily beneficial.[2] It all depends on the balance between **trade diversion** and **trade creation**. Trade diversion occurs if a customs union or free trade agreement forces a country to buy expensive products from a partner country rather than from the cheapest world source. Trade creation occurs if the participating countries now buy some products from lower-cost producers among the member countries rather than from more expensive home producers.

The benefits of free trade have often been disputed, most recently by the environmental movement. Obviously trade and therefore trade policies have an effect on the environment by altering the volume and location of global production and consumption. Some argue that trade increases consumption and is therefore detrimental to the environment. Others argue that trade helps the environment by raising incomes and living standards. With higher living standards there is usually more interest in, and more money for, the environment.[3]

More specifically, it can be demonstrated that if the production of a good generates pollution, and if trade allows a country to import that good, then trade is good for the environment in that particular country. On the other hand, if the country exports the good, trade worsens the country's environment, a loss in welfare that might outweigh the standard income gains from trade. The loss of welfare would disappear, though, if the country had pollution taxes (see Chapter 2). Similarly, if pollution is caused by the consumption of the good rather than the production of the good, the opposite is true. Thus the opening of trade improves the local environment if the good is exported and worsens it if it is imported, assuming there is no pollution tax (Anderson 1992).

The strongest theoretical challenge to the benefits of free trade has its origin in the newer trade theories:

If there were an Economist's Creed, it would surely contain the affirmations "I understand the Principle of Comparative Advantage" and "I advocate Free Trade." For one hundred seventy years, the appreciation that international trade benefits a country whether it is "fair" or not has been one of the touchstones of professionalism in economics. Comparative advantage is not just an idea both simple and profound; it is an idea that conflicts directly with both stubborn popular prejudices and powerful interests. This combination makes the defense of free trade as close to a sacred tenet as any idea in economics.

Yet the case for free trade is currently more in doubt than at any time since the 1817 publication of Ricardo's *Principles of Political Economy*. This is not because of the political pressures for protection, which have triumphed in the past without shaking the intellectual foundations of comparative advantage theory. Rather, it is because of the changes that have recently taken place in the theory of international trade itself. While new developments in international trade theory may not yet be familiar to the profession at large, they have been substantial and radical. In the last ten years the traditional constant returns, perfect competition models of international trade have been supplemented and to some extent supplanted by a new breed of models that emphasizes increasing returns and imperfect competition. These new models call into doubt the extent to which actual trade can be explained by comparative advantage; they also open the possibility that government intervention in trade via import restrictions, export subsidies, and so on may under some circumstances be in the national interest after all (Krugman, 1987, p. 131–32).

There are two cases made for interfering with free trade; one is the **strategic trade policy** case.[4] Assume that economies of scale are so large in an industry, for example aircraft manufacturing, that there is only room for one firm. If two firms enter the industry they will both incur losses. Therefore the firm that establishes itself in the industry will earn above-normal profits. If through government subsidies a country can ensure these excess profits are earned by its own domestic firm, then the country has raised its own national income, provided the initial subsidies are less than the discounted value of the excess profits. Attempts by governments to divert production to their own countries through selective subsidies are referred to as strategic trade policies.

The other case that is made for interfering with free trade is the **externalities case**, which rests on the presence of positive spillover effects. If an export industry has large spillovers on other domestic firms because of its large R&D activity, the market would operate more efficiently if the industry were subsidized.

Nevertheless, even though it may be advantageous in some special circumstances for a country to interfere with trade, interference is not always the best policy. In the first place, subsidization for strategic policy reasons is a form of beggar-thy-neighbour policy by which one country tries to gain at the expense of another; it is therefore likely to provoke retaliation,[5] and a subsidy war will make everybody worse off. That is why export subsidies are also illegal under the GATT rules. Second, the few studies of strategic behaviour in particular industries show that the potential gains are relatively small (Baldwin 1992). Third, because the gains depend on so much on the degree of market concentration and the behaviour of rival firms, economists are reluctant to recommend government intervention. Fourth, if it becomes known that a government is prepared to subsidize selected industries for strategic purposes, the government will be subject to pressure from various interest groups, and its choice of firms may be made in the interest of political gain.

The Development and Function of GAT T

Immediately after the Second World War, negotiations took place within the United Nations framework for new international cooperation in world trade.[6] The idea was to establish a formal international trade organization as a companion to the International Monetary Fund and the International Bank for Reconstruction and Development (the World Bank). Largely because of opposition from the United States, the new organization was never formed but much of the groundwork became part of the General Agreement on Tariffs and Trade adopted in 1947.[7] This is a multilateral treaty containing a set of rules that govern the trade policies of its signatories and the trade relations between them. It establishes the right of countries to sell their products abroad, and establishes the limits within which a country can restrict imports of goods and otherwise protect its domestic producers against foreign competition. While the basic rules are still intact, they have been amended and supplemented as a result of international negotiations. The main features are as follows:

- Each country is bound by most-favoured-nations (MFN) treatment to all contracting parties. This means that if favourable treatment is given to one member, it must also be given to all other members. Later, exceptions were granted for customs unions and free trade areas. Countries were also allowed to extend and continue tariff preferences for imports from developing countries.

- Each country is bound not to increase tariffs that have been agreed on through GATT negotiations. To increase tariffs, a country would have to reach agreement with all of its trading partners on compensation by reducing other tariffs and complying with specified procedures.

- No imported product may be treated less favourably than domestically produced products with respect to laws, regulations, and requirements ("national treatment").

- Quantitative restrictions (quotas) are prohibited except in special circumstances. The exceptions are for agricultural products where these are subject to government support programs that restrict the production or sale of the commodity; for serious balance-of-payments difficulties; to prevent "serious" injury to domestic producers; for products covered by the Multifibre Arrangement, that is, textiles; and for health and other reasons, ranging from protection of national treasures to the protection of public morals. Quantitative restrictions cannot be used as a "means of arbitrary or unjustifiable discrimination between countries where the same conditions prevail, or a disguised restriction on international trade" (Article XX).

- Export subsidies are prohibited, except for agricultural and primary products, while domestic subsidies are allowed provided GATT is notified. A country can impose a countervailing duty on a product subject to an export subsidy if it can prove it has suffered material injury as a result of the subsidy. An importing country can also impose anti-dumping duties if a product is sold at less than its normal value and if it can prove material injury. There are also general safeguard provisions that allow an importing country to impose tariffs or quotas if imports are causing or threatening serious injury.

- There is an elaborate mechanism for settling disputes, often through the use of independent dispute panels.

There have been eight successive rounds of tariff negotiations, the last of which (the Uruguay Round) was concluded in December 1993. The most successful in lowering trade barriers were probably the first round of 1947; the Kennedy Round, 1964–67, and the Tokyo Round, 1973–79. The framework for the negotiations has been determined partly by the authority given to the U.S. administration by Congress. For example, in the Tokyo Round, the U.S. negotiators had authority to negotiate reductions of up to 50–60 percent of U.S. rates.

The results of tariff reductions under the GATT have been impressive. It is estimated that for the United States the average tariff on dutiable imports was reduced from the 32 percent that prevailed during and immediately after Second World War to 12–13 percent between 1950 and 1965 and to 6 percent in 1980. The equivalent figures for Canada during the same period were 21 percent, 17–18 percent, and 14–15 percent (Stone, 1992, p. 60). Deardoff and Stern (1986) estimate Canada's average tariff in the mid-eighties at 5.2 percent, marginally higher than that of the United States, which was 4.3 percent.

After the conclusion of the Tokyo Round there was a general agreement that a new round of negotiations should follow, with an emphasis on non-tariff barriers to trade. That was because, after the lowering of tariff barriers, the member nations proved themselves adept at devising other barriers to trade that fell outside the GATT rules. This process, which has been referred to as the **new protectionism,** developed particularly during the late seventies and early eighties as a response to the slowdown in economic growth in most nations, as well as to the structural adjustments brought on by globalization. Established industries that find themselves in difficulties frequently call on governments to protect them from imports. Much to the dismay of Canadians, the United States seemed particularly prone to use its contingent trade laws on anti-dumping and countervailing duties and safeguard provisions to protect its own industries.

Another popular protectionist measure was the large-scale use of voluntary export restraints, particularly to force Japanese producers to reduce their exports of cars to the United States. This measure was first introduced by the United States in 1981, and Canada quickly followed suit.[8] But the Japanese turned out to be the gainers from this measure, for they capitalized on the resulting shortage of Japanese cars in the U.S. markets by raising their prices. This measure is estimated to have cost the U.S. economy almost $1 billion dollars a year, most of it as a direct transfer of money to Japan in the form of higher profits (Crandall 1985). Some other protectionist measures include local-content requirements, government procurement policies, export-credit subsidies, and various bureaucratic barriers.[9] The latest possibility is the use of environmental legislation as a barrier to trade.

The previous GATT negotiations had also left a legacy of unsolved issues, including restrictions on imports of agricultural products, especially meat, dairy products, wheat, eggs, sugar, and oil seed, by many industrialized countries, including Canada; restrictions on imports of textiles, clothing, and footwear; and restrictions imposed by the European Union (EU) on imports of television and electronic equipment from Japan, Korea, and Taiwan. A particularly sore point in relations between North America and the EU was the EU's agricultural policy. The policy had started as an effort to guarantee high prices for European farmers by undertaking to buy their produce if the prices fell below specified levels. But the support prices were set too high, and as a result the EU had to store large quantities of food. At the end of 1985, European stockpiles consisted of 780,000 tons of beef, 1.2 American million tons of butter, and 12 million tons of wheat (Krugman, 1991, p. 194). In an effort to get rid of the surplus, the EU started to subsidize exports. The result was depressed world farm prices and substantial hardship for farmers in countries that were not able to enter the subsidy war. In Canada, prairie farmers were particularly adversely affected.

The Uruguay Round

The Uruguay Round began in 1986. The ambitious agenda covered most of the unresolved GATT issues, including agricultural trade, with the exception of the compatibility of environmental legislation with GATT rules. In particular, the negotiations were intended to remove tariffs and non-tariff measures and to bring a large number of restrictive bilateral trade arrangements within the GATT framework. Another objective was to enlarge the GATT rules to include the growing trade in services, the protection of intellectual property, and barriers to foreign investment (Stone, 1992, p. 222). Fourteen negotiating groups set to work, each dealing with a different area: tariffs, non-tariff measures, natural resource-based products, textiles and clothing, agriculture, tropical products, agreements and arrangements pertaining to multilateral trade negotiations, safeguards, subsidies and countervailing measures, trade-related aspects of intellectual property rights (including trade in counterfeit goods, such as imitation Gucci watches), dispute settlement, trade-related investment measures, and the functioning of the GATT system). The negotiations, which were exceedingly complex, saw the formation of various coalitions of like-minded countries.

Canada was a member of the Cairns group, which consisted of fourteen countries trying to reduce obstacles to trade in agricultural products. The Cairns group did not include the United States, the European Union or Japan. In the negotiations Canada was caught between the need to serve the interests of the western grain producers and those of eastern poultry and dairy producers. Our government found itself in the untenable position of arguing for the continuation of marketing boards, which effectively impose a prohibited tariff on imports, while at the same time arguing in favour of trade liberalization for other agricultural products such as grains.

The negotiations were finally concluded on December 15, 1993; the treaty will come into force July 1, 1995. The main features of the treaty are the following:

1. The creation of a new international body: The World Trade Organization with stronger powers than GATT, particularly in the settlement of disputes.

2. Agriculture, textiles, and some services, with the notable exception of telecommunications, shipping, and financial services, were included.

3. A large section of the treaty set out the basic principles and rules of intellectual property rights; these go beyond existing world conventions on patents, copyright, and so on.

Environmentalists have been critical of GATT for its treatment of environmental issues. Their feeling that the GATT rules did not protect the environment resulted from a judgement by a GATT disputes panel in late 1991 that found the United States in breach of GATT rules in blocking imports of tuna fish from Mexico, which had used nets that also killed dolphins (*The Economist*, February 27, 1993). Under the U.S. Marine Mammals Protection Act, tuna was not to be imported from any country that had a weak policy on the protection of dolphins, or whose fishermen killed more than one and one-quarter times as many dolphins as the American fishing fleet did in that year. In its ruling, the GATT panel argued that imported products must not be treated any differently from domestic products. That is, the methods used in producing a product are not a reason to discriminate against it. The panel also ruled that although a country can restrain trade to protect animal health or natural resources in its own country, it has no right to do so to protect such things outside its own country. Furthermore, a country cannot restrict trade in one product to enforce unrelated environmental policies; therefore the United States cannot restrict trade in tuna to enforce policies related to dolphins.

GATT of course does not want countries to use technical standards as disguised barriers to trade. How a country chooses to produce a product is its own affair. Some countries choose to have strict pollution laws, and other countries have strict labour laws, but GATT officials argue that such rules should not affect exports and imports. Environmentalists object to GATT on the grounds that:

- Trade liberalisation encourages economic growth, and so damages the environment.
- GATT (and the proposed North American Free Trade Agreement), by limiting national sovereignty, limits the right of countries to apply whatever environmental measures they choose.
- GATT does not allow countries to keep out a product because of the way it is produced or harvested.
- GATT prevents a country imposing countervailing duties on imports produced under lower environmental standards than its own. It also discourages subsidies, which are one way to compensate producers for meeting higher environmental standards than their rivals.
- GATT will — if certain Uruguay-round proposals are agreed — encourage the harmonisation of product standards. This would expose higher standards on, for instance, food additives or pesticide residues, to challenge as trade barriers.
- GATT prevents countries imposing export bans, which they may want to use to protect, say, their own forests or elephants. American environmentalists want to ban the export of certain pesticides that are prohibited in the United States but sold to developing countries.
- GATT frowns on the use of trade measures to influence environmental policy outside a country's territory. Yet increasingly the issues that arouse environmental passion are those affecting what greens call the "global commons" — the oceans and atmosphere, animal and plant species threatened with extinction — that concern all countries.
- GATT may undermine international environmental agreements, through its prohibition of trade measures that discriminate against individual nations. Yet such measures may be the most effective way for countries that play by the rules of an international agreement to penalise others that do not.
- GATT resolves disputes in a secretive way, without allowing environmentalists to put their arguments and without making important papers on a case available to them.

"Bow your head, Adam Smith?"
(*The Economist*, February 27, 1993, p. 26).

However, it can be demonstrated that trade policy is not the most efficient means of minimizing pollution. For example, it can be shown that an export tax is less effective than a pollution tax. On the other hand, trade policies by which countries discriminate against countries that do not abide by the rules can be important in bringing about the multilateral cooperation needed to deal with trans-border environmental problems. The difficulty is to create incentives for countries to cooperate, and trade policies are seen as one of the few available instruments for encouraging cooperation (Anderson and Blackhurst, 1992, p. 5). The Montreal Protocol has a provision for trade sanctions.

GATT officials realize the need for some rules on environmental matters. For example there should be a set of defined circumstances in which trade measures would be permitted under international environmental agreements. Trade measures against non-signatories could be permitted if taken with the agreement of a specified quorum of countries and if there were an appeal procedure. (*The Economist*, February 27, 1993). However, *The Economist* (*ibid.*) argues that GATT can act only on a consensus among its members, and there is no consensus on the integration of trade and environmental issues.

Canada's Push for Free Trade with the United States

Historically, Canadian trade policy was to a large extent determined by the trade policies of her main trading partners, the United States and Britain. Between 1854 and 1866 there was free trade between Canada and the United States through the Reciprocity Treaty. The treaty was terminated by the United States in response to friction arising because of the American Civil War and the imposition of protective tariffs by the Province of Canada before Confederation. The United States then turned protectionist and was to remain so until the mid-thirties. In 1878 under Sir John A. Macdonald, Canada implemented its own protectionist policy (the National Policy) which was designed to protect its fledging manufacturing industries, and which in the process fostered east-west trade to keep the new country together. The building of the national railway capable of moving both goods and people east and west, was also an integral part of the National Policy.[10]

Britain, on the other hand followed a low-tariff policy that Canada tried to change through much of the period, to gain preferential access to the British market. Canada provided similar preferential access to goods from Britain and other countries in the British Empire.

The U.S. high tariff policy was changed in 1934 under the new Roosevelt administration. Congress delegated to the President the authority to lower tariffs by up to 50 percent in return for reciprocal tariff reductions and concessions by other countries. As a result both Canadian and U.S. tariffs were reduced.

After the Second World War, Canada came to be increasingly dependent on trade with the United States because of the erosion of traditional European markets due to the creation of the Common Market in Europe. In particular, the entry of Britain into the Common Market in 1973 was a serious blow to Canada's trade prospects outside North America. The interdependence of the Canadian and American economies was reinforced by the Defence Production Sharing Agreement of 1959 and the Canada-United States Automotive Agreement of 1965 (the Auto Pact), which established free trade in motor vehicles and parts.

During the seventies, the interdependence of the two countries became a major political issue. In 1972, the Secretary of State for External Affairs, Mitchell Sharp, outlined three possibilities for Canadian trade policy (see Economic Council of Canada, 1976, p. 6–7). The first option would maintain the current relationship with the United States, with only minimal adjustments to policy; the second option would move towards closer integration with the United States; and the third would pursue a long-term strategy of developing and strengthening the Canadian economy and other aspects of national life, in the process reducing Canada's dependence on the United States. Mr. Sharp chose the third option as the most likely to ensure Canadian sovereignty, independence, and distinctiveness.

In retrospect, it could be argued that the government followed the first option rather than the third. Admittedly, in 1976, Canada did sign an agreement with the Common Market for greater economic cooperation, an agreement seen at the time as a concrete example of the third option. But there were no preferential tariffs involved or any other specific agreements for enhancing trade between the two parties. Not surprisingly, an agreement for mere cooperation did not lead to any concrete results. On the contrary, since then Canadian trade with the Common Market has declined in importance.

However, in the late seventies and early eighties, a momentum in favour of free trade with the United States was developing, led by the Economic Council of Canada, the Standing Senate Committee on Foreign Affairs, and the C.D. Howe Research Institute. In addition, the Macdonald Commission in its *Report on the Economic Union and Development Prospects for Canada* (1985) argued forcibly that a free trade agreement with the United States was the only means of securing access to a large market.

Free trade was seen as a panacea for Canada's troubled manufacturing sector. Free trade would remove U.S. tariffs, thereby enlarging the market for Canadian products; producers would then be able to specialize and achieve longer production runs and lower the costs of production. Indeed, the European experience showed that free trade increases specialization to such a degree that trade within an industry increases. Free trade would also remove the protective barriers from many Canadian industries and force them to rationalize and become more efficient.

In view of the interest that the free trade issue has generated in Canada over many years, it is not surprising that there is an abundance of studies on the potential effects on Canada of free trade with the United States. Indeed, a number of Canadian economists made significant contributions to the study of customs unions. They include Young (Canada 1957) in a study for the Royal Commission on Canada's Economic Prospects, Wonnacott and Wonnacott (1967), Williams (1976), Boadway and Treddenick (1979), and Harris and Cox (1984). Particularly the pioneering work of the Wonnacotts and that of Harris and Cox differed significantly from studies done for other countries, in that the Canadian studies took explicit account of the gains to be achieved by exploiting potential economies of scale. The estimated income gains for Canada were therefore quite large. The 1967 Wonnacott study estimates the benefits to be approximately 10.5 percent of GDP (compared to some European and American studies, which arrive at gains from trade liberalization of 1 to 2 percent of GDP).

The Harris and Cox study was a large simulation study using a computable general equilibrium model to estimate the effects of multilateral free trade, bilateral free trade, and unilateral free trade on 29 industries. The gain in Canadian real income of bilateral free trade was estimated to be in the order of 10 percent. Both the Wonnacott and the Harris and Cox studies were based on pre-Tokyo Round tariff levels. Later studies showed much smaller gains. Hamilton and Whalley (1985) showed a gain of 0.7 percent; and Brown and Stern (1987) and Wigle (1988) predicted that under certain conditions there might be a welfare loss. The reason for the large differences in estimates are the different assumptions used by the modellers.[11] Not surprisingly, studies using the much lower tariffs in effect after the Tokyo Round as a benchmark also give low estimates. A study by the Department of Finance estimated the gains to be 2.5 percent of GDP (Government of Canada 1988).

The Canada-U.S. Free Trade Agreement

In September 1985, the Canadian government approached the U.S. government with a proposal to negotiate a free trade area with the United States; by October, the U.S. government had agreed to participate. Canada's negotiating objectives according to the Minister for International Trade, James Kelleher, were fourfold: security of access to the U.S. market, particularly by reducing the risks inherent in the U.S. system of anti-dumping duties, countervailing duties, and safeguard provisions; expanded access to the U.S. market to provide Canadian industry with a market large enough to realize economies of scale and specialization; a stable North American trading system to encourage an orderly transition to a more competitive economy and to provide an incentive to investments; and an orderly and more predictable system for managing the trade relationship and resolving disputes (Lipsey and York, 1988 p. 9–10). Canadians were particularly upset about the U.S. use of trade remedy laws under which Canada had to agree to a 15 percent export tax on softwood lumber to avoid the threat of a countervailing duty. Another countervail case resulted in a 5.82 percent duty on Canadian exports of East Coast groundfish; and an escape clause action resulted in a 15 percent duty on Canadian exports of shakes and shingles. Negotiations ended in the fall of 1987, and enabling legislation was passed in both countries for the agreement to come into effect on January 1, 1989.

The main feature of the agreement was that there was to be free trade in the majority of goods with some tariffs to be reduced immediately, some within five years and others within ten years.[12] The following goods were exempted: commodities subject to support under supply management schemes (that is, poultry and eggs), beer, and cultural industries. Export controls on unprocessed logs were maintained, as were Canada's export restrictions on East Coast unprocessed fish. The United States also maintained its cabotage laws that restricted coastal shipping in American waters to American ships. There was also provision for national treatment, under which each country undertook not to discriminate between foreign and domestic producers in any activity, and some government procurement was opened up. The agreement also provided for free trade in a number of services by including the right to establishment and the principle of national treatment. The main exception here was the cultural industries.[13] Special provisions for the energy sector prohibited export taxes of the type used by Canada as part in the National Energy Program in the early 1980s. If either country for whatever reason found it necessary to ration energy, it could not discriminate between U.S. and Canadian customers.

In 1972, the Canadian Parliament had passed a law requiring all foreign takeovers above a certain size to be screened to determine whether they were in the national interest. This law was substantially weakened when the Mulroney government came to power. Under the Free Trade Agreement Canada undertook to screen foreign takeovers only if they involved assets of more than $150 million.

The agreement contained an elaborate dispute settlement mechanism. The two countries agreed to negotiate a mutually acceptable set of trade remedies, such as countervail, anti-dumping, and safeguards, and to agree on what constituted an unfair subsidy. In this they failed, mainly because it was not in the U.S. interest to reach an agreement. Since only 25 percent of U.S. trade is with Canada, therefore any rules that limited the way in which subsidies could be used for U.S. firms, for many of which trade with Canada was of only marginal interest, were unacceptable (Whalley, 1990, p. 124). Instead the Americans agreed to develop such laws over a five-to-seven year period.[14] In the meantime the agreement outlined a mechanism for solving trade disputes. "The binational dispute settlement mechanism" has two functions: one is to act as a legislative watchdog, and the other to replace the existing appeals procedure (Lipsey and York, 1988, p. 95–97). For the first function, there was a bilateral review of any proposed changes in the current regulations of either country. For the other function there was provision for a binational review panel in place of domestic judicial review.

Under the rules, each country continued to apply its own trade remedy laws. Any appeal against the use of these laws would go first to the domestic trade authority. If decisions by the domestic authority were challenged, a binational review panel consisting of five members, two chosen by each government, and the fifth chosen by the four members previously selected, would determine whether domestic laws had been applied correctly and fairly. The decision of the panel would have to be made within a specified time.

Apart from the inclusion of the cultural industries, American negotiators also wanted an agreement on intellectual property rights, the reason being a dispute over pharmaceutical patent protection. Canadian patent law permitted the federal government to compel patent holders to license their pharmaceutical inventions to Canadian manufacturers at a low royalty rate (Bill C-22). The justification for doing so was that patents often gave foreign firms excessive profits at the expense of consumers (Hufbauer and Schott, 1992, p. 179). After a bitter debate, Canada acceded to U.S. demands for change in 1993, and the law was repealed.

Was the free trade agreement a good deal? It is probably too early to assess its economic effects, and given the small decreases in tariff barriers possible after the Tokyo round, those are likely to be small. The timing of the treaty was unfortunate, coinciding with a high Canadian dollar, the introduction of the GST, and a worldwide recession, creating an impression that free trade was to be blamed for our high unemployment. Wilson, Dungan, and Murphy (1994), using the FOCUS macroeconomic model, do not attribute the recent recession to free trade. According to their estimates, the recession can be fully explained by the U.S. business cycle, the zero inflation policy, and tax increases.

The Free Trade Agreement guaranteed Canada better access to the U.S. market, albeit at the price of some major concessions in our control of foreign investment and energy. The limitations on our ability to screen foreign investments may not be in our long-term interest, given the unusually large proportion of foreign ownership in Canada. We should note, Porter's comments in Chapter 7 that Canada doesn't appear to get the maximum benefit from foreign investment. Relatively few companies use Canada as the home base where research and product development take place. Similarly, for environmental and other reasons, the limitations on our ability to manage our energy resources may be a serious handicap in the future. Wilkinson (1991) also argues that the difference in size between the two economies gives the United States a considerable leverage over Canada.

The failure to agree on a common approach to trade policy laws has turned out to be serious. While there is some evidence that the binational panels have speeded up the settlement of disputes (Horlick and DeBusk 1992), the number of disputes has been a continual source of frustration.[15] After the agreement was signed, there were several countervail cases, including a countervailing duty on pork (which was subsequently decided in Canada's favour); a ruling that Hydro-Quebec's pricing policies constituted an unfair subsidy; and a new attempt by the United States to impose a countervailing duty on softwood lumber.

The North American Free Trade Agreement (NAFTA)

In June 1990, it was announced that the United States and Mexico intended to negotiate a bilateral free trade area. This announcement was followed by the so-called *Enterprise for the Americas Initiative*, which proposed a series of new free trade areas between the United States and other countries in the Americas (Hufbauer and Schott, 1992, p. 24). Faced by that possibility Canada had to choose between joining the negotiations or being relegated to being one of the spokes in a U.S.-centred free trade system. Wonnacott (1990) argued that if Canada was not part of the hub, most of the benefits would accrue to the United States. Each of the spoke countries (Canada and Mexico, and other countries at a later date) would continue to face barriers in each others' markets, while trade preferences earned in the U.S. market would be eroded by increased competion from the other spokes. Therefore the decision of the Bush administration to seek a free trade deal with Mexico did not leave Canada with any option apart from participating in tri-lateral negotiations. Failure to do so might have jeopardized some of the gains Canada had earned under the Canada-U.S. Free Trade Agreement. In February 1991 there was a joint announcement by the three countries that they would begin negotiations; these negotiations came to a successful conclusion in 1992. NAFTA was ratified by all three countries in 1993 despite vociferous opposition in the United States by labour and environmental groups, which successfully argued for the inclusion of side agreements relating to labour and the environment.

According to d'Aquino (1993), NAFTA contains the following improvements over the Canada-U.S. Free Trade Agreement: clearer and more predictable rules of origin;[16] liberalization of access to U.S. and Mexican government procurement; more stringent obligations regarding energy regulation; inclusion of land transport and specialty air services; inclusion of an intellectual property chapter; higher content requirement for American auto assembly and parts producers; and a commitment to implement NAFTA in a manner consistent with environmental protection and the promotion of sustainable development. Cadsby and Woodside (1993), however, argue that some of the provisions are not necessarily improvements on the Free Trade Agreement. The rules of origin make it more difficult for Canadian apparel manufacturers to compete, and the investment safeguards may grant foreign investors rights denied to Canadians. And though the changes to the dispute settlement mechanism might lead to more effective solutions of trade disputes, the broadened grounds for access to so-called

Extraordinary Challenge Committees could lead to increased harassment of Canadian producers. In the authors' view, the side agreements on labour and environmental cooperation are largely symbolic.

NAFTA is a free trade area equal in population and GDP to the European Union or slightly larger. In 1989 Canada, Mexico, and the United States had a combined GDP of U.S. $5,932 billion and a population of 357 million, compared to the combined GDP of the European Union of U.S. $5,784 billion and a population of 358 million. Studies of the effect of NAFTA on real incomes show that Mexico would gain between 5 percent and 8 percent of GDP, Canada would gain approximately 0.1 percent of GDP because of the small volume of trade involved, and the United States would have marginally larger gains, (Copeland, 1992, p. 202–203). According to Watson (1992), Mexico accounted for only 1.25 percent of Canada's total imports and only 0.45 per cent of its exports in 1983. Thirty-four percent of imports from Mexico already enter tariff-free. Tariffs on the other imports rarely exceed 10 percent. One can therefore argue that Canada is already quite open to Mexican goods.

The most important concern for Canada is whether the inclusion of Mexico in the free trade agreement will displace some of Canada's existing trade with the United States. This is quite possible. Watson (1992) estimates that the value of all Canadian exports subject to competition from Mexico in the U.S. market amounted to $59 billion, which is substantial, compared to the paltry $1.7 billion value of Mexican exports to Canada in 1989.[17] However, increased competition from Mexico could not have been avoided even if Canada had refused to join the agreement.

Unlike the European Union, NAFTA is dominated by one country, the United States, which accounts for 85 percent of output and 70 percent of the population. The largest economy in Europe, namely Germany, accounts for only 25 percent of output and 22 percent of the population (Hufbauer and Schott, 1992, p. 4). Because of the difference in size of the member economies of NAFTA, there is obviously an imbalance of power that does not exist in the European Union. However, some Canadian defenders of NAFTA point out that NAFTA is an improvement on the Free Trade Agreement in that the addition of

Mexico redresses the balance somewhat. Furthermore, the purpose of NAFTA is not to achieve the close integration aimed for in Europe, such as a common currency and centralized regional and social policies. NAFTA does not even include free mobility of labour or a common external tariff. However, Wilkinson (1991) argues that in some other respects, in particular integration of capital flows and harmonization of product standards, the integration of Canada and the United States has proceeded further than the integration of the European Union.

The prospects of free trade with Mexico raised far more opposition in the United States than the free trade agreement with Canada, the main reason being the disparities in wages between the two countries. It was also feared that lack of environmental standards in Mexico would lead to a deterioration of the environment. Canadian opposition also concentrated on these two issues. In 1988 the average hourly wage in Mexico was U.S. $1.57 compared to $13.58 in Canada and $13.92 in the United States (Copeland, 1992, p. 207). Again trade theory would predict that the wages in the participating countries would move closer together. However, this process is already underway in the world economy because of liberalized multilateral free trade. Canada and the United States are facing competition not only from Mexico, but also from most of the world's low-wage countries. In fact, most empirical studies in the United States agree that the real wages of unskilled labour are in decline, a process that will probably accelerate under NAFTA (Hufbauer and Schott 1992).

Labour unions have also opposed NAFTA on grounds of inadequate labour laws and working conditions, particularly in the **maquiladoras**. A maquiladora is a processor of goods to be returned to the original producer for resale. Thus, under "in-bond" arrangements, imported components enter Mexico duty-free, provided the importer posts a bond guaranteeing that the assembled products will be exported and not sold domestically. If the product is sold in Mexico, import duties will be collected from the posted bond (Hufbauer and Schott, 1992, p. 91). The maquiladoras have been remarkably successful. The first 12 were established in 1965, and by March 1991 there were 1,900 plants operating. Hufbauer and Schott (1992) argue that the program worked for Mexico much as the Auto Pact worked for Canada in allowing duty-free imports of components as an incentive for national production. Both also served as foundations for wider free trade arrangements.

The maquiladoras account for only 5 percent of Mexican GDP and 1 percent of value-added. They account for 60 percent of non-oil exports to the United States. Most of the workers are female. Examples of child abuse and sweatshop conditions have been reported as well as appalling environmental conditions caused by pollution and hazardous wastes. It is thought that some U.S. and Canadian plants cannot compete against Mexican-based enterprises that can escape expensive pollution standards. Therefore "good" production facilities would close down and be replaced by "bad" facilities in Mexico.

It is obvious that differing environmental standards affect competitiveness. The question is by how much. Would it be serious enough to lead to plant closures? *The Economist* (February 27, 1993) quotes a 1985 OECD study which found that pollution-control measures in France, the Netherlands, and the U.S. may have reduced total exports by 0.5–1 percent. But there is little evidence that strict environmental measures by themselves cause companies to relocate. Factors such as the costs of labour and transportation, access to markets, and political stability are far more important. *The Economist* (March 20, 1993) also claims that NAFTA goes further to safeguard the environment than any previous trade agreement. NAFTA also encourages the participation of environmental groups in the settlement of disputes. In addition, there is an agreement between Mexico and the United States to spend more than $4,700 million over three years towards cleaning up the border area.

Conclusions

In this chapter, we first examined the case for free trade, which is still strong despite recent challenges by environmentalists and strategic-trade theorists. In the case of the environment, trade policies are usually second-best policies for dealing with environmental matters. Pollution taxes or tradable emissions are more efficient. Trade policies could however have a place as a sanction in trans-boundary pollution questions such as the destruction of the ozone layer. Strategic-trade policies suffer from the same problems as the unilateral imposition of tariffs: they are beggar-thy-neighbour policies and therefore leave the country open to retaliation.

I also pointed out that trade liberalization has implications for distribution of income. Even though it can be shown that the nation as a whole becomes better off, some groups will lose and others will gain. If the distribution of income becomes more uneven as a result of free trade, a country's well-being may be adversely affected.

The chapter also examined in some detail the trade liberalization effort under GATT, including the achievements of the Uruguay Round. The interest in Canada in free trade with the United States was examined, together with the Free Trade Agreement concluded in 1988. I argued that the net benefit to Canada of the agreement is probably marginal because of the substantial concessions we had to make in the control of energy and foreign investment and the failure to get an agreement on the use of trade remedy laws—countervail, antidumping duties, and safeguards. As a result, even after the agreement was ratified, Canadian exporters were still harassed by the aggressive application of U.S. trade laws. This chapter also examined NAFTA. Given Canada's small volume of trade with Mexico, NAFTA is unlikely to have much effect on Canada. But I argued that it was in Canada's interest be part of NAFTA to safeguard what we had already achieved in our bilateral treaty with the United States.

TOPICS FOR DISCUSSION

1. Did we have the option of not joining NAFTA?

2. There has been much attention in the media to restrictive U.S. trade policies and continual harassment of Canadian exporters. The most recent issue has been the allegation that Canadian exports of durum wheat to the United States are subsidized.

    What do you think about Canada's record as a free trader? Name a few cases in which Canada has been accused of intransigence and of not acting in good faith.

3. Do you think trade should be used as a weapon in international politics to make countries (for example China) improve their

human rights record or their environment? What are the advantages and disadvantages of such policies?

RECOMMENDED READING

For an easily follwed summary of the initial free trade agreement with the United States, read *Evaluating the Free Trade Deal: A Guided Tour through the Canada-U.S. Agreement* (Lipsey and York 1988). The differences between NAFTA and the Canada-U.S. agreement are outlined in *Assessing NAFTA: A Trinational Analysis* (Globerman and Walker 1993). For information about the trade issues in Mexico and the United States, read *North American Free Trade: Issues and Recommendations* (Hufbauer and Schott 1992). If you want to explore the social, cultural, and environmental issues surrounding NAFTA, *Ties beyond Trade: Labour and Environmental Issues under the Nafta* (Lemco and Robson 1993) and *North America Without Borders? Integrating Canada, the United States and Mexico* (Randall 1992) are good sources.

References

Anderson, Kym. "The Standard Welfare Economics of Policies Affecting Trade and the Environment." In *The Greening of World Trade Issues*, eds. Kym Anderson and Richard Blackhurst (1992): 25-49.

Anderson, Kym and Richard Blackhurst eds. *The Greening of World Trade Issues*. London: Harvester Wheatsheaf, 1992.

Baldwin, Robert E. "Are Economists' Traditional Trade Policy Views Still Valid?" *Journal of Economic Literature* 30 (June 1992): 804-30.

Boadway, Robin and John Treddenick. "A General Equilibrium Computation of the Effects of the Canadian Tariff Structure." *Canadian Journal of Economics 12* (1979): 424-46.

Brown, Drusilla K. and Robert M. Stern. *US-Canada Bilateral Tariff Elimination: The Role of Product Differentiation and Market Structure*. Research Seminar on International Economics, Department of Economics, University of Michigan, 1988.

Cadsby, Charles Bram and Kenneth Woodside. " The Effects of the North American Free Trade Agreement on the Canada-United States Trade Relationship." *Canadian Public Policy-Analyse de Politiques* 19 (December 1993): 450-63.

Canada. Government of Canada. *The Canada-U.S. Free Trade Agreement: An Economic Assessment*. Ottawa: Department of Finance, 1988.

Canada. Government of Canada. *Royal Commission on Canada's Economic Prospects, Canadian Commercial Policies*. Ottawa: Queen's Printer, 1957.

Copeland, Brian R. "Regional Trading Blocks and Canadian Trade Policy." In *False Promises: The Failure of Conservative Economics*, eds. Robert C. Allen and Gideon Rosenbluth, Vancouver: New Star Books, 1992: 179-209.

Crandall, Robert W. "What Have Auto-Import Quotas Wrought? *Challenge*. (January/February 1985): 40-47.

D'Aquino, Thomas. "Why We Need NAFTA." *Policy Options* 13 (January-February 1993): 21-24.

Eastman, H. C. and S. Stykolt. *The Tariff and Competition in Canada*. Toronto: Macmillan, 1967.

Eden, Lorraine and Maureen Appel Molot. "Comparative and Competitive Advantage in the North American Trade Bloc." *Canadian Business Economics* 1 (Fall 1992): 45-60.

Eden, Lorraine and Maureen Appel Molot. "Canada's National Policies: Reflections on 125 Years." *Canadian Public Policy-Analyse de Politiques* 19 (September 1993): 232-52.

Globerman, Steven and Michael Walker eds. *Assessing NAFTA: A Trinational Analysis*. Vancouver: The Fraser Institute, 1993.

Hamilton, Bob and John Whalley. "Geographically Discriminatory Trade Arrangements." *Review of Economics and Statistics* 67 (1985): 446-55.

Harris, Richard G. "Innis Lecture: The New Protectionism Revisited." *Canadian Journal of Economics* 23 (November 1989): 751-79.

Harris Richard G. and David Cox. *Trade, Industrial Policy and Canadian Manufacturing*. Toronto: Ontario Economic Council, 1984.

Hazledine, Tim. "Why Do the Free-Trade Gain Numbers Differ So Much? The Role of Industrial Organization in General Equilibrium." *Canadian Journal of Economics* 22 (November 1990): 791-807.

Horlick, Gary N. and Amanda F. Debusk. "The Functioning of FTA Dispute Resolution Panels." In *Negotiating and Implementing a North American Free Trade Agreement*, ed. Leonard Waverman, Vancouver and Toronto: The Fraser Institute and the Centre for International Studies, 1992: 1-27.

Hufbauer, Gary Clyde and Jeffrey J. Schott *North American Free Trade. Issues and Recommendations*. Washington D.C.: Institute for International Economics, 1992.

Krugman, Paul R. "Is Free Trade Passé?" *The Journal of Economic Perspectives* 1 (Fall 1987): 131-45.

Krugman, Paul R. and Maurice Obstfeld. *International Economics: Theory and Policy*. 2nd edition. New York: HarperCollins Publishers Inc., 1991.

Lemco, Jonathan and William B. P. Robson eds. *Ties Beyond Trade: Labour and Environmental Issues Under the NAFTA*. Toronto: C.D.Howe Institute and the National Planning Association, 1993.

Lipsey, Richard G. and Robert C. York. *Evaluating the Free Trade Deal: A Guided Tour through the Canada-U.S. Agreement*. Toronto: The C.D. Howe Institute, 1988.

Randall, Stephen J. ed. (with Herman Konrad and Sheldon Silverman). *North America without Borders? Integrating Canada, The United States, and Mexico*. Calgary: The University of Calgary Press, 1992.

Stone, Frank. *Canada, the GATT and the International Trade System.* 2nd edition. Montreal: The Institute for Research on Public Policy, 1992.

Watson, William G. "North American Free Trade: Lessons from the Trade Data." *Canadian Public Policy-Analyse de Politique* 18 (March 1992): 1-13.

Wigle, Randall. "General Equilibrium Evaluation of Canada-US Trade Liberalization in a Global Context." *Canadian Journal of Economics* 21 (August 1988): 539-65.

Wilkinson, Bruce W. "Regional Trading Blocks: Fortress Europe versus Fortress North America." In *The New Era of Global Competition, State Policy and Market Power,* ed. Daniel Drache and Meric S. Gertler. Montreal and Kingston: McGill-Queen's University Press, 1991: 51-83.

Williams, J. *The Canadian-US Tariff and Canadian Industry: A Multisectoral Analysis.* Toronto: The University of Toronto Press, 1978.

Wilson, Thomas, Peter Dungan and Steve Murphy. "The Sources of the Recession in Canada: 1989-1992."*Canadian Business Economics.* 2 (Winter 1994): 3-16.

Wonnacott, Ronald J. "US Hub-and-Spoke Bilaterals and the Multilateral Trading System." *Commentary.* Toronto: C. D. Howe Institute, 1990.

Endnotes

1   It can be shown that the optimum tariff equals the reciprocal of the foreign export supply elasticity.

2   A free trade area is the loosest type of regional trade grouping. Its aim is usually to remove tariff barriers between participating countries. A customs union is a free trade area where the participating countries have agreed on a common external tariff. A common market is a customs union with free mobility of labour and capital.

3   For a discussion and analysis of the related issues, see Anderson and Blackhurst (1992), and also "Trade and the Environment: The Greening of Protectionism" in the February 27, 1993 issue of *The Economist.*

   Hufbauer and Schott (1992, p. 131) quote some studies that show that pollution is positively correlated with per capita GDP up to a certain level of GDP. When this level is reached, there is a negative correlation between pollution and per capita GDP.

4   The strategic-trade-policy argument was developed by James Brander (a Canadian) and Barbara Spencer in a serious of articles in the mid-eighties. For a discussion, see Harris (1989).

5   The case for subsidies for research in high-technology industries is a sounder one where national welfare could be increased without adversely affecting welfare in other countries. Even in this case, however, one has to be careful as subsidies can be used to promote inefficient activities (Baldwin, 1992).

6   Much of this section relies on Stone (1992).

7   It is interesting to note that in the GATT agreement concluded in December 1993, a new international body, the World Trade Organization, was created following the idea of the proposed International Trade Organization.

8   The European Union has also negotiated voluntary export restraints with many countries, covering steel, autos, electronics, and textiles. It is believed that 20 percent of world trade in steel is regulated by such agreements

9   An amusing example of a creative trade barrier was the Japanese refusal to allow imports of foreign skis on the grounds that Japanese snow was different from foreign snow, and therefore foreign skis could be dangerous.

10 Eden and Molot (1993) provide an interesting analysis of Canada's national policies. They delineate three national policies, the first covering the period between 1867-1940 coinciding with what is usually referred to as the National Policy. This period is characterized by "defensive expansionism" with its emphasis on constructing a national entity. The second national policy covers the period 1941 and 1981 and is described as a policy of "compensatory liberalism" with a commitment to liberalized trade through GATT, Keynesian policies, and the building of the social safety net. The third policy starts in 1982 and is a policy of "market liberalism" characterized by market-based policies, free trade with the United States, and fiscal restraint.

11 Hazledine (1990) constructed a model to demonstrate how sensitive the results were to the varying assumptions about pricing behaviour and entry barriers. He modelled five different assumptions about pricing behaviour, including the Eastman-Stykolt hypothesis (used by the Wonnacotts and Harris and Cox), a monopolistic competition hypothesis, a market share pricing hypothesis, a competitive hypothesis, and a mainstream industrial organization hypothesis. Depending on which hypothesis is chosen, estimates for welfare gains vary between 0 and 7 percent with the high estimates resulting from the Eastman-Stykolt hypothesis. The Eastman-Stykolt hypothesis (after Eastman and Stykolt,1967) assumes that a tariff on imports forces colluding domestic oligopolists to raise their prices to the world price plus the tariffs. The resulting high profits attract new entrants which because of scale economies will operate at high costs. Excess profits (rents) will disappear.

12 The synopsis is taken from Lipsey and York (1988) and also from the excellent discussion in Copeland (1992).

13 The exemption for cultural industries is permissible under GATT rules. The restrictions prevent U.S. firms from exploiting copyrights, particularly through the use of TV channels. There is considerable pressure in the U.S. that this exemption should be removed on grounds that the protection of culture is an excuse for economic protectionism and has little to do with content but more with who will profit from the exploitation of American copyrighted materials (Hufbauer and Schott, 1992, p.180).

14 Negotiations had not even started in 1993, pending the outcome of the Uruguay Round.

15 Horlick and DeBusk (1992, p. 11) also found that the Panels had been impartial with no link between the nationality of the panellist and the decision.

16 A free trade area differs from a customs union or a common market in that the participating countries do not need to harmonize the tariffs imposed on non-member countries. Canada can therefore maintain a different tariff on Japanese products from the United States and Mexico. If Canadian tariffs are lower than US tariffs, it would pay Japanese exporters to ship goods destined for the United States via Canada. Rules of origin are necessary to prevent this from happening.

17 Note, however, that Eden and Molot (1992) in a study of Canada's comparative advantage in NAFTA show that the Mexican and Canadian economies are complementary rather than competitive which would weaken Watson's argument.

11

Social and Investment
Policies

After reading this chapter together with the other chapters in this volume, you will understand the necessity of reforming our social policies and also our investment policies particularly as they pertain to education. You will also be able to discuss the many and various proposals for reforming our policies on unemployment insurance, welfare, and education.

The last two chapters surveyed our fiscal and monetary policies and our trade policies. Given the rapid integration of the global economy, it was in Canada's interest to seek a free trade agreement with the United States and to be part of NAFTA. The jury is probably still out on whether we got a good deal. There is no doubt that we made significant concessions without receiving much in return. While the dispute settlement mechanism is an improvement, we are still being constantly harassed by the aggressive application of trade laws in the United States. Our fiscal and monetary policies have landed us in a situation that threatens our social policies, which many see as the glue that keeps the country together. So far our social policies have been unable to eradicate poverty, in particular child poverty, where our record is worse than that of most other rich countries.

A United Nations committee has sharply criticized the Canadian government for allowing poverty and homelessness to persist at disturbing levels in one of the world's richest countries.

Despite its vast wealth, Canada has made "no measurable progress" in alleviating poverty over the past decade, the UN committee said in a strongly worded report yesterday.

More than half of all single mothers are living in poverty, thousands of children are poor, hungry families are dependent on food banks, many adults are homeless and discrimination against poor people is widespread, the report says.

The criticism by the UN committee, which includes members from 18 countries, is believed to be the harshest attack it has ever launched concerning the performance of an industrialized nation.

Earlier this month, the committee listened to two days of testimony by Canadian government officials and social groups. It gathered statistical data and studied photographs of homeless people in Toronto, lineups at food banks, and native people at Indian reserves.

Canada has an "enviable situation" in its economic resources, yet the problem of poverty is persisting, the UN committee said.

It criticized the federal government for slashing its contributions to cost-sharing agreements for social assistance.

The committee also attacked the government's failure to take adequate steps to solve the poverty problem.

A further subject of concern for the committee is "the evidence of hunger in Canada and the reliance on food banks operated by charitable organizations," the UN report said.

It cited evidence of Canadian families "being forced to relinquish their children to foster care because of inability to provide adequate housing or other necessities."

The government does not seem to make any effort to keep track of the extent of homelessness in Canada, the committee said, adding that it was surprised by the low percentage of the federal budget that is spent on social housing. "UN Body Chastises Canada on Poverty" (*The Globe and Mail*, May 29, 1993).

We obviously need to do more, though in a fiscal climate where taxes are already high and where government expenditures have to be cut rather than increased, it appears that the electorate is now obsessed with the debt and is in favour of government cutbacks in many areas.

Valaskakis (1990) argues that the indiscriminate reduction in the size of government is not necessarily desirable because deregulation may lead to unregulated oligopolies or monopolies, rather than free competition, if the experience in the airline industry is anything to go by. There is quite likely more danger of abuse from an uncontrolled private monopoly than from a democratically elected government. An example of "undesirable indiscriminate downsizing" is the situation facing the municipalities. While the municipalities have the responsibility for providing water supplies, sewage treatment, and waste collection, they have not been given the financial resources to do so properly, in fact federal and provincial governments have reduced funding for these services (Olewiler, 1993, p. 394). A deteriorating infrastructure and in some cases no infrastructure — sewage treatment in Victoria, Halifax, and Montreal comes to mind — will require a large amount of money. It is not clear where the money is going to come from. User fees and property taxes are regressive in their incidence and can probably not be relied on to provide sufficient capital.

The management of the environment and of social dissension will be the main difficulties for future governments. The conflict between the demands of the so-called knowledge sector and the demands of the traditional service sector with its low-paying jobs will have to be resolved. If the state is to take the necessary responsibility, Valaskakis argues, we have to have a productive public sector, a socially responsible private sector, and a growing relationship between the two.

Courchene (1992) argues that Canada is totally unprepared for the new global economy and that we are on the route to a low-wage and therefore a low-transfer economy, that is, a U.S. social system with Scandinavian tax rates. We are in a danger of re-commodifying labour by treating our workforce as equipment which can be discarded at will, and of trying to compete in products requiring unskilled labour at the bottom end of the labour market. The trouble is that there will always be somebody somewhere with a lower end. In Courchene's view the answer is

> To move towards a society where we are competing with the middle and upper parts of the labour market on the one hand, and to provide both citizen upward mobility in terms of skills enhancement and an industrial system geared to high-value-added production. This is the only route back towards a high-wage and, if we wish, a high-transfer economy . . . What this means in practical terms is a wholesale rethinking and restructuring of the social envelope, including primary, secondary, and post-secondary education and R&D on the one hand and, relatedly, the integration of welfare, UI, apprenticeship training and the transition from school to work on the other (Courchene, 1992, p. 770–71).

In this final chapter we will see what might be done. We will first search for efficiency gains in the economy, gains that could be had at virtually no cost and that could be used to provide more resources for other areas. Then we will look at the possibility of creating jobs for people, because without the prospects of a more buoyant job market, it is unlikely that we can make the structural changes necessary to compete and survive in the new global economy. We will also look at ways to invest in the future so we can leave a legacy to our children that we can be proud of.

Potential Efficiency Gains

Our review of the environmental and resource sectors indicated that there is potential for some efficiency gains here. In Canada we tend to solve our environmental problems through a command-and-control approach where the burden of the proof to show that environmental damage has occurred rests with the regulatory agency.[1] Chapters 2 and 3 showed that a command-and-control approach to environmental problems is unnecessarily costly. Admittedly at the provincial level there are some market incentives, such as excise taxes, user fees, and a deposit refund system. But at the federal level there are none, despite much discussion of their desirability. While recycling has been embraced on a large scale by consumers and municipal governments, it appears to be expensive, because of the lack of markets. It is possible that market-based alternatives would be a better solution.

It also appears that our environmental assessment procedures do not work well because of inconsistent application and federal-provincial conflicts. It is likely that further study would find that our policies for forestry mangagement and hydrodevelopment are inefficient and should be changed.[2] In general, our record in the management of our renewable resources has not been good. We need to do more and better research into the condition of natural resources and how they should be managed. As was pointed out in Chapter 1, the inclusion of resources in the national accounts would make sense. Despite commitments made under the Green Plan it does not appear that the federal government is allocating the necessary resources for environmental research and clean-up.

Another sector where substantial efficiency gains are possible is agriculture. Study after study has demonstrated that the marketing boards that regulate the production of milk, eggs, and poultry through quotas raise prices for consumers, increase profits for the initial quota holders, and lead to inefficiencies. Later the profits become capitalized in the value of the farms, thereby inflating farm prices.[3] Marketing boards were exempted from the Free Trade Agreement with the United States, and they figured prominently in Canada's negotiations in the Uruguay Round because marketing boards have the same effect on trade as a prohibitive tariff. Canada found itself in the untenable position of simultaneously defending marketing boards and condemning barriers to trade in other kinds of agriculture such as grains. As a result of the negotiations, Canada agreed to replace the quotas by explicit tariffs of more than 300 percent, which are to be lowered gradually.

Both federal and provincial governments recognize the need to remove interprovincial trade barriers, but so far little has been done. Because of their effect on competition, these barriers lead to inefficiencies. All the provinces have barriers against out-of-province competition. Quebec is reputed to be the worst offender in such areas as government procurement and labour mobility. Firms bidding on a Quebec government contract must have a base in the province unless they are granted a special exemption (*The Globe and Mail*, May 31, 1993). Local firms are given a 10 percent price advantage against outside bidders, and if more than three local firms have submitted bids, out-of-province firms are excluded. It is almost impossible for out-of-province construction workers to work on Quebec construction sites. In retaliation, New Brunswick recently introduced regulations preventing Quebec firms from supplying goods, services, and labour for any government work. In the spring of 1994 efforts were being made by the provinces to work out a trade deal which would guarantee more open trade within Canada.

By avoiding duplication between various levels of government substantial economies could probably be achieved. Indeed, decades of constitutional debates have produced reams of studies recommending the streamlining of government services, but with no results. The need for better coordination of provincial and federal fiscal policies was pointed out in Chapter 9. Better coordination in all policy areas is obviously necessary.

The Challenge to Reduce Unemployment

In my survey of employment and unemployment I noted that unemployment as measured by the official statistics has been rising, not only in Canada but also in other countries. I also noted that the proportion of part-time jobs is increasing and that the gap in pay between jobs requiring high skills and those requiring low skills, particularly in the service sector, is widening. The demand for labour will not necessarily increase at the same rate as economic growth.[4] Unless the economy can generate more jobs, the conflict between jobs, competitiveness, the debt, and the environment is going to be formidable.

While job creation is necessary, there is also a need to make the labour market more efficient both by offering stronger incentives for people to work and by creating better matches between the need of employers and the skills of workers. One of the prime candidates for reform is the unemployment insurance system; which is reputed to be the most generous in the world. A survey of some of the empirical studies in Chapter 5 showed that unemployment insurance has increased the unemployment rate in Canada. To qualify for benefits a claimant has to work for at least 14 weeks in regions of low unemployment and 10 weeks in areas of high unemployment. The duration of payments also varies with the region; in high unemployment regions up to 52 weeks of benefits are paid. The benefits vary with the number of weeks of insurable employment and are equal to 60 percent of average weekly earnings to a maximum amount. There are extended benefits for those undertaking approved training or participating in approved work-sharing or job creation projects. There are also special benefits for self-employed fishermen.

It appears that the system is too generous and that some of the vast amounts of public money used for unemployment insurance could be more profitably channelled into other programs, such as child-care or low-income housing.[5] The Newfoundland Royal Commission in its summary report (Newfoundland, 1986, p. 406–09) has the following to say about unemployment insurance (UI): (1) It undermines the intrinsic value of work; it undermines good working habits and discipline because of the apparent meaninglessness of some of the make-work projects possible under section 23 of the Unemployment Insurance Act. (2) It undermines the importance of education, since it is as easy to get the 10 weeks work to qualify for UI with a Grade 8 education as with a university degree. Furthermore, the system penalizes people for aspiring to further their education because benefits are cut off if they become full-time students. (3) It is a disincentive to work. If one earns more than 25 percent of benefits they will be cut off. Another requirement of UI is that one must remain available for work. It is therefore safer to do nothing than to work. (4) UI discourages self-employment and small-scale enterprise:

Seasonal fish-plant operators have had to adapt to the ten-week syndrome by hiring many more plant workers during the season than would otherwise be needed. Workers expect to get laid off to give someone else a chance once they get their 10 stamps. This is a rational adaptation from the point of view of the community: it shares out the available work, qualifies the maximum number of people for income stabilization payments (UI benefits) during the off-season and thereby maximizes both household and community incomes. For the fish-plant operator, however, it means higher operating costs due to labour turnover, lower productivity and difficulties in finding workers during the fall and winter; plant operators also find that it is difficult to get fishermen to continue supplying fish plants in the fall, once they have qualified for UI . . . Other small businesses, such as hotels, restaurants and various other service industries also experience inefficiencies and periodic labour shortages due to the UI system. Waitresses, for example, are reluctant to work for one or two days a week during busy periods, because it could disqualify them for UI for the whole week . . . The UI system also biases the local economy towards working for other people as employees, rather than starting a small business or co-operative enterprise for oneself. People running small businesses (for example in the tourist industry) who may be making little money themselves, are ineligible for UI (Newfoundland, 1986, p. 407).

(5) UI encourages political patronage in its make-work system because projects tend to be allocated according to political criteria rather than economic ones. (6) UI distorts the effects of local development groups and is vulnerable to manipulation. In testimony to the commission, Newfoundlanders were concerned about the practice of job rotation whereby all of the workforce in an area is rotated through the jobs to qualify for UI; about employers who submit records for higher salaries than they were paying so that their laid-off employees would not have their UI reduced; about social service departments that provide short-term jobs for recipients of benefits so that the burden of looking after them can be shifted to the federal government. [6] The list goes on.

There have been many suggestions for reform. The Macdonald Commission (Canada 1985) recommended that industries with a higher record of lay-offs would pay higher premiums. It also recommended lowering the benefit rate to 50 percent of earnings; lengthening the qualifying period to 15–20 weeks; tightening the link between the maximum benefit period and minimum employment period; and eliminating the regional variations in benefits. It also proposed a full-scale reform of the whole income-maintenance system in Canada, such that the money saved from UI reform could be used for a guaranteed annual income system and special training programs.

The Forget Commission (Canada 1986) proposed that the regional variations in benefits and qualifying period should be abolished because it was fundamentally unjust to treat unemployed workers in similar circumstances differently. The money saved from these changes should be used for human resource programs tailored to meet the needs of the individual, including training and community development. The job search requirement should be rescinded for persons undergoing training, and insurance should be extended to part-time workers. The Commission also proposed returning the program back to an insurance basis such that the minimum entrance requirement would be 350 hours (approximately equal to ten weeks) and the benefit level would be based on average earnings over the previous ten weeks. It also proposed the phasing out of the job creation part of unemployment insurance. The commissioners rejected the idea that industries with high lay-off records should pay higher premiums on the grounds that it would unfairly penalize seasonal industries.

The Newfoundland royal commission agreed with the previous two in proposing an overhaul of income security programs in Canada, recognizing that the intention of UI has shifted from income maintenance to income security and income support. The Newfoundland commission also proposed that UI should be restored to its original purpose of income maintenance for people on short-term lay-off or between jobs. The commissioners argued that some of the current functions of UI should be taken over by a guaranteed income scheme (a guaranteed basic income system combined with an earned income supplement).

Large-scale reform of the UI system has proved to be politically impossible because of the complexity of the program and the number of people it benefits. Cousineau (1988) points out that in order to be re-elected, a government will change a program only if one or more of the following conditions hold: (1) the change will improve everybody's welfare; (2) the change will improve the welfare of some without changing the welfare of others; (3) the change will improve the welfare of some, and will worsen the welfare of others, but the latter group will receive compensation; (4) the change will improve the welfare of a small concentrated group and diffuse the cost over a large unorganized group. The proposed UI changes do not fulfil any of these conditions. Pal (1988) argues that for change to be possible the political process has to be made more open and the government must be prepared to engage in negotiations with affected groups.

There have, however, been minor adjustments to tighten up eligibility. In 1993, people who quit their jobs became ineligible for UI, and as of April 1, 1994, the benefit ratio was reduced from 60 percent to 57 percent.

There are other proposals for lowering unemployment. Weitzman (1984) argues that profit sharing is likely to reduce lay-offs in recessions. Under the current system, if demand for a firm's products declines, the firm will be forced to lay off workers, who will not be rehired until either demand picks up or wages fall. Under profit sharing a firm would pay the worker a relatively low wage, say half the going rate. In return, the workers would be entitled to a share of the firm's profits. In a downturn, compensation would automatically fall and therefore lay-offs would be reduced. An additional advantage is that workers might take more interest in the profitability of a firm, thereby increasing productivity. Weitzman argues that one of the reasons why employment in Japan is more stable than in North America is that most Japanese workers receive a substantial part of their pay in the form of year-end bonuses. Profit-sharing arrangements are more common in the United States than in Canada. The Macdonald Commission recommended that they should be supported on a voluntary basis.

Daly and Cobb (1989, p. 313–14) propose that society should guarantee everyone a job. If a government employment centre is unable to offer a worker a regular job, it should offer three options: job training that would have the possibility of leading to long-term employment;

help in homesteading in the countryside; or an immediate low-paying job, either full-time or part-time.[7] The job could be community work, such as helping the elderly or cleaning up highways or parks. The person could also be offered the possibility of designing his or her own job. They argue that the pay should be very low (below current minimum wages). There would be no possibility of advancement, but a good work record could lead to a proper job. They also propose a modest guaranteed annual income. With such a scheme, minimum wages would be unnecessary since the guaranteed income would set a floor for living standards.

Two other ways of increasing employment would be through shorter working hours and work-sharing. Reid (1986) examines three types of policies. The first is legislated or negotiated reductions in the standard work week; the second is voluntary work-time reductions, with proportionate reductions in pay, through job sharing, longer vacations, sabbatical leave, and early retirement; the third is short-time compensation in which layoffs are avoided by using unemployment insurance benefits to compensate workers for temporary reductions in the work week. As an example, he uses the 1982 recession. From 1981 to 1982, total hours worked per week dropped by 3.8 percent. The drop was accomplished through a reduction of employment resulting in a rise in unemployment from 7½ to 11 percent. If, instead, the average hours worked had been reduced by 1½ hours a week, unemployment could have remained at 7½ percent. While the majority of workers are in favour of the status quo according to some American surveys, it is likely that a policy of work-time reductions during recessions would have net social benefits. It would save society unemployment insurance premiums and possibly social assistance. It might also help to prevent hysteresis, where laid-off workers lose some of their hard-earned skills. However, reduced hours may in practice not be very effective in reducing unemployment. Evidence from Europe, for example, shows that for many firms marginally shorter work-weeks increases productivity to such an degree that new hiring will not occur. A reduction in hours of labour is not in general supported by management and is only a secondary goal for labour.

There have often been suggestions that the government should engineer comparative advantage and therefore create "good" jobs through the aggressive use of industrial policies (strategic trade policy). Indeed, the literature surveyed in the previous chapter indicates that in some circumstances such policies may be beneficial. "We tend to produce dynamic and enterprising economic dwarfs to do battle with equally dynamic and enterprising economic giants abroad; these giants, in addition have their governments fully behind them" (Valakaskis, 1990, p. 216). However, the fact that these types of policies may have worked in other countries, such as Japan, does not mean that they will work in Canada. We have a different culture and different institutions. A number of failures of government-sponsored projects, including Dome Petroleum, the Bricklin sports car, and others, show that we are not very adept at doing this. Given our political structure, any attempt to create comparative advantage through subsidies would leave itself open to political patronage and the influence of interest groups. It would appear that the creation of good and interesting jobs requires a long-term commitment to investment in human and physical capital, and in knowledge, which we will turn to below.

Reform of Social Policies

During the constitutional debates and the debate about free trade, many Canadians described themselves as different from Americans in that we are more compassionate, as manifested in our generous social programs. Almost all Canadians believe that everyone has the right to medical care, and nine out of ten believe that people have a right to incomes adequate to live on. Seven out of ten think that Canadians are generous (Bibby, 1990, p. 112). But Bibby points out that we also think that looking after people is the job of the government and should be done by specialists. Canadians as individuals are not particularly generous. The proportion of our incomes that we give to charity has declined for both individuals and corporations. In 1985, individual Americans gave three times as much to charity as Canadians, and American corporations 4.4 times as much as Canadian corporations (*ibid.*). The Canadians who give the highest percentage of their incomes to charity are farmers, followed by pensioners and self-employed professionals. People in the Atlantic provinces are more generous than those in other regions.

Though it is our governments that are expected to look after people, most governments will be unable to continue previous generous levels of support because of high debt and high tax rates. Most of our social programs were designed and expanded during the fifties, sixties, and early seventies. The sixties saw the development of Canada and Quebec pension plans, the guaranteed income supplement for the elderly, the Canada Assistance Plan, equalization, medicare and hospitalization, and the current structure of unemployment insurance. Banting (1985, p. 9) argues that in general the programs were motivated by a quest for security, predictability, and social rights rather a desire to narrow the gap between the rich and the poor. Because of rapid economic growth and despite the increased expenditure on policies, there was a cumulative federal fiscal surplus of $2.75 billion over the 1965–74 period (Courchene, 1991, p. 131).

Courchene argues that there are three challenges to social policies in the nineties: **the fiscal challenge, the economic challenge** and **the socio-demographic challenge**. The fiscal challenge, which has already been alluded to, is that our social programs are crowded out by deficits and debt servicing. The federal government is attempting to pass some of the costs on to the provincial governments, at the same time as the traditional tax base of the provinces has been eroded by the GST. The economic challenge is to make social programs help to ensure our survival in the global economy by promoting efficiency and flexibility. The socio-demographic challenge is for social policy to adapt to the new groups that are in need in the 1990s. We have already discussed the needs of single-parent families in Chapter 6. Serving these needs requires investments in day care and policies to close the gender gap in earnings.

Our survey in Chapter 6 also showed that we have succeeded quite well in alleviating poverty among the elderly. It would make sense if old-age pensions were "clawed back" in a similar fashion to child tax credits; this money could be used to provide more subsidized day-care places.

We noted in the previous section that two of the royal commissions recommended that the reform of the UI system should be coupled with a reform of the whole income-support system, including the introduction of a guaranteed annual income. The Macdonald Commission recommended that the existing federal tax and transfer programs including GIS, family allowances, child tax credits, married exemptions, and the federal share of social assistance programs, should be replaced with a universal income security program. It recommended that the guaranteed level should be relatively low and should be supplemented by social assistance payments by the provinces if necessary. The Newfoundland commission proposed that Newfoundland could be made a pilot project for a new income-security system where all individuals would receive basic income support through a guaranteed basic income, set at half the minimum income established by the Statistics Canada's low income cut-offs (and roughly equivalent to social assistance in Newfoundland). In addition, it recommended an earned- income supplement that would subsidize earned income through the tax system on a decreasing scale up to a specified limit. Such a system would provide both minimum income security and incentives to work. The Forget Commission also recommended that any savings from reforming UI should be used for job training or better programs for the less well-to-do. The federal government has moved in a piecemeal way towards a guaranteed annual income system in its use of tax credits in the income tax system, and the phasing out of the family allowance.

As governments cut back and taxes rise, the call for workfare will probably become stronger. Some newspaper columnists appear to devote a fair amount of time to revealing every welfare scam. Even left-wing provincial governments appear to favour the idea of workfare as a way for people on social assistance to form some attachment to the labour market. The evidence from our discussion in Chapter 6 shows that workfare can be beneficial to the individual and can cost society less money than the current welfare programs. It is also clear that these programs should be targeted because not all individuals will benefit. Evans (1993) argues strongly that for these reasons workfare should not be compulsory, though compulsory programs may work in countries where there is a commitment to full employment. She asks why people should be forced into training or workfare if there are no prospects for long-term jobs.

Investment Policies

In order to create high-paying jobs we have to invest in people, new knowledge, machinery and equipment, and infrastructure. Part of the investment will have to be publicly funded or subsidized and part privately. The balance between public and private funding should depend on the externalities generated.

In order to finance the required private investments, the savings rate will have to be increased, or we will have to borrow even more from abroad. Future borrowing may be very expensive, given our high debt levels which have made foreign investors reluctant to buy Canadian bonds, and the competition for investment money from eastern Europe. To encourage domestic savings, the move towards consumption taxes, such as the GST, is desirable because consumption taxes, unlike income taxes, do not tax savings. To finance the public investments, other programs will have to be cut, or government operations will have to be more efficient. I have already offered some suggestions on how this could be done. Nevertheless, it will be difficult for governments to find money for the necessary investments in infrastructure. There is a danger in relying on user fees for financing infrastructure because they can be highly regressive. In particular, the needs of the municipalities and their difficulties in raising money have to be recognized. It may be desirable to change government accounting practices to make it quite clear to the public when government is borrowing for investment rather than for current consumption expenditures.

Canada has consistently lagged behind other countries in investments in the generation of new knowledge, that is, R&D. One of the reasons is that our economy is based on natural resources. Traditionally, resource-based companies have not done much R&D. However, for our resource sector to survive and to meet the environmental and other challenges, it is essential for it to engage in R&D. Some would argue that R&D is not necessary because knowledge is transferable, and we can get it for free by borrowing from other countries. But Macdonald (1991) points out that technology transfer will not work unless the technological capacity of the recipient equals or exceeds that of the donor. Therefore the recipient must be engaged in R&D. The competitiveness of a knowledge-based economy rests with the quality of the scientific and technological knowledge base in the country. He argues that it is essential for it to be resident within the industrial infrastructure and to have strong links with science research in the universities. R&D should be supported by tax subsidies, as is the case at present. The government should also continue to subsidize research in the universities.

The majority of Canadian students enter the social sciences or humanities, and an MBA is seen as the most essential requirement for success in business. It seems important that more students should take courses, science and engineering, not necessarily for the purpose of a career, but to create awareness about science and what it can do. Similarly the education of science students should include languages and other cultures. We should turn multiculturalism into an asset and encourage an exchange of ideas between the various cultures in Canada. Indeed the policy should be trans-culturalism rather than multiculturalism. Our many cultures should not be allowed to exist inside walls as cultural enclaves. We should benefit from them in their ability to make us question the way we do things.

Investing in people involves investing not only in education but also in day care. Day care is important for two reasons. One is that it is vital that good day care be available not only to the children of the well-to-do, but also to children from low-income families. Good-quality day care could make up for deficiencies in the home environment and give less privileged children a better chance of success in school. The second reason for investing in day care is that it improves the possibilities for women to succeed in the market place and in that way would go a long way towards alleviating the poverty of single-parent families. We certainly spend sufficient money on education, but we do not seem to spend it well, judging by the performance indicators we looked at in Chapter 7. In its report *Education and Training in Canada*, the Economic Council of Canada (The Canada Communication Group 1992) recommends a closer integration of school, work, and training and more accountability. Each province should set clear goals, including specific results in literacy and numeracy tests and a reduction in dropout rates. Interprovincial and international comparisons of the results, should be published, together with the participation rate of females and members of minorities in different school programs. There should be a complete overhaul of apprenticeship systems and vocational programs. Few students choose these programs, partly because the schools emphasize their academic programs, thus short-changing the majority of students, who are not destined for university. It might be useful to raise the minimum school-leaving age as an additional means of combating the high school drop-out rate, thereby forcing students to stay at school.

The universities should receive more funding, but it may be more efficient to give some of the money to the students directly in the form of tuition vouchers.[8] The rest could be given to the universities as subsidies for research. The universities could be free to set their own fees but would be required to offer scholarships to a certain proportion of students. At present, because of provincial government restrictions on fees, students in expensive programs like medicine pay virtually the same fees as arts students, even though we have a surplus of doctors. This is a socially wasteful practice. In order to attract more students into science and engineering, the governments could give larger vouchers for these subjects.

Conclusions

This brief survey showed that there are no shortage of solutions to some of Canada's problems, solutions that have been suggested again and again. Included here is a reform of unemployment insurance and our income support-policies to make them less biased against work. Unfortunately such reforms do not appear to be politically attractive for governments, and the result is that reforms are being made on too small a scale and in too piecemeal a fashion. There is also a need for an extensive reform of our education system. This appears to be politically popular but may be difficult to achieve because education is a provincial responsibility. A full-scale reform of the system in line with the suggestions of the now defunct Economic Council of Canada would require a commitment from all provincial governments.

TOPICS FOR DISCUSSION

1. This chapter advocates investments in human capital and a revamping of our education system. Are you in favour of selected subsidies to investments in advanced technologies, for example, telecommunications technology? What are the arguments for and against such subsidies?

2. It is sometimes argued that it is very difficult to change the education system because of resistance from people with a vested interest in the status quo — teachers, professors, and the educational bureaucracy. Do you think our universities need to change, and if so, in what way? Do you think tenure should be abolished?

3. The increasing cost of health care has been a serious problem for provincial governments. Discuss the advantages and disadvantages of user fees as a way of curtailing costs.

RECOMMENDED READING

Excellent discussions of the issues involved in changing our social policies are found in *The Case for Change: Reinventing the Welfare State* (Watson, Richards, and Brown 1994). Courchene's "Path-Dependency, Positive Feedback and Paradigm Warp: A Schumpeterian Approach to the Social Order" (Reynolds 1993) is also well worth reading. Eden and Molot (1993) provide an interesting perspective on investments policies by being in favour of a new national policy based on free trade, investments in human capital, and the building of a national telecommunications infrastructure.

References

Banting, Keith. "Universality and the Development of the Welfare State." In *Report of the Forum on Universality and Social Policies in the 1990s*, eds. Alan Green and Nancy Olewiler. Kingston, On: Queen's University, John Deutsch Institute for the Study of Economic Policy, 1985.

Bibby, Reginald W. *Mosaic Madness: The Poverty and Potential of Life in Canada.* Toronto: Stoddart Publishing Co., 1990.

Canada. *Commission of Inquiry on Unemployment Insurance. Report.* Ottawa: Ministry of Supply and Services, 1986.

Canada. Communication Group. *Education and Training in Canada.* Ottawa: Ministry of Supply and Services, 1992.

Canada Royal Commission on Employment and Unemployment *Building on Our Strengths: Final Report of the Royal Commission on Employment and Unemployment* St. John's, Newfoundland: Queen's Printer, 1986.

Courchene, Thomas J. "Toward the Reintegration of Social and Economic Policy", In *Canada at Risk?* eds. Bruce G. Doern and Bryne B. Purchase (1991): 125-49.

Courchene, Thomas J. "Presidential Address: Mon pays, c'est l'hiver: reflections of a market populist." *Canadian Journal of Economics* 25 (November 1992): 759-92.

Courchene, Thomas J. "Path-Dependency, Positive Feedback and Paradigm Warp: A Schumpeterian Approach to the Social Order." In *Income Security in Canada: Changing Needs, Changing Means*, Elisabeth Reynolds. Montreal: The Institute for Research on Public Policy, 1933: 43-83.

Cousineau, J.-M. "Le rapport Forget et l'economie politique de l'assurance-chomage." *Canadian Public Policy-Analyse de Politiques* 14 (March 1988): 1-7.

Daly, Herman E. and John B. Cobb Jr. *For the Common Good: Redirecting the Economy toward Community, the Environment and a Sustainable Future.* Boston: Beacon Press, 1989.

Doern, Bruce G and Bryne B. Purchase eds. *Canada at Risk? Canadian Public Policy in the 1990s.* Toronto:C.D.Howe Institute, 1991.

The Economist. "Where are the Jobs?" May 22 1993.

Eden, Lorraine and Maureen Appel Molot. "Canada's National Policies: Reflections on 125 Years." *Canadian Public Policy-Analyse de Politiques* 19 (September 1993): 232–52.

Evans, Patricia M. "From Workfare to the Social Contract: Implications for Canada of Recent U.S. Welfare Reforms." *Canadian Public Policy-Analyse de Politiques* 19 (March 1993): 54-68.

The Financial Post. "B.C. forest plan wins kudos," April 16, 1994.

The Globe and Mail, "Provinces at war over trade. Fed up New Brunswickers challenge Quebec's labour laws," May 31, 1993; "UN body chastises Canada on poverty," May 29, 1993.

MacDonald, John S. "Science and Technology Policy" In *Canada at Risk?* eds. Bruce G. Doern and Bryne B. Purchase (1991): 194-204.

Olewiler, Nancy. "Environmental Quality and Policy in a Global Economy." In *Productivity Growth and Canada's International Competitiveness*, eds. Thomas J. Courchene and Douglas D. Purvis. Proceedings of a conference held at Queen's University 18-19 September 1992. Kingston ON: John Deutsch Institute for the Study of Economic Policy, Queen's University, 1993.

Pal, L.A. "Sense and Sensibility: Comments on Forget." *Canadian Public Policy-Analyse de Politiques* 14 (March 1988): 7-15.

Pedersen, George. "The Challenge for Universities" In *Canada at Risk?* eds. Bruce G. Doern and Bryne B. Purchase (1991): 179-94.

Reid, Frank. "Combatting Unemployment Through Work Time Reductions" In *Policies for Full Employment*, eds. Duncan Cameron and Andrew Sharpe Ottawa/Montreal: Canadian Council on Social Development, 1988: 173-89.

Reynolds, Elisabeth B. ed. *Income Security in Canada: Changing Needs, Changing Means*. Montreal: The Institute for Research on Public Policy, 1993.

Valaskakis, Kimon. *Canada in the Nineties: Meltdown or Renaissance*. Ottawa: The World Media Institute, 1990.

Veeman, M.M. "Social Costs of Supply-Restricting Marketing Boards", *Canadian Journal of Agricultural Economics* 30 (March 1982).

Watson, William G., John Richards, and David M. Brown. *The Case for Change. Reinventing the Welfare State*. Toronto: C.D. Howe Institute, 1994.

Weitzman, Martin L. *The Share Economy*. Cambridge, Mass.: Harvard University Press, 1984.

Endnotes

1   For a good discussion of the Canadian situation in a global context, see Olewiler (1993).

2   In response to public opinion, the Government of British Columbia plans to introduce new legislation controlling clear-cutting. The government has also announced a forest renewal plan, using revenue from stumpage fees to promote tree farming and investments in high value-added manufacturing ventures in forestry products (*The Financial Post*, April 16, 1994).

3   See for example Veeman (1982).

4   Optimistic scenarios can of course be painted. *The Economist* (May 22, 1993) claims that" technology and global competition will eventually put more people to work than it makes redundant". There are three reasons for optimism. One is that despite record numbers of unemployed in OECD countries, more people are now at work than ever before, because of increases in the participation rate. Another is demographics. The number of people of working age will fall or grow more slowly in most rich countries.Thirdly, experience so far has shown that labour-saving technological innovations have not led to a decrease in employment.

5   According to Courchene (1993, p. 54) UI payments were $5 billion in 1984 and increased to nearly $20 billion in 1992.

6   Following Courchene (1992), p. 144.

7   Daly and Cobb argue that current agricultural practices are environmentally unsustainable and should be changed toward a more labour-intensive type of agriculture. This would also help to revitalize rural communities.

8   See for example Pederson (1990).

Summary and Conclusions

This book has outlined some of the global changes affecting Canada and the world and the way in which they threaten our well-being as Canadians. The changes facing Canada and the world in the political, technological, environmental, and economic spheres reinforce each other. In the political arena, there appears to be a general lack of confidence in the ability of governments to solve today's economic, social, and environmental problems. This lack of confidence, combined with the diminished power of governments because of globalization and decreased deference to authority, has led to political disintegration in many parts of the world and heightened tension between various interest groups in others. The diminished power of governments and decreased deference to authority can be attributed to improvements in education and the enormous changes in communications technology. Other changes in technology that affect us are advances in biotechnology and materials technology and the use of computers in production.

The changes in technology have in turn led to fundamental changes in the structure of the global economy, which is now based on knowledge rather than on materials. There are far-reaching implications for the organization of production. Firms have become increasingly footloose, moving production to where there is cheap labour if they need cheap, unskilled labour. If some of the firm's operations require a pool of highly trained specialized labour, those operations will be located where such labour is available. Financial capital, equally footloose, moves across borders in search of the highest return. The rewards to knowledge will increase, leading to larger income disparities between people with advanced training and education, and those without.

We examined our well-being from several angles: per capita income, the environment, employment, and income distribution. We also looked at the sustainability of our current well-being. We concluded from our analysis in Chapter 1 that, compared to most countries in the world, Canada is doing very well, rating second on the United Nations Human Development Index. I argued, however, that given the growth rate of our national debt, our current standard of living is not sustainable. An examination of our environment in Chapter 3 revealed that our control of pollution could be much improved. Our water quality problems in particular appear to be serious. Like other nations we are also confronted with the problems associated with the destruction of the ozone layer and global warming. The resource aspect of our environment was examined in Chapter 4, where we concluded that our renewable resources, in particular forests and fish, had been mismanaged to such an extent our the resource base is jeopardized.

The survey of employment and unemployment in Chapter 5 showed that the nature of employment has changed with the growth of service jobs and non-traditional jobs such as self-employment and short-term and part-time work. Globalization has contributed to a greater segmentation of labour markets between the amount of training and experience required and therefore between the salaries earned. The chapter also indicated that unemployment has gradually increased. Many studies point toward our generous unemployment insurance as a contributing factor.

The survey in Chapter 6 of the distribution of income and the incidence of poverty showed that we have proportionally fewer poor people than the United States but far more than many European countries. We have a particularly high incidence of poverty among single parents, most of whom are women. This is particularly worrying because of the potential long-term adverse effects on the children.

Chapter 7 noted serious weaknesses in our competitive position. Productivity growth has been poor, particularly in our resource industries, where our comparative advantage appears to lie. We spend less on research and development than most other industrialized countries, and our record of research and development as measured by the number of patents and the number of scientists and engineers employed in research is worse. We are also less likely than other countries to adopt new technologies in production and though we have spent more on education than most countries, there is some evidence that the money has not been well spent, judging by the quality of output, particularly in the schools. Unless we correct some of these weaknesses, our living standards will not improve.

Chapters 9, 10, and 11 surveyed our major economic and social policies as they have developed over the years. To overcome the many problems we have outlined, we need a new set of policies:

- We need to eliminate deficits both at the federal and provincial levels for reasons outlined in Chapter 9. As taxation is already very high, deficit reduction would require large cuts in government expenditures.

- We need to reform unemployment insurance and social assistance in favour of retraining and upgrading. Indeed, for many people workfare may be appropriate.

- We need to reduce child poverty by enforcing child support payments from the non-custodial parent, by offering more subsidized day-care places to low-income families, and by making child tax credits more generous for low-income families.

- We need to abolish agricultural marketing boards and the costly interprovincial barriers to trade.

- We need a full-scale reform of our education system to raise standards and introduce more accountability. Our universities should be deregulated to make them more responsive to market conditions. Any deregulation of tuition fees should be accompanied by a revamped student loan system in which repayment is contingent on income. There should also be closer links between universities and industry in R&D and technology transfer.

- Market incentivies should be introduced for pollution control. Statistics Canada should introduce enviromental accounting into our national accounts. Costs-benefit analysis should be used by all levels of government as an aid in making decisions on resource management and extraction. More research should go into the management of renewable resources.

- Given the increased importance of the service sector to the economy, attempts should be made to raise productivity in that sector.

The solutions suggested here are hardly radical, but they will of course be difficult to achieve because of the continued tension between the federal and provincial governments and between Quebec and the rest of Canada. I repeat, however, the observation from the introductory chapter that we are blessed with a variety of natural resources, we have a relatively clean enviroment, and we have a culturally diverse, highly educated population, capable of generating a wealth of ideas and solutions to our own problems as well as to the problems of the world at large. We should be abe to rise to the challenge.

Index